The Red Line

'The way to heaven out of all places is of length and distance.'
Thomas More, *Utopia*

To Ann & Daniel

The Red Line

A Railway Journey Through the Cold War

Christopher Knowles

PEN & SWORD
TRANSPORT

First published in Great Britain in 2017 by
Pen & Sword Transport
an imprint of
Pen & Sword Books Ltd
47 Church Street
Barnsley
South Yorkshire
S70 2AS

ISBN 978 1 47388 744 2

Typeset in Ehrhardt by
Mac Style Ltd, Bridlington, East Yorkshire
Printed and bound by Replika Press Pvt. Ltd.

Pen & Sword Books Ltd incorporates the imprints of Pen & Sword
Archaeology, Atlas, Aviation, Battleground, Discovery, Family History,
History, Maritime, Military, Naval, Politics, Railways, Select, Transport,
True Crime, Fiction, Frontline Books, Leo Cooper, Praetorian Press,
Seaforth Publishing and Wharncliffe.

For a complete list of Pen & Sword titles please contact
PEN & SWORD BOOKS LIMITED
47 Church Street, Barnsley, South Yorkshire, S70 2AS, England
E-mail: enquiries@pen-and-sword.co.uk
Website: www.pen-and-sword.co.uk

Contents

Preface

In April 1981 I set out from London on a train journey that, many weeks later, would bring me to Hong Kong. With me were a half dozen paying customers, whose welfare was notionally my responsibility. Our route would take us through East Germany, Poland, the Soviet Union, the Mongolian People's Republic and the People's Republic of China – a substantial part of what was then the Communist world. From our vantage point today it may seem surprising that these countries were regarded with at best suspicion and at worst with visceral terror. That was the nature of the Cold War.

Over the following years, I was to make that journey some twenty-four times. Although this was how I earned my living, this route was one I chose to repeat time and again for two reasons. First, I became fascinated by what most people would have regarded as the eccentric dystopias east of the Berlin Wall; totalitarian, sometimes despotic regimes founded on oppression and violence, where Western ideas of freedom were largely absent, where daily life was exhausting and frustrating and yet where a kind of old-fashioned gentility was preserved. Second, the journey itself was perhaps the greatest adventure possible in conditions of safety and security. We travelled on a series of ordinary trains, mixing with people whose lives were alien to our own, on almost the world's longest possible continuous railway route.

Travellers were, quite naturally, apprehensive at entering our enemies' lairs. That first journey I, too, was apprehensive (because I had no clue what I was doing) but soon discovered that as foreigners, and particularly as tourists, there was nothing to fear. If you were in an organised group, you were somehow immune to suspicion; a pretty good cover for a spy, I would have thought.

We did not know it at the time, but all of those countries were on the brink of great changes, with China leading the way, and Poland close behind. Now, compared to that time, in many aspects they are unrecognisable, even if China remains nominally a Communist state and Russia's interpretation of democracy is ambiguous in the extreme. But in 1981, those changes were some way off. Hundreds of millions of citizens across Europe and beyond the Urals, through Asia to the southern tip of China continued to live under highly bureaucratised and frequently oppressive governments and many of them had just emerged from decades of terror and abuse.

That is why the story of these journeys is worth telling. What follows, combined into a single imaginary journey, is a selection of the events that occurred over the years, featuring many of those sometimes demanding but always spirited people who travelled with me at different times. All of the events are true and with the exception of the incarceration in Ulan Bator, which was the unfortunate fate of another, most happened to me; but I have taken the liberty of occasionally taking them out of their original context in order to preserve the narrative flow. They express my wonderment at everything we saw, from the awe-inspiring to the downright depressing.

Acknowledgements

My thanks to Christian Wolmar for his enthusiastic help in ensuring that this book was published; to commissioning editor John Scott-Morgan; to editor Carol Trow for her light touch and subtle suggestions; to Voyages Jules Verne, the travel company that made these journeys possible; to all the passengers who made life so interesting; to the local people we met along the way, who often had to work in difficult circumstances; and to my fellow guides, for the good times we shared.

Above all I thank my family and friends, near and far, for their love.

Hook of Holland, Netherlands to Ulan Bator, Drive 8,759 km, 110 h
Ulaanbaatar, Mongolia

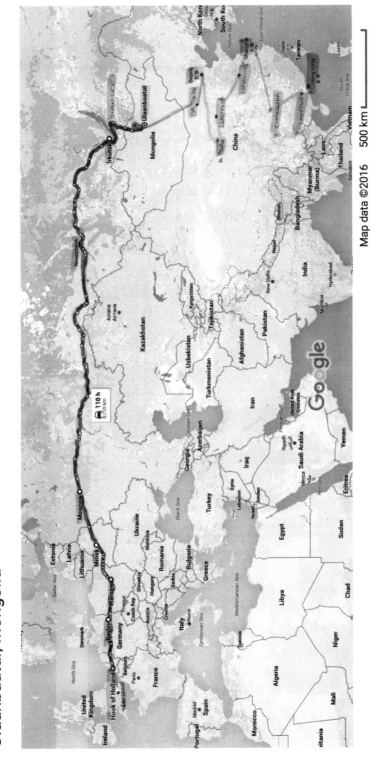

Map data ©2016   500 km

Chapter 1

First Steps

It all started in 1981. I was living in London then and had found myself at a loss. I was young but not so young that the expectations on the back of an expensive education did not weigh heavily on my shoulders. Seduced by the charms of the 1960s, I had lived a bit of a rackety life in early adulthood, a series of jejune enterprises and dead-end jobs in various European backwaters had left me with the knowledge of several languages, experience of some aspects of the world and not much else.

A friend of mine from school, like many others I knew, had moved effortlessly through the rest of his education to land a lucrative job with a bank in the Far East, in Hong Kong. With little in common beyond our shared school experiences and despite the altogether different trajectories of our lives since, we had nonetheless remained in touch. When, on one of this friend's occasional visits home, we met for a drink in the City, he suggested that if I had nothing better to do with my time then I might consider looking at China, which was just then, after decades of conflict and self-administered impoverishment, beginning its first cautious consorting with the west. The friend, convinced that China would now inevitably become integrated into the wider world and knowing of a company searching for enthusiastic and sensible recruits to represent them there, had noted their contact details and duly passed them on to me.

My first reaction was irritation, because it seemed like a lofty piece of advice from one who was already doing well in life to one who was feckless. That was just my state of mind at the time. But as I thought a little more about it, the more the idea enchanted me. China! In my mind there lodged an image that must have been in a book we used at kindergarten school. There was an impossibly wide river, the Yangtse Kiang as were taught to call it, dotted with junks, with those characteristic sails that reminded me of bat wings (a bat, I learned later, is a symbol of happiness in China), made of bamboo matting and bamboo battens. It is remarkable, the power of an image, how it can colour our judgement for ever. And then there was all that recent history – the Cultural Revolution, the Gang of Four – that had in some almost indiscernible way impressed itself upon me whilst simultaneously seeming so distant and so exotic as to be unknowable and out of my reach. I don't think that it would ever have occurred to me to think of going to China, then, a place that seemed threatening and remote, had it not been for that letter. Yet, when what was a kind of invitation arrived, it seemed irresistible.

Well, I wrote to them and within a fortnight, there came a reply. There are three things that I shall always remember about that letter: the stamp, with its strange script and picture of an ape (it was the year of the monkey); the name of the company, with its echoes of trade winds and adventure; and the last line of its content, written by a certain Mr. Whitacker. He said: 'Address your enquiry to our head office, in London. I think the address will interest you.'

It did, very much. It was the street where I lived.

Of course, it seemed to me that I was being shown my destiny. No matter that the job was not for would-be swashbuckling entrepreneurs, as I had pathetically imagined, but to be a guide, in charge of parties of tourists into the newly opened China market. A part of me felt a certain ignominy in applying for such a position, and, in particular, through the assistance of a former school friend who was earning a small tax-free fortune in a glass tower in Hong Kong whereas I was floating, adrift, rootless. But, the allure of China, the prospect of going all that way – and being paid for it! I could not bear to sacrifice an opportunity like that to convention. That would have been the more sensible way but I ignored it and there it is.

I remember the first time I went to the office of the company. It lay on the extension of my street that I rarely passed, since it was not on the route to either the railway station or the bus stop. I nearly always turned left, when it lay to my right. Nonetheless, I must have passed it many times without noticing it. That was its genius. There was its seduction. You have to remember that at the period I am talking about travel had become an industry consisting – if you remove the wealthy – who can always do what they want anyway – and a handful of adventurers – of chartered aeroplanes crammed with customers in search of cheap holidays in the sun. Travel was an unsubtle business drained of adventure and wonderment. A travel agency was a shop window covered in labels screaming cheap deals to purpose-built resorts in southern Europe. The office of this company was the exact antithesis of what typified for most people the notion of travel.

I looked at this office, with its artfully constructed anonymity and I saw something quite different. Instead of a travel agency, I saw a mysterious emporium. Above all, I was reminded of an old-fashioned bureau, where travellers would book their passage across an ocean to an outpost of empire. I could smell the brine and feel the salt on my skin and see the palm trees hanging still and limp in sultry, tropical air. When I looked up, there was the reason. Above the door, as if it were a pub, there was a sign.

I kept a sporadic diary, then, and this was what I wrote at the time:

'Would it be fanciful to liken the threshold of a travel company office with a frontier? By passing from a wind-scoured London street in the winter of 1980 into a room of palms, Chesterfield sofas, model locomotives in glass cases and seductive travel posters from the golden age of travel, before the internet, mobile phones and last-minute travel had reconfigured notions of time and distance, I seemed, with a single step, to move from one world to another. This was no run-of-the-mill travel agent. A painted placard, like a pub sign, depicting an ocean liner and a steam locomotive, swung above the entrance to an anonymous office. No garish stickers featuring cheap fares to the Costas or to Florida, just an opulent waiting room to an exotic emporium hinting at romance and exploration.

'It was stagecraft, a brilliant piece of theatre that enchanted me, like a child in a toyshop. Like a child, I saw only adventure and a foxed album of faded, tantalising images: a steam locomotive and its train unfurled along the platform; and a long, long journey east, around the globe to China.'

I was utterly bewitched by the discretion of the operation. You had to be wiser than I was to regard it as anything other than a fable come to life. When it came to it, I was as gullible as the rest of them. But how happy I was to be able to suspend reality. That was its beauty.

I was interviewed by the owner of the business. An enigmatic man, with a quiet manner and the childlike eyes of the visionary. He was a man of commerce but one who understood that theatre was the supreme tool in the sales kit. There was more to the job than I had expected. Of course, I had no realistic conception of what the work entailed, imagining with breath-taking naiveté that I would be leading parties of awe-struck customers around exotic cities and lecturing them in the subtleties of an ancient culture – a sort of mild Indiana Jones. It did not occur to me that my ignorance of the language and my complete absence of any proper understanding of the nature of China could perhaps be obstacles.

As it turned out, none of this mattered. No, what came as a surprise to me was the revelation that China was to be at the end of the line. My job was to take a party of paying customers from London all the way to Hong Kong by train.

Perhaps, now that travel to distant places is taken for granted, it is not easy to fully grasp the significance of such a journey, for we have lived most of our lives in an epoch when the division of the world into two ideological camps has, for the time being, passed. We have all heard of the Cold War and the Berlin Wall, but even within this short passage of time they have become names from academic history, much like Waterloo or the American Civil War. But this conflict of ideas was still the great talking point of the time. More than that, wars in distant corners of the globe were fought over it all – left versus right, communism versus capitalism. For those in charge of this mess, it was portrayed as the struggle of ideas. The ugly truth is that it had little to do with ideas and everything to do with power and alliances and self-justification. All that absurd posturing seems now as remote as a medieval religious war.

In the west, we were afraid of them, as they were afraid of us. The fear was palpable, by which I do not mean that we passed each day as if it were our last so much as we felt it more than ever important to take pride in our precious freedom. A journey such as this, by train to China, across a divided Germany, a Poland already in turmoil, the USSR and Mongolia, was more than a jaunt. On the one hand, it was a well-trodden trail – it was certainly not an expedition – on the other, it was a journey into the unknown. Some would consider it an odd undertaking, even an eccentric one. Bumping along thousands of miles in uncomfortable trains for weeks on end does not, any longer, seem very alluring. But notwithstanding the tensions of the Cold War, we rejoiced in a confident optimism about our own lives compared to those of the poor benighted enslaved on the other side of the Wall, together with a sneaking curiosity. It never occurred to me that it could be otherwise, and so it was with a mixture of trepidation and excitement that I took the job when it was offered to me. What did I know of Russia and the Soviet Union? Of China? And, of all places, Mongolia? Nothing: nothing but stereotypical images, the jetsam from news bulletins and kindergarten history.

Chapter 2

The Berlin Line

My train was to depart in April of that year. In the end, I was offered the job for the unlikely reason that I spoke Italian! The thinking went that since tickets for the journey could be purchased by anyone from anywhere, the requirement for an Italian speaker might arise should any Italians, in those days unlikely to speak English, choose to join. In the end this ability went unneeded for the party, consisting of Britons, Americans, Australians, and a small contingent of French, was a small one, but as is the way of these things, filled with contrasting personalities. I met them on the eve of departure at the Great Eastern Hotel, attached to our departure point, Liverpool Street station. Now it has been turned into a 'boutique' hotel, trading on its associations with the romance of the railways – just, of course, as my new employer was doing in 1981 – but its appeal then was purely utilitarian, a workaday relic. I suppose that the average hotel reflects the country that spawns it. The average hotel in the England of that period still reeked of cabbage, served against the dulled gleam of Sheffield plate; the dusty tombs of empire. The Great Eastern's bedrooms were at the end of a process of constant, half-hearted adaptation to the fashions and innovations of the decades since its construction in the late nineteenth century by the son of the architect of the Houses of Parliament. A kettle in the room and a little basket of instant coffee, teabags containing the finest black dust, and sachets of powdered milk, were offered as facilities. It had the finesse and pretensions of a Victorian pub and its clients were commercial travellers and tourists in search of a bargain. I fell in love with it, I think for its complete absence of glamour and the knowledge that we were stepping out from it the following day onto a platform not for a commuter train to an office or to a weekend in the country, but to East Berlin and Moscow.

After all these years I remember it so clearly, that meeting, that evening. My employer came too, to step in at the inevitable moments when the look of bafflement on my face would betray my complete lack of experience – remember these were paying customers, expecting some sort of expertise! Ridiculous, when you think of it, to imagine that in those days anyone could know the details of such a trip, except in their imagination. It was a rain-sodden night, when the yellow of headlights blurred into the muddy gleam from uneven pavements and I was very nervous, conscious of a certain deceit and too callow to know that nobody minds deceit, if sincerely expressed.

As it turned out, although they must surely have detected my lack of experience, most of them were polite enough not to comment on it. The one exception – there is always one, the one that wants to be different – insisted to me that I find him a room in his preferred hotel in Moscow. What could I say? One thing I knew was that the luxury of choosing where to stay in Moscow, or anywhere in the USSR, was out of the question. In a country where state control reached into every aspect of life, no matter how trivial, such matters were out of our hands. This man was called Archie and was not what you might call a man of the people – he was the sort whose loathing of communism was … visceral, so visceral that you might ask why he had chosen to immerse himself in the slough that was the source of everything he found disgusting. I could see that the others, who were almost unnaturally calm about the road ahead, were raising their eyes heavenwards in despair at the prospect of several weeks in the company of what they regarded as the voice of unmitigated prejudice. Of course, this cheered me up immensely. I sensed, I suppose, the charm of the management technique of 'divide and rule', because a disruptive Archie would make the others overlook my failings. The Famous Writer, who was on assignment and who would be an occasional spectral presence throughout the journey, cast a jaundiced eye over his fellow travellers and made his excuses.

Early the next morning, taciturn with apprehension, beneath the great roof designed by the same engineers that supplied the roof of the Albert Hall, we gathered on the platform built on the site of the original Bethlem Royal Hospital, the original 'Bedlam', the world's oldest psychiatric institution. Nearby was a huge marble plaque, like an altarpiece, listing those employees that had died in the First World War. Unveiled in 1922 by one Sir Henry Wilson, he was killed on his way home from the ceremony by an IRA sympathiser. All of these historical currents had their confluence at this one frothing pool of unheeding commuters. I don't know why that realisation struck me as poignant, any more than the imminence of departure from an antique railway station was peculiarly evocative of the essence of travel. I wonder if at that moment we did not all feel ourselves like time-travellers, suspended in eternity; immortal, invisible among all those people going about their daily routines? Great stations are gathering places in a way that an airport can never be, if only because in ancient cities they are usually in the centre, a palimpsest. Each of us was there for different reasons – each of us was a pilgrim, in a way.

First, before joining our train to East Berlin, where we would interrupt the voyage for two nights, we had to cross the North Sea, as there was no Channel Tunnel yet. In the meantime, it was pleasant to amble through the suburbs of London and then gallop through the Essex countryside to the port of Harwich. We were travelling First Class. The journey was advertised as First Class - once we boarded the train in Holland, First Class would be merely a technicality, but across the south of England, and across the North Sea, there was space and comfort. We could read our newspapers for the last time (there would, assuredly, be no *Daily Telegraph* in Moscow) and glance up to look through streaming windows with sentimental affection on cosy English pastures. If anyone asked, we could say that we were on our way to Hong Kong. 'Oh, really? How fascinating! China, too! And Mongolia! Good heavens - are you flying from Luton?' 'No, we are taking the train this time …' And so we boasted a little, with all the insouciance we could muster and we liked to think that everyone who heard us thought us liars or fools.

By the time we reached the Dutch coast at Hoek van Holland, darkness had descended and so had the rain, falling lightly, like moist dust. The Dutch passport officers sat up high, on raised stools, looking down at us with professional severity before, as they did in those days, stamping our passports. Then we had to claim our suitcases and find our train. Here, a foolish moment of panic almost brought my new career to an early and ignominious end. One of the passengers, Joe, young, bearded and idealistic, had overslept, so arriving at Liverpool Street too late to register his bag to Hoek van Holland. Impulsively, I suggested that he simply leave it in the baggage van with all the others, trusting with idiotic optimism that the guard would realise what had happened and add it to the others. Of course, when we went to the baggage hall at the Hook, his bag was not there; it was still awaiting collection at Harwich. Miraculously, given that he was conceivably without a change of clothes as far as Hong Kong, Joe accepted the situation with astounding equanimity. We all knew (if our media was to be believed) that it was impossible to easily buy items like clothes east of Berlin. Fortunately for me there was no time to dwell much on this, as the most important task was to catch a train.

This marked the real beginning of the journey because we were searching for the Russian train for Moscow. I had no idea what to look for until there it was on the timetable above our heads, the magic word 'Moscou', and the platform number. We left the dazzle of the baggage hall and hastened into the damp, ill-lit platform area. The trains were marshalled in lines, humming and crackling with electrical discharge, seal grey in the dim light. Were it not for the red lanterns at their rear, twinkling like ruby stars, they would have been almost invisible. As we drew closer, the colours and motifs of their countries' railway systems became clearer, their destinations – Copenhagen, Marseilles, Athens, Salonika – written across their flanks on detachable tin boards. Inside the carriages, as we walked past accompanied by a porter with his trolley carrying our bags, lights flickered on in compartments as people found their seats. Tired faces sighed with relief, as luggage was stowed and seats secured. We walked on and on in silence behind our luggage trolley, beset by a ridiculous anxiety. It seemed as if the train for Moscow was exiled to some special part of the station reserved for fools and delinquents.

That was how the world was, where the battle for supremacy between east and west manifested itself, in petty snubs masquerading as policies, according to which that train could have been exiled to the furthest reaches of an international transportation hub either by the Soviets themselves, as a defence against contamination by Western values or, possibly, by the local authorities in some forlorn retaliatory gesture. Or, just as likely, it was nothing more than coincidence – who knew? That was it, you see, one never could tell the truth of anything. One thing was certain and rather useful to me; it added to the mystique of everything Russian.

The Moscow train turned out to be a single Soviet 'international' carriage, tacked onto the end of a long chain of carriages belonging to various national railway companies that would gradually disperse over the coming days, our own carriage detached at intervals and reattached to another composition of carriages until it was home in Moscow. Naturally, our carriage was quite different from all the others, from the strange pitch of its roof, which was out of kilter with that of its neighbours, to the Cyrillic lettering on its side, which since I had not taken the trouble to learn it, acted as yet another symbolic barrier.

Two men awaited us on the platform beside the carriage. They were in uniform, not of the faintly reassuringly shabby, ill-fitting type associated with railway staff around the world, but of a more military cut, with caps that, as well as bearing the inevitable hammer and sickle on a red background, were of a singular shape: a wide brim surmounted by a broad, flat crown that bore a passing resemblance to something I could not at that moment pinpoint, but which I was to learn was a material echo of a time when Russia was in thrall to the 'Tartar-Mongol yoke'. It was at that moment that I was gripped by an existential panic that I find hard to convey to you in words because it was entirely irrational. At first, this arose from something fairly banal, which might be best described as bureaucratic obstructionism, with all its attendant frustrations – the long perusal of the ticket, the detailed inspection of our various visas, the catechism of questions in Russian that I could not understand or answer – except that there on that damp, murky platform, in the form of two uniformed men, we were confronted by the absolute power of the Soviet state. They were perfectly nice, bluff, genial teddy bears, the two of them. Yet had they chosen to refuse us passage, there was nothing I could have done about it. Who would I have complained to? There was nobody and, anyway, no time. Naturally, it would not have happened but the point is that what had seemed to me unthinkable was far from it because these two men – Yuri and Andrei as we came to find out – were patriotic believers in the rightness of a cause even down to the trivial business of boarding a train. For them, we were not merely foreigners but class enemies, by definition suspicious. Don't ask me what a class enemy was, or is – it is a meaningless confection dressed as philosophy. They didn't understand it either. So, at that moment, for the first time in my life, I felt the discomfort of something beyond my understanding.

Our carriage was surprisingly comfortable, with fold-down beds eventually made up by our two attendants. Each compartment boasted a sink, into which streamed a thin flow of cold water. Like almost every carriage we travelled in between the coast of Holland and the south of China, it was manufactured in East Germany. On board, a thousand miles from its frontier, we had already crossed into the Soviet Union. I cannot explain this sensation exactly and, in any case, the realisation came only later on closer acquaintance with the Russian character. We had been kidnapped in a way, smuggled over the border into a sweaty, airtight world to become, in varying measures, resentful and awestruck honorary Soviet citizens. Yuri and Andrei visibly relaxed once we were all locked up and under way. They felt safe among the homely odours of crude disinfectant and stewing tea. It was shocking to discover how easy and, on reflection, how disconcertingly pleasurable is the sensation of resignation. It had nothing to do with political conviction, but there was something perversely comforting in the brutishness of daily life in the east, as the spirit submits to the rough Russian embrace.

I had hoped that there might be a dining car somewhere on the train. In those days, when we depended on the admirable printed Thomas Cook timetables for information about train composition, some details remained unclear. According to the timetable, some kind of dining service was provided on the train, but after persuading Andrei and Yuri to unlock the carriage door so that I could explore, and after walking the whole length of the train, nearly every compartment dark and empty, save for here and there splashes of yellow neon and single passengers slumped in seat corners in exhausted dejection, as if we were travelling on a ghost train, I found no dining car. Only on the way back did I notice a uniformed man half asleep in a compartment surrounded by plastic boxes, similar to those handed out on aeroplanes. He protested that he needed to keep some back for others, until I pointed out that there were few other passengers, most of whom were asleep, at which point he relented and I bought the lot. They contained a doughy croissant, some butter and jam, and an apple, enough to sustain us until the following morning when we were to have breakfast in East Berlin. Over the next few weeks, there were moments when that waxy-skinned apple, watery and tasteless, became in our imagination the epitome of the best and freshest of foods.

We raced through the night. What I recall in particular were the names of some of the Dutch stations – Amersfoort, Hengelo – where we paused beneath canopies lit up by dazzling neon, to be objects of curiosity for the last few exhausted commuters on their way home, to whom what they took to be Russians peering longingly out at the 'free' world was the highlight of their day. Then across West Germany – Germany was two countries then – to the border with its dysfunctional twin, East Germany, or, as it preferred to be known, the German Democratic Republic, the GDR, or in German, the DDR.

We slept. Then my compartment door was flung open and the light snapped on. Planted in the doorway was a stout man in a uniform and the inevitable peaked cap. From somewhere on his person, a polished hammer and sickle caught my eye. On his large belly rested a small tray, supported by a halter around his thick neck. He exhaled a mist of cold night air. I fumbled for my watch – it was close to two in the morning.

'*Passportern*!' the creature bellowed, and his demand was repeated along the corridor like an echo, as his colleagues among the GDR border guards, all short and squat, or tall and thin, like members of a troupe of comedians, shouted the same thing into each compartment, with weary, oafish synchronicity.

'Look at them,' Archie growled to me along the corridor from his compartment. 'Bloody Prussians. Commie Nazis – that is all they are. Isn't that right, Fritz?' he said mockingly to the officer dealing with his passport.

The officer, who didn't understand English, certainly recognised the scornful tone. But he had met the likes of Archie a million times before. 'Fritz' held his pen poised above the form and raised an unsmiling face to stare steadily into Archie's eyes. He muttered something, as he lowered his eyes to continue writing, and his colleagues broke into loud laughter. Archie blanched; and yet again, I experienced the worst feeling in the world, which is that of powerlessness.

Everything that was bizarre and tragic about that time is symbolised by a little diagram. It is a passport stamp for the GDR. In that little two-tone rectangle filled with figures and images is all you need to know about the way in which the resources of a country founded on an ideology were poured into circumscribing with fetishistic meticulousness the movements of any visitor and of every citizen. In the top left corner, the ubiquitous national symbol consisting of the workers' hammer, the compass of the intelligentsia and the rye of the farmers. In the other corner, a cute, toy-like locomotive, to indicate how we entered the country. Across the middle a series of figures that seemed to partially but, mysteriously, not completely, correspond to the date. In the bottom right corner, a number that I guessed was personal to the officer wielding the stamp. And then the two colours, the combination of red and black or green and purple or yellow and purple, which changed not only according to the location but according to an unpredictable calendar, with the aim, I imagine, of dissuading would-be fugitives from attempting to counterfeit them. Of all the many visas that in those days filled my passport, some of which were lavish affairs taking up an entire page, those miniature masterpieces of meretriciousness were my favourite.

At the time I regarded the bovine border guards as rather amusing. It was only many years later that the suspicions entertained by the likes of Archie turned out to be well founded. These men – always men – were the *Grenztruppen der DDR*, a military force among whom there lurked more than a few members of the 6th Main Department *(Hauptabteilung VI)* of the GDR state security service, the *Ministerium für Staatssicherheit der DDR*, better known now, infamously, as the 'Stasi'. The Stasi officers worked among them covertly, wearing the same uniform, keeping a watchful eye on those guards regarded as possible defectors. Under no circumstances was a guard permitted to be alone; and if one should foolishly attempt flight, his colleagues were under instructions to shoot him without hesitation. Here was a country run on the principle of scientifically enhanced paranoia.

Sleep was elusive and before long I gave up the struggle, dressed and stood in the corridor. Outside, the darkness of the German Democratic Republic was profound; there was almost no electric light, beyond the occasional street lamp casting a brassy glimmer on damp pavements, or the feeble beams from the headlights of a solitary car, as it bumped slowly, like a toy with a failing battery, along a country road. I did not see anyone else – everyone was sleeping in order to be fit to continue building a socialist society. Our train rolled on, passing at speed through empty, ramshackle stations, their names printed in the black Gothic script of pre-war Germany. At dawn, we briefly re-entered the western world. The neon glare of West Berlin, with its homely vulgarity, came as a welcome surprise after the oppressive darkness of East Germany. The divided city of Berlin lay in the middle of the GDR like an island run by two warring tribes, with one side permanently in shadow. Carved up into zones at the end of the Second World War, the western part of the city, though a West German outpost, was notionally administered by the Americans, the British and the French. The other, eastern, part was the Soviet zone, or 'democratic' zone, which in an act of brotherly love was eventually returned by the Russians to the new East German state not as East Berlin, as it was called in the west, but simply as Berlin, the *Hauptstadt der DDR*. According to the GDR, there was no West Berlin, only Berlin. If in 1981 in the GDR you had bought a map of the city, it would have shown all the streets of East Berlin, featured all its landmarks and indicated the city limits with an inoffensive purple line. Beyond the purple line there appeared to be nothing other than a couple of unmarked roads and a lonely underground railway station in the middle, apparently, of an uninhabited desert. And yet you would have seen printed across that emptiness not WEST BERLIN, in acknowledgement of its existence, no matter how unpalatable to the Soviet Union and its acolytes, but WESTBERLIN, as if it were at best a vague idea for a yet to be built suburb; at worst some kind of impenetrable wilderness – a wasteland.

Of course in a way they were right! For East Germans, West Berlin did not exist; the map was correct. Yet the more I thought about that purple line, the more sinister it seemed to me. What purpose did it serve, when there was nothing beyond it? A purple line; even as an administrative symbol it was a deceitful, nasty little joke. That pretty little line, so precise, so bureaucratic, failed to indicate one very ugly fact, that it marked the presence of something almost beyond comprehension; an unbreachable wall, encircling West Berlin and built by the East Germans themselves. West Berlin did not exist for them and yet they built a wall to blot the chimera out. According to the manufactured logic of Soviet thought, the Western world was founded on a gigantic lie, and therefore had been consigned not even to the past, not even to history, but to the indignity of obliteration.

I stood at the carriage window staring with a kind of longing at the winking lights, the dazzle of the shop windows, the first commuters on their weary way to the station. Theirs was a sort of drudgery, but it seemed to me, at that moment, an appealing one. I felt like a prisoner looking from his cell into a notion of freedom.

We pulled into the main station of West Berlin, Berlin Zoo. The station interior simmered and hummed in the white glare and beneath the lights a couple of immigrant cleaners swept the platforms among the early commuters with languid, rhythmic flicks, as if they were sowing seeds beneath a beating sun. Then we were off again, slowly, stuttering and clanking eastwards. This short journey eastwards into the *Hauptstadt der DDR* was, in a peculiar respect, the most memorable of any that I made throughout my life. Before we knew it, we met the purple line. As the train approached the Wall itself, the street lights dimmed once more and we entered a zone of darkness. We could have been crossing the Styx into Hades. Some way raised above street level, the railway line seemed to trace a winding course along the top of the Wall itself. Progress was painfully cautious, but inexorable. To our right, almost abutting the Wall, there was the Reichstag, in West Berlin but only by a few metres, with the West German flag stubbornly illuminated by spotlights, billowing with what I took to be a kind of defiance. Behind it, the purple line crossed the river Spree to continue describing its erratic course across the boundary between the two halves of the city. Beyond the Wall itself – and even now, long after the whole disgusting apparatus has been dismantled, I find it extraordinary – which was the boundary marker, the purple line made material, there was a gamut of motley defensive mechanisms: crash barriers; then a wide strip illuminated by a line of glimmering lamps, for all the world like an abandoned street, with who knows what horrors planted beneath its surface: anti-tank traps; two further rows of fences; and in the middle of it all a watch-tower. We could see the guards at the top of the tower training their binoculars on us from behind their no doubt bullet-proof glass, as we screeched painfully on. For all its theatricality, I felt afraid to even think of raising a camera to record the moment; and yet, he went on, even now the recollection is as clear to me as if I were looking at a photograph.

The others awoke, slid open their compartment doors and stood yawning in the corridor, trying to work out the peculiar geography of the two Germanys and the two Berlins. Yuri and Andrei brought us glasses of hot, bitter tea, and Russian sugar cubes parcelled in paper decorated with pictures of locomotives and aeroplanes in illustration of Soviet mastery of technology. We stood in silence, fascinated, disbelieving and shivering, in a kind of awe of what lay below us. Each of us felt like a spy finally unleashed in enemy territory. The fact that we were just a bunch of tourists slipped our newly collectivised minds. It seemed inconceivable to me that the construction of a wall – a pile of concrete – could act as a barrier between two sets of millions of people that shared the same language, history, culture, outlook. But, of course, the wall was merely the expression of those that thought it up and who connived in it and complied with it.

We were to spend a couple of nights in the *Hauptstadt der DDR* before going on to Warsaw and Moscow. We had been told that we were to leave the train at East Berlin's main station, known as Berlin Ostbahnof and which translates as Berlin East Station (with the built-in implication of the existence of a Berlin West Station, which, of course, according to the GDR line, could not exist), where we were to be met by a representative of the state travel agency, which, named with suitably utilitarian absence of glamour or imagination, was simply the *Reiseburo*, or the Travel Agency. Yet as it turned out, we were unable to continue to Ostbahnof, as we had been assured we could and should, because when the train came to rest in the preceding station, Friedrichstrasse, where we remained in our seats in expectation of a few more minutes of jolting towards the east, we were ejected with some impatience onto the platform, together with our oversized suitcases, by a platoon of East German soldiers making their way through the carriages, who disregarded my protestations with the aggressive contempt that they were used to inflicting on their comrades.

Here, my understanding of the artifice that went into the construction of a divided city (one half of which, remember, did not exist) failed me. This station, Friedrichstrasse, lay wholly in East Berlin. Yet, even if according to the GDR there was no West Berlin, it had implicitly to acknowledge the presence of the West Berlin S-Bahn, the suburban train service, and its underground sibling, the U-Bahn, both of which operated through Friedrichstrasse, by actively denying access to it to its own citizens. Thus, when we were left on the empty platform early that morning, minutely surveyed by soldiers armed with sub-machine guns on loggias bolted high up against the station walls, whilst their colleagues, leashed to their sleek Alsatian dogs, patrolled the platform around us, we were in limbo. I subsequently discovered more about the peculiar layout of this station. Between certain platforms, a metal-glass barrier had been constructed with the express purpose of severing this place of arrival and departure in two quite isolated partitions, both fully under armed control, the one for people within East Berlin and the other for transit travellers, all within one station building with a maze of connecting hallways, barriers, numerous cameras, armed guards with sniffer dogs, and plain-clothes agents.

I hardly noticed the train as it accelerated out of the station into the morning, and when I did, looking at the last carriage curve away with that grace that trains attain once they have achieved their momentum, I felt quite bereft. I can honestly say that I was almost overcome with panic because, through the great grimy windows of the station, the blurred skyline of the city was taking shape in the early etiolated sunlight. A pair of soldiers, stormtrooper-like in their jodhpurs and high polished boots and in leanness of build and in zeal and commitment clearly a cut above their oafish comrades at the border, approached and without a word sternly directed us to an unmarked flight of stairs down which we dragged our suitcases until we finally reached the passport and customs area.

I won't go into the long and tedious procedures (the detailed perusal of each passport and visa; the indifference to the difficulties in manhandling luggage up and down the various staircases) to which we were subjected in order to enter the German Democratic Republic for a single day, but after an hour or more we found ourselves on a street corner beneath the station in a state of some bewilderment. Naturally the *Reiseburo* representative was nowhere to be seen. Today the problem would be solved with a telephone call but we had no phone. We had no local currency (it was unobtainable outside the GDR), so even if I could have located a public telephone I would not have been able to use it. Needless to say, we had no map. There was no-one to ask and even if there were they could or would have been of no assistance, since consorting with westerners, certainly in the shadow cast by the Wall, was conceivably a risky undertaking for East Berliners. I, with the optimism of innocence, worried less about the eventual outcome than about satisfying the concerns of my charges, who, as paying customers themselves, suffered a form of self-delusion by confusing payment for a service with its efficient delivery in impossible circumstances and whose major concern, apart from being not arrested by the secret police, was the desire for a hot bath. People want adventure without the associated discomforts. Delusion was not confined to the world beyond the Wall.

In the midst of all this confusion, and burgeoning desperation, I noticed in a dark corner of the street a car with a taxi sign on its roof. My first reaction was less relief than intrigue at the discovery that it was a Mercedes-Benz, a marque that I presumed in a socialist utopia would be a cipher for western sybaritic excess, especially as it was manufactured in the capitalist hell that was West Germany. Then again, with the contorted logic that appeared to prevail beyond the Wall, perhaps the presence of such a car reflected a kind of parallel patriotic pride. Still, after a great deal of haggling, eventually the driver agreed to transport us to the hotel, four at a time, on the understanding that he was paid an exorbitant sum in West German marks for each journey. Given our numbers, in the space of a few minutes he was about to become rather well off by local standards and, in order to show the value that he attached to our well-being, he spun the wheels impressively as he accelerated away at high speed towards the city centre. The smell of scorched rubber lingered and then he returned and repeated the exercise until we were all in our hotel, which, by the way, was an unexpectedly luxurious affair known, I was to learn much later, as the 'Stasi nest'. This hotel, designed by a certain Mr Kiss, was built in the bland international style of the epoch, a style that was supposed to proclaim, by its very existence 'you are in a modern city, in a modern, sophisticated country'. In a small, stifling, deadened way, it succeeded. There was a bar where drinks unobtainable anywhere else in the GDR were sold for West German marks (or dollars of sterling or indeed almost any currency that was not the local one). In fact, everything in that hotel had to be purchased using Western currencies, which meant that the hotel was closed to the average East German citizen, another of those curious arrangements that seemed to my naïve mind to sit oddly with the professed philosophies of our hosts. But then, as I was to discover over the coming weeks, inconsistency was simply another element in the seemingly endless elasticity of Soviet logic.

The Palast Hotel, with its plush reception area and general air of sleek contemporary opulence, as if through yet another quirk of the city's political and physical geography we had inadvertently found our way to West Berlin, was one of those places, it seems, where some of the more implausible pieces of Western propaganda were close to the truth. Some rooms were monitored. There were microphones here and there and the Stasi did have a permanent presence among the staff, listening and watching for … well, for what? But none of this occurred to me at the time, bewildered as I was at the nature of this Soviet utopia, in which, as I soon discovered, emotions were not wholly suppressed when it came to the GDR sense of slight. As we stood in the leatherette lobby, a coach pulled up outside, from which descended the *Reiseburo* representative that we were to have met at Ostbahnof. Pale with anger, he harangued me at some length for failing to disembark as instructed at Ostbahnhof. 'But why did you not stay on the train?' he asked repeatedly. 'The timetable says very clearly that your train terminates at Ostbahnof!' No answer would satisfy him. No matter how often I described to him the impossibility of resisting the bidding of the guards; that we were compelled to pass through border control at Friedrichsrasse for fear of being executed by what I thought looked like people highly trained in the use of firearms and ever alert to the danger of revolution or invasion, he would not believe me. To actively believe something so demonstrably false indicated to me either that we were dealing with an extreme case of delusion or that the entire country was deluded. But of course he did know the truth – he, of all people, must have recognised the power wielded by the state – it was just that he wanted, desperately wanted, my story not to be true. I will never forget him, for part of me felt rather sorry for this pathetic, fearful young man; the other part of me thought him an insufferably cocky shit, especially when failing to obtain satisfaction from me, he appealed to the others, as if to say 'your leader is a fool'.

The thing that annoyed me most was that the members of my party, including Archie, whom I might have expected in this case to have been on my side, given his attitude to Communism, turned their exhausted faces towards me in attitudes of silent reproof as if this local expert knew what he was talking about. These same people, who at home would have laughed nervously at the very thought of confronting a customs or passport officer at Dover, never mind in Berlin, and who would have had no truck whatsoever with any claims made east of Osnabruck, were prepared to give this lackey the benefit of the doubt.

Once he had calmed down, the man from the *Reiseburo* introduced himself as Hans. I recall him with particular vividness. Very thin and short, with the trace of a limp and the unhealthy shiny pallor of old cheese, he was in his early twenties and one of those people for whom I felt an instinctive sympathy and an immediate dislike. Each of us has at best a tenuous control over our destinies. Hans had far less control than most over the course of his life and yet he remained unyielding in his insistence that his country would be a terrestrial paradise were it not for the perfidy of the Western world. The slightest criticism from me, or the most casual enquiry about life in the GDR, was met with a fusillade of angry ripostes or replies that at home would have been supplied by party 'strategists'. I had no desire to undermine his life or beliefs; my questions arose simply out of curiosity, for at the back of my mind I kept wondering, 'Am I missing something here? Is life here better than it seems? Has my upbringing blinded me to an unrevealed truth?' As I contemplated East Berlin's tinny landscape, notwithstanding such fleeting doubts, I felt that I could trust my instincts. The way life was ordered in the GDR might suit some, but it would not have suited me. Perhaps it suited Hans, in which case I was unable to locate the source of his aggression – was it indignation or frustration? Or was it, after all, jealousy? And then, towards the end of our stay, in a moment of weakness, when we were alone for some reason or other, so that he did not need to perform in his usual manner, he confided to me in his belligerent way that of all the music in the world, above all, he loved jazz. I must admit to having been taken aback, not least because I had presumed that jazz, along with pop music, was pretty much frowned upon as an example of

Western decadence, even if, at least in the case of jazz, it might be interpreted as the expression of an oppressed people. Well, as it turned out, after years of futile discussion on whether it met the criteria laid down for cultural excellence as decreed by the various sages and committees of the Communist Party, jazz was more or less tolerated in the GDR. Who can predict the vagaries of Communist party logic? But Hans could not obtain the recordings he craved of the great American musicians, because, he informed me bitterly, of a western embargo on their export to the socialist world. Frankly, I did not believe this but then again, anything was possible in the jejune battles of the time. I could not know whether Hans' professed love of jazz was anything more than a pose but it did indicate to me that there was in him, at least, a desire for personal fulfilment that would for ever remain unrequited for as long as he believed it possible for foreigners to disembark at Berlin Ostbahnof.

The highlight of our morning was to be a guided tour of the *Hauptstadt der DDR*. The guide was not to be Hans but a specialist, whom we were to collect from the *Reiseburo* headquarters located somewhere in the centre of the city. A coach duly took us there and, after several minutes idling in front of the tall, anonymous building on Alexanderplatz, a portly, rather florid middle-aged man in a shapeless suit. emerged from it. As we set off to rejoin the wide, decongested avenues of East Berlin, he took his place at the front of the coach, grasped the microphone and for some time said nothing. Nothing at all.

Meanwhile, we looked around us for the first time. East Berlin had a metronomic quality about it. The little cars, which carried the celebrated and infamous brand name of Trabant, criss-crossed the dead-straight boulevards like clockwork toys, leaving oily spurts of smoke in their wake. All around us was a sense of gloomy grandeur, whether the rows of identical blocks of flats or the great buildings left over from that other Germany that existed before the Second World War, the magisterial domes and towers, the black bricks, like an incomplete museum, or a work of art left unfinished. There was a profound sense of emptiness. I realise we have certain ideas of how cities are but surely the whole point of them is as a place of congregation, where people go to invent and grow, not merely be. The *Hauptstadt der DDR* was without vitality or colour, with almost no sign of commerce but none either of relief or laughter or urgency or hope.

I recall nothing of the details of the commentary when finally it came and I don't believe I ever knew the name of the guide; perhaps, in keeping with state policy, he did not introduce himself. All I remember is the peculiar monotony of his delivery style, which was not a drone but a lifeless parody of a North American accent, uttered in the booming declamatory manner of one who intones the countdown of a rocket launch at Cape Canaveral. 'Good AFternOOOOn and WELcome to BerLIN, CApital of the GDR, the GERman DEmoCRAtic RePUblic. The PROgramme for this MORNing is as Follows.'

We were all taken aback at this, in this most un-American of places; apart from the Americans in the party, who presumed that was the way everyone spoke throughout the world. He was, this guide, an intriguing character. He wore his air of professional reserve as if it were a shield against sunlight – his detachment was almost physical. That he was certainly a member of the Communist Party and therefore a pillar of the ruling class, both attracted and repelled us. His personal integrity had been subsumed into the state apparatus and he had the strained, impoverished air of a disappointed and exhausted teacher. The tour took us to Unter den Linden, still elegant, if rather forlorn, culminating in the Brandenburg Gate, a poignant symbol of disunity, located in desolate, deserted Pariser Platz, from where we enjoyed the curious sensation of acknowledging to ourselves the invisible, unheard bustle of the other, disowned Berlin on the far side of the wall. Curious is perhaps an epithet too anodyne to describe the sense of dislocation one felt. Entrapment is more like it. For those East Germans not taken in by the pretences of their government, who knew perfectly well what lay on the other side, the strain of living a daily lie, whatever its benefits, must have been harrowing.

We stopped here and there; in particular, I remember watching the changing of the guard at the Memorial of the Unknown Soldier – or was it called the Memorial to the Victims of Fascism and Militarism? I can't remember which it was, but what I remember with perfect clarity is that the ceremony was performed using the very same chilling goose step that in West Germany had been banned for its associations with Nazism. It was impossible not to be impressed by the flawless precision and stony discipline of the exercise. As if hypnotised, a crowd gathered to watch; an onlooker with a camera, trespassing right into the path of the unstoppable march, had to be yanked back into the throng. Apart from the rousing march music that accompanied the spectacle, and the rhythmic stamp of the sentries' boots as in perfect synchronicity they met the ground, awestruck silence prevailed. Just once throughout the performance did I hear a suppressed titter; otherwise, nothing. We were all fascinated. Some of us were fearful. Others were enthralled. I did not trust this clash of martial theatre and sentiment for the dead; it felt intimidatory. Although our anonymous guide batted away the inevitable interrogations on the subject from those like Archie who rejoiced in the contradictory aspects of life in the east, I remember thinking that behind this pious charade was surely the dead hand of Moscow. Respect for the dead was one thing; turning it into a national cause quite another. Of course, that is only my opinion; I do not know all the facts. But together with the nearby Wall, this little event reflected a state of mind that existed all the way from Berlin to Canton.

Midway, we stopped at a coffee house for a break. The coffee house was in a pavilion situated in a garden somewhere near the River Spree. There was very good coffee, cake and beer, all on sale for Western currency and therefore unavailable to the average East Berliner, who, with the exception of beer, potatoes and tinned goods from fraternal socialist states, had much of the time to put up with *ersatz* versions of almost everything. Outside, citizens lay on the grass in the spring sunshine, with mute gratitude timidly enjoying the benevolence of the state. The result was unsettling rather than restful. There was no joy, no noise, and no laughter. It was as if all these citizens, taking a break from work with their families, escaping their mean apartments, had been anaesthetised, their children placed under a spell that prevented the flow of tears or the exercise of their lungs. There was calm but an unnatural one that seemed to speak, silently, of exhaustion. Our guide sat with us but remained inscrutably saturnine. In such circumstances, he could not easily deflect our curiosity and so he made it his business to insinuate into the conversation one or two points that placed the onus for justification onto us. He had learnt English, it transpired, as a prisoner of war in the north of England, an experience he had found demeaning, not least because of the 'imperialist' attitudes of the English; and then, more tellingly, he informed us that a Communist Party member from Great Britain had once denounced him to his own authorities for failing to criticise Trotsky during his commentary. He was shocked, not at the accusation itself, but at the perfidiousness nature of Western democracy. It was no wonder that he cultivated an unapproachable manner – he had a lot to lose.

Whilst we were doing our best to extract from the poor man some crumb of criticism of life in the GDR, there occurred an event of such unbearable poignancy that ever since I have been beset by a terrible shame.

Among those in the party was an Australian man. With his German name – Hermann – and a completely bald skull, he resembled the war criminal of the popular imagination. Indeed, with his baggy shorts, the preoccupied air of the loner and his Australian slang uttered in a still impenetrable German accent, he was for his fellow travellers a rather comic figure. The truth was altogether different, for Herman was a figure of tragedy, a victim of 'ideology'. When, in 1961, the division of Germany came, like the descent of the guillotine blade in the night, Hermann, who had gone west in search of work, found himself on one side of the Wall, the rest of his family on the other. Before he could see her again his wife died, at which point, with little hope of being reunited with his daughter, by now married and with children, he emigrated to Australia. They corresponded, but she could not leave and he was afraid to make a visit that could create difficulties for her and embroil him – so he felt – in a dispute about his nationality. He feared that he might be reclaimed.

As the rest of us took coffee at the pavilion, Hermann, in the twenty minutes at his disposal, discreetly slipped away to the post office that he had located in advance and from where he would despatch a parcel of presents and delicacies for his daughter and grandchildren. Sending a parcel from Australia was useless – it would have been impounded and created problems for her. His mannerisms, together with the accent and language of a Prussian peasant farmer, would go unnoticed in a post office. His flapping shorts may have provoked sniggers among the staff behind the counters – as in all controlled societies, contempt for the foibles of others was commonplace – but he would have been adjudged a bumpkin visiting the big city, metropolitan superciliousness being as much a feature of life in the socialist east as it was in the capitalist west. Yet for all his planning and painstaking efforts, the chances are that it was all for nothing; the Stasi kept a room above most post offices where they could sort mail before it was delivered. His daughter would not even have realised that a parcel had been sent to her.

I had a photograph of Hermann, standing alone in his shorts, staring directly into the camera lens with an expression at once irritated and uncomprehending. Behind him was a summery blue haze, like you might see against the sea on a hot day. Flowers lined the path on both sides. To me, Hermann looked like somebody's grandfather unwillingly towed along on a family holiday, out of place, eager to be at home in his armchair. This photograph was taken in Siberia, above Lake Baikal, many days after we had left Berlin. You see, for most of us Hermann was a figure of fun, but then, only I knew of his escapade in East Berlin. At the time, I saw his gesture merely as romantic bravado – a good story, a minor episode in the game that was the Cold War. To my shame, I completely overlooked the human implications: the dismemberment of a family; the guilt; the regret; the relief at his own good fortune and the longing that must have tormented them all throughout their lives. Is there anything more inhumane than this, unless it is to forcibly remove children from their parents for a misunderstanding or incorrect diagnosis? To divide people in the name of a monstrous ideology is worse than war. It is a form of lifelong mental cruelty. Death is easier to face than the knowledge that you cannot embrace the living. Now, it seems to me that he was a simple man who had been brought up in a world where disruption and catastrophe were part of everyday life. In his lifetime there had been a long, terrible war, followed by the disgrace and ignominy of defeat; then, his devastated country had been pounced on by the Russians and finally, there had been the disintegration of his family. He had become accustomed to deferring to events outside his control, so much so that there appeared to be no outrage in him. And so he had moved on, becoming not quite Australian, no longer entirely German; now old and lonely, in no man's land.

In a day of ironies, the next was at our final stop before lunch, at the Soviet Cemetery, which commemorated 5,000 of the Russian soldiers that died in the capture of Berlin at the end of the Second World War and was dominated by a grotesque statue of a Russian soldier cradling a German child, its virtues extolled straight-faced by our German guide in his theatrical American drawl. If the Germans were grateful to the Red Army in 1945 for helping to bring an end to what the Russians called the Great Patriotic War, their gratitude soon faded with the imposition of the Stalinist form of Communism that bore only a faint resemblance to the better life they had presumed would at last be theirs.

There was one further irony that day; after lunch, another coach unexpectedly arrived to take us for a tour around West Berlin! So we were to leave the *Hauptstadt der DDR* to cross the purple line for a visit to a place that did not exist – WESTBERLIN – before returning that evening to the real world that was East Berlin. Hans, of course, simply disappeared, leaving me a note to say that he would see us the following morning for our transfer to the railway station. Our world was not his to acknowledge.

So we went through the rigmarole of passing through the heavily armoured frontier post at Checkpoint Charlie; the mirrors on trolleys placed beneath our West Berlin coach in search of contraband or escapees, the passports collected with rigorous solemnity. All this to rejoin our fellow capitalists for one last lingering glimpse at the gimcrack vessel we were giving up for a holiday in the east. In fact, the tour of West Berlin was almost as strange as that of its estranged twin, a faintly desperate experience with the guide, in her more exuberant way every bit as sententious as her colleague had been earlier in the day, eager to advertise the miracle of isolated capitalism that was her home. And there was the Wall, following us everywhere, its westernmost face tangible in a way that it was not on the other side. In the west you could run your fingers over it, even at certain points see over it from purpose-built platforms through a telescope, much as you might do at a seaside resort to survey the horizon; only here you saw a maze of barbed wire, tank traps and watch towers and buildings which in places had become part of the wall's fabric and which were still hollow from the final bombardments of the Second World War. Blank windows, from which no-one had gazed for almost half a century, gaped eerily back at us. The Wall haunted West Berlin. It ran a random course across the city, through buildings, across water courses and railway lines. West Berliners, living their lives as best they could in its shadow, affected nonchalance. The effect for visitors was of a city that had resorted to artifice in order to preserve its sanity, and its sense of identity. The description of people leading lives of quiet desperation was as appropriate for West Berlin as it was for its eastern counterpart, except in the east, the struggle to maintain self-respect was an entirely interior matter, as self-expression was a criminal offence. At least westerners had the consolation of being able to voice their opinions, no matter how vile they might be, for the judgement, no matter how critical, of their fellow citizens. This, I thought, is the one precious thing we had that they did not – and which we must never give up.

Now that, apart from a commemorative remnant, and a route of markers embedded in the pavement, this abomination that was the Wall has gone, it is worth retelling its history. On the afternoon of 12 August 1961, the leader of East Germany, Walter Ulbricht, an earnest Stalinist of whom even his fellow Communists said, 'You really get cold just looking at him,' announced the closure of the Berlin checkpoints between the Soviet sector and the sectors run by the Americans, British and French. The following day, at midnight, the construction of barriers began. Then the Brandenburg Gate was closed and, by August 26, it was no longer possible for the citizens of what was now West Berlin to cross into East Berlin. Only in December 1963, more than two years later, was the border reopened to westerners who could then make brief visits to relatives and friends.

What possible reason could there be for this, after a crippling war against a common enemy? In summary, it happened because the alliance between the Western powers and the Soviet Union during the Second World War was a temporary expedient with the single aim of overthrowing the Nazis. It was agreed at the Yalta Conference that as part of the process of reconciliation and 'de-nazification', a defeated Germany would be occupied, according to the military position at the moment of victory, with the aim of the eventual restoration of democracy to a united Germany. The USSR thus occupied the area that was to become East Germany, but it was not long before the relationship between the four occupying powers soured. In an effort to insist on Soviet cooperation, the American, British and French sectors united to create West Germany, which led to the withdrawal of the USSR from the Allied Control Council and the foundation of the German Democratic Republic. The capital, Berlin, parcelled out into sectors under Allied control, found itself encircled. Instead of a single state with a democratically elected government, Germany became two countries, allowing the Soviet Union, in a vengeful and opportunistic act, to advance its influence into the heart of Europe.

Initially, the borders between the two new states remained open, but East Germany haemorrhaged skilled workers, who went west in search of a better life, an exodus which in 1952 led to the virtual sealing of the frontiers – except, because of its peculiar division into four sectors, in Berlin, from where people continued to flood westwards across the barbed wire. Out of a population of seventeen million, more than two and a half million quit East Germany between 1949 and 1961. The Russian solution was not to wonder at the reason for this, but to make it impossible for it to continue by the construction of an insuperable barrier – the Berlin Wall. The crudeness and scale of the plan was Russian; the thoroughness with which it was carried through, German. On Monday, 14 August 1961, local people would have approached the border between the Allied and Russian sectors and found themselves permanently separated from relatives and friends on the other side. They would surely have had to pinch themselves. Even if they had watched uneasily as the political gulf widened between the Allied and Soviet sectors, they could not have believed, just as they were beginning to put a catastrophic war behind them, that a dividing wall would be planted in the middle of their city.

Later, I came across the celebrated photograph of one Conrad Schumann, an East German border guard, who in 1961, only a few days after the construction of the wall, when much of it still consisted of coils of barbed wire, coaxed by waiting onlookers on the western side of the divide, took his chance and leapt to freedom, arms spread wide like a bird balancing in a pocket of air, shouldering his rifle, which he then flung from him before being driven away in a West German police car. Many years later, the wall razed, Germany again one country, he hanged himself in the orchard of his house in the town where he had eventually settled. Perhaps he was built that way, but I would guess that he had never succeeded in shaking off a kind of grief.

And then, returning east after our tour, we breached it one more time, as if we had passed through a mirror into the land of utopia, where dreams of socialist nirvana coexisted with the banalities of stunted lives; where small victories were fought for interminably in the shops and factories; where hopes were nurtured and invariably disappointed. Where sanity was like mercury. Where, somehow, life went on.

Chapter 3

The Moscow Line

When we left Berlin early the next morning, it was, of course, from Ostbahnhof. Hans saw us to the platform, vanishing without ceremony as the Moscow train drew into the station. By now, I had gained the impression that deference to everything Soviet and ambivalence to everything Western more or less was the thread that ran through the administration of the GDR.

We had a long day ahead of us, and a long night to follow. Our carriage was a replica of the one we had travelled in from Hoek van Holland. Only one day had passed and yet it seemed as if we had lived through a page of history! Our duo of carriage attendants was similar to Yuri and Andrei, if a little bulkier. As we pulled out of Ostbahnhof and trundled through the railway yards, all flaking brick, pools of oil and rust, overlooked by rows of identical regiments of flats, one of them handed out the glasses of black tea to us, looked out the windows and with a look of ineffable disgust simply said '*Niemetski*', which, I later discovered, is Russian for 'German'. At that moment it became very clear to me that as we sped eastwards, we were passing back through time towards 1945.

Steam locomotives still in use in Eastern Europe in goods yards.

Then we were in the countryside, finally and firmly behind the purple line, passing trains laden with Russian tanks and sallow-faced commuters, past farms and villages that would have been almost picturesque were it not for the eerie tranquillity that hovered in the fields and around the forlorn churches. In the airless compartments of the neighbouring carriages, filled with migrant Polish workers returning home, there prevailed the pungent smell of eastern cigarettes and, even at that hour, the stale paraffin fumes of cheap vodka. Now that we were safely behind the Iron Curtain, our carriage attendants were more easily persuaded to unlock the carriage doors so that we could wander at will along the corridors. The Poles, in their plaid shirts and newly-purchased jeans, at first looked at us with a mixture of puzzlement and amusement, before one asked with a straight face in English whether we had decided to abandon the iniquitous West for the immeasurable pleasures of the socialist East? After which we were invited in to share their breakfast of greasy cured sausage and oily vodka. For many Americans, entering the communist world was an act of courage. The modern idea of tourism is invariably associated with Americans and yet comparatively few Americans possess passports. For those that did in the early 1980s, their vision of travel was preponderantly one that was characterised by promises of comfort in exotic locations. Sharing a smoke-filled compartment with the enemy was not on the travel agenda. For one thing, neurosis about cigarette smoke was an American invention and smoke exhaled from communist lungs was the worst kind of passive smoking imaginable. Two poisons in one day. What a way to go.

'Well,' they would say resignedly, when there was no easy remedy for some minor irritation, 'I guess we just have to ro-o-o-ll with the punches!', a self-pitying remark with a hint of venom, which seemed, in the circumstances of the lives of those around us, maladroit and insensitive.

The journey from Berlin to the Polish frontier was brief, a matter of an hour or so. We arrived at the border at Frankfurt (Oder).

'Is this the same Frankfurt?'

'No'.

The question exemplified the indifference to the political geography of the world prevalent in some quarters, a trait that I found both exasperating and endearing. It is not as if the USA is entirely unfragmented. There is Hawaii, there is Alaska. Nor did they appreciate that it was one of their former presidents, who thought he understood Stalin, that was instrumental in the disposition of the borders to the east of Berlin.

There are two Frankfurts, but in every respect apart from their shared name – which means 'Frankish town by a ford' – they could not have been more different. 'Poles apart' as the irritating Guppy, who happened to be within earshot, muttered maliciously. Frankfurt-am-Main was the flourishing hub of West German business. Frankfurt (Oder) was a run-down former Hanseatic port, a border town only from the end of the Second World War, when the Oder became the demarcation line between the states of Poland and Germany. Naturally, I knew nothing of this at the time; as far as I was concerned, Germany had always been Germany and Poland always Poland. As I learnt later, the frontiers of Central Europe had constantly shifted over the centuries like ebbing and rising waters. Yet, the territory east of Frankfurt (Oder) for some distance had been historically German – it was only the convenient presence of the River Oder which enabled Stalin to demand of his wartime allies an agreement that would present a portion of eastern Poland to the Soviet Union, whilst Poland, in cynical recompense, would be handed the chunk of Germany east of the Oder. In my ignorance I, too, made no connection between where we were and what had happened only thirty-five years before. We were passing through; there was nothing to see here, nothing to photograph, nothing to remember. We were tourists! Where was the glamour in this anonymous terrain, these rolling fields of green and brown, these dull towns filled with put-upon, defeated people? But the story of these lands is vivid when you think of it and the memory of earlier tumults for the people living in them more vivid still. We had crossed a river, that was all; and just like that the towns where once you would have heard nothing but German in the churches, in the shops, in the schools – at the whim of one man, it all changed, other people, another language. Is that not incredible? Stalin, Uncle Joe Stalin. Everything from now on was the work of Uncle Joe.

The Polish passport and customs control post was at Kunowice, a suburb of the new Polish town, Slubice, that a few decades before had been Dammvorstadt, a district of Frankurt (Oder). Poland in 1981 was at the beginning of a struggle for freedom that would eventually bring down its government, so I rather presumed that everything about Poland would be somehow easier and more welcoming. But border guards and policemen are the same the world over and it was there at a seemingly sleepy frontier post that we lost the first of the group. Well, not at that very place, but effectively, we lost him there. What gave rise to this was his Polish visa, that sacred security device that decides our fitness to enter those countries that demand them, whilst earning said states a bit of useful foreign currency and which, since it had been obtained by the Company from the Polish Embassy before leaving England, I had naturally presumed to be in perfect order. In fact, the one advantage to a visa is precisely that it acts, in theory, as an official *passepartout*, if not an official welcome to the country in question.

The irony of all this was that the person metaphorically dragged off the train was Perkins. This was not his real name but the one given him by Archie, with whom he was compelled to share a room whenever we stayed in hotels, single rooms for tourists being considered a bourgeois luxury and therefore unimaginably expensive. It turned out that Perkins had been a conscientious objector during the Second World War! And in one of those random acts of providence, he had ended up sharing a room with Archie, of all people, who had been a military man in the war and who behaved throughout the journey thus far as if he had unfinished business with it.

Our passports and visas were taken away for inspection. An hour must have passed before the guards returned, accompanied by an English-speaking character in a brown suit and a tie decorated with large olive spots. I could not help but notice that his trousers were flared in the way that had been fashionable at home fifteen years before. He was perfectly courteous in his quiet, steely way but quite resolute in his announcement to me that Perkins was not welcome in his country and that in the circumstances he would have to travel under armed guard as far as Warsaw, where we were all to disembark and remain until a flight home could be arranged for him. He assured us that we would be on our way to Moscow the following morning. There was no gainsaying this arrangement. Naturally, as notional leader, I argued his case, for, as we were merely in transit across Poland, it was hard to imagine what possible mischief he could do. Whatever I said made no difference, just as it would not had I remonstrated with a British immigration official. There was alarm among the participants but far less than had this happened in the GDR, for Poland was not considered to be in the same league of dark and terrible.

We continued at breakneck speed across the Polish flatlands, the carriages swaying with the sustained effort. As the wheels clattered across the points; as we clung to any available purchase in the corridor; as the interval between click and clack became shorter and shorter; as the engine roared during rare moments of deceleration, it was hard to suppress unworthy thoughts about the quality of maintenance. An American in the party, who had in a former life worked on the railways, assured me that the rails and the system in general were all in fine condition. The railways behind the Wall

View from the train of a Polish farm, where for all the vaunted achievements of socialism, the old ways prevailed.

were among the few enterprises that had retained a Revolutionary sense of purpose. In the west, the train was part of a nostalgic yearning for the age of elegant travel. In the east, it was synonymous with a momentous period of change and patriotic fervour, when it was a workhorse for the distribution of labour and the dissemination of revolutionary ideals. Trains, there, were sacred carriers of arms and men. Because they had some sort of strategic value in the battle against western imperialism – no doubt unfounded in the nuclear age – they worked. Of course this became clear to me, like so many things on this journey, only once we had entered the holiest of holies, the USSR.

Perkins sat in a compartment whilst the guards stood chatting in the corridor. I sat with him, Archie having abandoned him as if he were the carrier of a brand of peacenik contagion. He told me that he was at a loss to understand why it was that he, of all people, had been singled out for disqualification, not from setting foot on Polish territory but even from merely using it as a kind of bridge; all the more so as he had been in his youth a full member of the British Communist Party, refusing conscription because of his belief that the communist movement stood for brotherhood and peaceful cooperation. Even then, at the time of our journey, he ran a bookshop that specialised in socialist literature in some provincial south-eastern English town, through which, I deduced, he must have made a good living if was able to afford to take the train to Hong Kong. Like each of those in that party who stood out for one reason or another, I recollect quite clearly his baby face and his threadbare curtain of long, thin silvery hair. I remember, too, the unaccountable ambivalence I felt towards this quietly-spoken, well-mannered man, whose convictions at a time when the patriotic tide would have been overwhelming, would have required significant reserves of moral courage; still greater reserves were required to withstand the scorn of the likes of Archie, who was not a man of subtle opinions. I think now that my ambivalence arose from an unease at the conflation of moral conscience with a political belief that was so evidently founded on violent suppression of dissent. In Perkins, behind the reasonable, humble façade, there lurked a coldness that, in the name of peace, would through deliberate inaction have abetted in murder. In the end, I was torn between admiration and suspicion, which in a way is the dilemma of daily life. One ends up making choices based on impossible and frequently errant judgements. I never did find out why Perkins was considered so objectionable by the Polish authorities but as the years have passed, and as I have discovered more about the chaos and duplicity in eastern Europe that marked the years between 1917 and 1945, I have come to understand how it could be that a sympathiser to a cause as dogmatic as Soviet communism could also be considered a dupe and a traitor. Odd, but there it is.

The journey across Poland to Warsaw took all day. In some ways, what we saw was a perfect reflection of the Polish dilemma. Through one window we might have looked out onto roads filled with Mercedes-Benz cars, bought with foreign currency earned by Poles working abroad; and through the other onto fields where

View from the train – old-fashioned horse power in contrast with the electrified railway system.

horses and carts worked the fields in what looked like a vision of Arcadian bliss were it not for scarlet banners draped across walls with the word '*SOLIDARNOSC*' or the slogan 'FOR OUR FREEDOM … AND YOURS' emblazoned across them in dazzling counterpoint to the flat, drab landscape and the broad, grey sky, to the domes and spires of Catholic churches prominent in every village and town drifting by. The train hardly rested but on one of the rare occasions that with a great roar it slowed, wheezing and gasping in the purlieus of some industrial dystopia or other, I found that I was staring through the window at the image of a dwarf stencilled onto a splintered concrete post. For a few moments the vision did not register, so that I almost thought that it was just the happenstance of a few smudges, much as a conjunction of clouds might remind you of a map of Europe or of a swan in flight. As we lingered it started to take shape, turning into the crude outline of an elfin figure beneath a floppy, Noddy hat, and then I realised that the depiction was indeed the work of man, intending quite deliberately to obliterate traces of print, of which I could just read the single word 'Stalin', that echoed the policies of the much-despised Polish government. Given the country's wretched circumstances at the time, when the clash between a growing protest movement and its orthodox enemies risked turmoil, the light hearted nature of this palimpsest astonished me. And then I thought, well, in the circumstances that is a pretty brave act to spray a cartoon character over a stern government proclamation. And then I wondered: what inspired this character and how in what was effectively a police state did its creator find the time and materials to make the stencil, and why? Because I presumed that graffiti, as a form of self-expression, would have been considered an anti-revolutionary act, which, to boot, despoiled the People's property. So why bother? Why take the risk, when the Solidarity movement itself risked bringing upon it the wrath not only of its own government, but the implacable wrath of the USSR? At least the Solidarity supporters formed a united mass movement, whose numbers offered a certain amount of protection. This solitary stencilled figure appeared to be the act of a lone joker, out of sympathy with everything around him.

Then, each time the train dawdled at the outskirts of a town, so that the blurred world outside the carriage window separated into crystals of visible detail, I began to see these stencilled dwarves everywhere, on fences, gates, station walls, the flanks of blocks of flats; and I realised that this was not the suicidal eccentricity of a single person but the symbol of a piece of comedic subversion, the silent, mocking commentator that undermined state pomposity. There, an officious pronouncement ignored by all, on top, a childish, sketchy figure that by its presence mischievously pointed out its absurdity. Years later, when Poland finally found peace, I learnt something of the philosophy of the man that started this movement. He said, 'Can you treat a police officer seriously, when he is asking you: "Why did you participate in an illegal meeting of dwarfs?"'

Our fellow travellers among the Poles did not, I noticed, have much to say to us about events in Poland. Mostly they looked out in mournful contemplation of the country as we sped through it. From the way they talked among themselves, I could see that differences of opinion would surface from time to time, to subside gently away to nothing almost as soon as they had arisen. Change was desired by most, but revolt was not for everyone.

While the sun was sinking, the train finally pulled into a nondescript suburban Warsaw station. As we descended wearily onto the platform in the evening chill, the presence of a handful of shifty-looking characters was obvious and we – or those of us with unnaturally colossal suitcases – stood out very clearly as pampered foreigners. Most of the pallid, nervous-looking individuals hovering about the platform looked at us from the corner of their eyes out of curiosity and perhaps a little hostility; but the gaze of others fell addictively onto our bags and their imagined delights within, which would have sold well on the black market. Elsewhere in communist Europe foreigners were almost completely immune to petty crime – it was one of the benefits of holidaying in police states – but in Poland, the entrepreneurial spirit had never been successfully extinguished. That was a great comfort, even if it demanded a little extra vigilance.

We were met by a pair of serious looking security officers, like their colleague at the border dressed in suits that might well have been designed and stitched in a local version of Carnaby Street. With a shrug of the shoulders and surprisingly little in the way of visible regret, Perkins left us in their company as they escorted him into a waiting car that would take him to the airport. I rather think he sympathised with their point of view, sensing that in some abstruse way he had failed to keep to the Party line. I know that he returned safely to England as the Company soon after received a request from him for a refund of the unused portion of the journey, a cheeky request that was politely rejected.

The rest of us were looked after by a representative of the state tourist agency, who escorted us to our hotel, which, like the Palast in Berlin (East), had been built in partnership with a Western company and boasted the same plastic sophistication. With the assurance that we would be on a fast train to Moscow the following day, on the whole everyone's spirits were high, even elated at the thought of seeing something of the Polish capital and postponing arrival at Moscow, the prospect of which, I would say, terrified and attracted in equal measure. In the meantime, we were given dinner. After a day like that, with Perkins banished and the country-wide unease we had witnessed from the moment we had left Berlin, who would have thought that a cup of coffee could provoke a row? Everyone there knew, the whole world knew, that fresh, aromatic coffee was a luxury outside the experience of any Soviet ally's citizens. Its absence was, to Western eyes, at least in some quarters, a touchstone of the Communist failure. I innocently presumed that the universally acknowledged hardships endured at the time by the Poles would have commanded a degree of empathy among those, like us, who after a few weeks of minor discomforts and inconveniences would return to our comfortable existences in the West. Empathy was surely the least that should have been expected of us. Instead, one among us, when asked to pay in US dollars for the second cup of coffee he had requested, erupted in a torrent of furious indignation. 'Where I come from, coffee is a courtesy,' he shouted. 'We do NOT pay for coffee! And, anyway, why can't I use your lousy Polack currency?' The pale, tearful waitress rushed out of the room; after a minute there entered the restaurant manager, who, with admirable dignity, calmly poured the man his second cup, gave a jack-knife of a bow and left, refusing payment from any of us. I can see it now, the red plastic seating, the embroidered table cloths, the fierce lighting, the desire and the expectation to be regarded as equals. And there we were, passing through, comfortable, put to a little trouble; whilst outside the millions were waiting patiently for when they, too, could sit in hotel restaurants and demand a second cup of coffee.

The contrast between the careworn world outside the hotel walls and the cosy world inside them was an unnatural one. A conventional tower block of the type found in any western city, it conveyed an illusion of cosmopolitanism, until you looked across the road to the Stalinist Palace of Culture & Science. A 'gift' from Stalin in 1952, a massive, gloomy, tower in grey stone that tapered to a spire, it was the tallest building in Poland. Its architecture was supposed to reflect the ideological tropes of Marxism; to most it would seem more accurately to conform to the ideology of a megalomaniac. It was accurately described on its completion as 'a drunk confectioner's nightmare' and among local people was universally despised. To see the two buildings together as neighbours – a modernistic international hotel and a Russian fortress – neatly summed up the Polish predicament. As for our hotel, the State, by pandering to what it thought was Western taste, tried to make fools of us. Some fell for it. Above all, and most insidious, was the perturbation that crept up on a few from the moment that we arrived in East Berlin. At first, the soldiers and police and general air of danger was thrillingly picaresque. As we penetrated deeper into Axis World, and looked across the tired landscapes, the grubbiness and despair and pretence and, above all, the pointlessness of it all, gnawed away at the nervous system. One of the more highly-strung travellers among us had worked himself into a state of such trembling agitation at the 'abduction' of Perkins and the sight at the borders of 'all those guns' that I feared for his sanity and at dinner he had drunk himself into a neurotic stupor. I wondered how he would deal with Russia.

Of all the peoples I encountered on that journey, the Poles seemed most careless of expressing their bitterness. There was a latent effervescence in their character at odds with the popular conception of the Slavs as lumpen, dark and brooding. Had they conformed to our hackneyed assumptions, it would not have been surprising, for the Poles, you see, were among the most unfortunate of peoples, stranded like leaves in a vortex set spinning and spinning by their powerful neighbours. They had 'rolled with the punches' for centuries. Yet their inherent optimism that all would eventually be well permitted a generous and thoughtful attitude to the past. They no longer aspired to the return of their ancient frontiers, which had for long been pushed back or extended at the whims of others and which, in any case, were always uncertain and temporary. Their only demand was for their national identity and to this they clung with a quiet but determined pride. There was a certain old-fashioned swagger in their demeanour, a touch of the dashing officer dancing a fast *mazurka*.

Before setting out on this journey, I had only the sketchiest conception of the country. It was the same old story – Poland was just a name and a set of vague clichés that I could easily have carried around with me all my life. In part, that ignorance was a reflection of the constantly shifting borderlands of central Europe, as well as an inevitable hint of jingoism. But it was still ignorance. I discovered that for some 200 years from 1573, Poland, together with Lithuania, had been at the heart of a Commonwealth, within which was implicit a faint notion of early democracy. Geographically, it had encompassed an area of over four hundred thousand square miles and ruled over a population of some eleven million, of many races and creeds. Most tellingly, given the *Solidarność* movement, the banners of which we had seen all day from the train, it differed significantly from all of its neighbours of the era; built into the commonwealth constitution there was a check on monarchical power, summed up as 'The King reigns and does not govern'. As is the way of these things, under the pressure of internal bickering and threats from its neighbours, all of whom were profoundly suspicious of any tendency that might undermine the absolute power of the monarch, it collapsed and disappeared completely, but not before, in 1791, in an attempt to save itself from oblivion, it had formed the first codified constitution in modern European history. How ironic that Poland should henceforth find itself almost continuously at the beck and call of others. It was too late, because within five years of the ratification of this constitution, Poland was a country no more, its freshly minted vision of the future dissolved by its neighbours, who, used to relying on Polish feebleness, regarded this renaissance as a threat to their hegemony. By 1795, Russia, Prussia and Austria had dismembered the Polish state. Poor Poland! Not that the Polish state was itself without some of the disagreeable prejudices that were features of the age – perhaps it would be better to say 'poor Polish peoples'. Yet in 1918, after the First World War, it regained its liberty, becoming an independent state once again, only for Uncle Joe to ride to the rescue of the oppressed and steal it for himself as a little compensation for Soviet lives lost in the battle against Fascism.

Poland is not just a land of emigrants. It has a history and culture that is but poorly celebrated in popular history. Although its period of greatness extended into the modern era, for most of the centuries that followed the commonwealth's demise, Poland's fate lay with others, in particular first with Tsarist Russia and finally the USSR.

That evening, after dinner, I went to the bar. Again I experienced the sensation of leaving one world and entering another, stepping from the anodyne semi-sophistication of the hotel lobby into the home of the totalitarian mob. The best thing about the hotel was its bar, a sleazy honey pot for local gangsters and hookers and for dealers and riff-raff from the obscurer fringes of the political world. This was where the spirit of enterprise, denied its normal manifestations, was cornered into a back-room bazaar. This was the city market-place trading in nocturnal essentials, dense with a fug of yellow cigarette smoke laced with the combustible fumes of vodka, abuzz with the murmur of conspiracy. Men with moustaches and black eyes, in ill-fitting, strangely coloured suits, sat hunched earnestly on the edges of black leather chairs, their women beside them blonde and beautiful and silent. Arms dealers and spies, envoys from the remoter corners of the Soviet empire, tense and watchful. As I came to learn, this was the Soviet universe writ small. When, at midnight, the door was flung open to reveal, inexplicably, a kilted Scotsman in bearskin and full military regalia who, cradling his pipes, stood squarely on the threshold to bellow out some ballad or other – very loudly – there were no smiles or quizzical brows; nobody there had the capacity for surprise or pleasure, or, if they had, none dared reveal it. Instead, uncouth faces registered mild irritation at the interruption, nothing more. Once the piper had withdrawn back into the outer world, the absorbing business of racketeering resumed, heedless and insensible.

Our hotel bar might have been gloriously sleazy, but it was a library-like retreat for quiet reflection compared to the other foreign owned hotel in town, the Inter-Continental. The barman whispered to me, 'Have you heard? About the assassination attempt?' He was speaking of Abu Daoud, the terrorist behind the massacre at the Munich Olympic Games of 1972, who liked to stay at the Victoria when in town and who had five bullets pumped into him in its lobby.

Perry was a rarity – a member of the party younger than thirty. An aficionado of low-life, he spent the evening with me in the bar and as closing time approached – this was the kind of bar you felt would never close – found himself in conversation with an attractive young woman, who agreed, at Perry's insistence, to take us to another bar that she knew to be open. A sprint by taxi in the usual unnecessarily enthusiastic manner through dim, deserted streets and across the river brought us to an empty room in the Praga district on the banks of the Vistula. My head, filled with vodka, took in little except the worn red velveteen fabric on the bar stools. Then, as the end approached, Perry snapped back his head in horror from nuzzling the girl's neck.

'Pay for it! You must be joking.'

She turned to me. 'You know, don't you … nobody does anything here except for money?'

To some extent this was true, as denial made people uncharacteristically avaricious. She was not a hooker so much as an opportunist – ordinary events became transactions. It was just normal; it was how you lived. So it was that Abu Daoud could mastermind mass murder in the name of anti-Zionism; and in Warsaw he could spend his days in the western-inspired luxury of the Victoria Intercontinental.

In the morning we walked around the Old Town. The heart of the Old Town was the Old Town Market Place, an ancient square with, on all sides above the glistening cobbles, high terraces of handsome townhouses, elegantly proportioned, subtly ornate, decorated in warm shades of russet, violet and red. The upper floors had been built with

Lenin rules, even in Warsaw, just as the Solidarity movement was taking flight.

a Renaissance sense of space and light; below them what I took to be medieval arched doorways accorded to each house a settled, solid aspect. The picture thus was one of permanence and continuity. Except almost every building we saw here, and everywhere throughout the Old Town, and indeed throughout the entire city, was pretty well brand new. Not a pastiche or an imitation but a loving reconstruction.

Here there was beer and ice cream. There was always ice cream in the Soviet east – efficient train services and ice cream and circuses. Were it not for the absence of shops and of hubbub and clamour of visitors and residents alike; were it not for a certain hush – not the deadened hush of East Berlin but a wariness that was almost conspiratorial – it could almost have been a square in any venerable central European town. Although the pause in joy and laughter was the sign of the times in Poland, the Poles of Warsaw had their glowingly beautiful town to cherish, possible only by a miracle of determination that grew out of anger and sorrow. For, by the end of 1944, except in spirit and in documents and in ruins, Warsaw was not there. It was essentially a street plan. In what was one of the most atrocious examples of deliberate demolition, through a pointless act of calculated revenge, one of the great European capital cities had been reduced to rubble, a stinking, fetid, slaughterhouse. As one of the residents said, emerging from the carnage when the ceasefire came, 'Not a single intact building as far as the eye could see.'

Let me summarise what happened, if only because this tragedy sometimes is overshadowed by all the many other tragedies of the time. By July 1944, it seemed clear that the Nazis were beaten. Confronted by Uncle Joe's apparently uncontainable Red Army, they appeared resigned to abandoning Warsaw and retreating westwards. Then, at the insistence of Hitler, by now clinically insane, they counter-attacked. The Polish Resistance Army in Warsaw, which had been waiting for years for the opportunity, had to make a choice; rise up then and there, counting on the imminent arrival of Soviet and Allied aid, or hold back until the rapidly approaching Soviet forces were within the city precincts. This was a dilemma. Long experience had taught the Poles to fear the Russians, who, as everyone suspected, concealed motives unconfined to the defeat of the Nazis. The Poles feared that if they hesitated, the Russians would conveniently accuse them of consorting with the Fascists. There was something to be said, therefore, for ensuring that the Poles placed themselves in the strongest possible position before the Russians arrived. On the other hand, the Nazi forces were far too powerful for an ill-equipped underground army, no matter how courageous, to defeat.

On 1 August 1944, the uprising went ahead anyway. As the Nazi reaction was initially slow, the Poles had some success. Within a few days everything changed. Instead of the Wehrmacht, who were engaged elsewhere in trying to repel the Russian advance, charge of the revolt's suppression was handed to Himmler's SS. Irregulars consisting of criminals and simpletons from the Ukraine and Azerbaijan who knew no better were drafted to perform untold acts of wanton cruelty. Hitler had for a long time wanted to be rid of Warsaw, which he regarded as a barrier to German influence to the east, so, when the insurgents occupied much of residential Warsaw and it became clear that hand to hand fighting was inevitable, the order came to level the city and kill every occupant. To set an example!

The spree began on 5 August. On that day alone, at least 8,000 – possibly many, many more – were murdered. The massacre went on throughout August and into September. The Allies – Britain, the USA, and expatriate Poles – made some mostly futile attempts to drop supplies, hampered by Uncle Joe's refusal to allow their planes to land on Soviet soil. Eventually, when the ceasefire came, the pitiful groups of citizens that remained emerged from the cellars, where they had hidden in unspeakable conditions, and filed out from among the ruins. As they left, Nazi soldiers marched in the other direction and razed anything that was left of the city. It was a thorough job, the slow, methodical equivalent to the work of an atom bomb.

The Red Army divisions, meanwhile, remained on the east bank of the Vistula, an artillery shell's flight from the mayhem. In the first days of the uprising they were too preoccupied with fighting the Nazis to have come to the rescue of the stricken Poles, as they, too, had not reckoned on the strength of the counter attack. When finally they were in a position to help, they did nothing. Instead of making their way into Warsaw, they simply halted. The conclusion reached by all but the Soviets themselves is that in order to enter Warsaw as saviours, they preferred to await the insurgents' defeat; for then, with the offices of the NKVD, forerunner to the KGB, they would be perfectly placed to ensure that the next Polish government would not be, as the majority of Poles desired, in the style of a Western democracy but would rather be effectively controlled from Moscow. Of course, one can speculate endlessly on such matters. But I would say that crucial hesitation on the Vistula is in keeping with what I came to know of Russia. What the Nazis did was genocidal. What the Russians failed to do was despicable.

The greatest miracle of all is that Warsaw was rebuilt. By the end of the war, with 85 per cent of it destroyed, it was quite literally a field of dust. In putting together a plan for the city's reconstruction after 1945, it was decided to rebuild the Old Town more or less exactly as it had been, a decision that must have taken some doing in the circumstances, and possibly the only genuinely popular one made by the Moscow-run Polish Government. By 1953, the project had been completed (the Royal Palace, being antithetical to everything that communism stood for, was completed after much debate only in the 1970s) to the point where a returning pre-war resident would have found everything familiar. Meticulous though the reconstruction was, using as sources aerial photographs, surviving architectural plans and even eighteenth century paintings by Canaletto's nephew Bellotto, and the result was wonderful, the Old Town, surrounded by streets of Socialist Realism, in 1981 was a brilliant gem in a tin setting.

It was odd but at the time none of this seemed to make much impression on us. Perhaps we were distracted by the edginess that seemed to have insinuated itself into our guide's commentary. The Solidarity movement, even at an early stage, brought hope to many who, for fear it would shrivel to nothing, dared not discuss it. Instead, we were led off the square to a small room to watch a film, which told the story of the Warsaw Uprising as the Soviet propaganda machine wished it to be interpreted. Notwithstanding protestations from some among us, we were not obliged to attend; it was perfectly possible, as some did, to instead bolster the ailing Polish economy by exploring the neighbouring streets to barter with the latest generation of beleaguered Varsovians for stamp collections featuring the head of Adolf Hitler.

Poland, like all communist countries, was ingrained with the smell of poverty – not the stink of ordure that could overpower in a slum, but a rankness that came with poor diet, boredom and oppression. The reek of cheap disinfectant emanated from doorways like a miasma, as if the elimination of bacteria was the answer to all humanity's problems. In Warsaw, only the churches, rich with the musky perfume of incense, offered a sanctuary. All the churches were busy. Our presence in them was an intrusion, because these buildings were more than sacred – they were refuges, often convenient cover for Solidarity meetings. Worshippers looked at us with scarcely concealed annoyance. We did not consider ourselves as tourists but in the eyes of those on their knees we were voyeurs.

That afternoon we were back on the train, again in the Soviet womb that was our accustomed single green sleeper carriage with its high roof, amid the pale blue livery of a long line of Polish State Railways rolling stock. By now we regarded our compartments as a dog regards its old basket, with its comforting smells and familiar form but on this occasion we had to fight for it. A snake of determined pickpockets, no doubt forewarned of the presence of a group of westerners, by definition wealthy, weaved their way among us as we struggled chaotically to embark. There was a lot of pushing, followed by a gravelly growl from one in the party of, 'Watch out! the bastards are after your wallets!' after which the gang, unprepared for the reserves of self-preservation innate to elderly Americans, emerged, dazed and bruised, jumped to the ground and made swiftly off through the crowds. Our new carriage attendants proceeded, with studied nonchalance, to sell us tea.

It was to be a long afternoon, followed by a long night. The train ran underground the length of the city to emerge at the Vistula and as we crossed its wide expanse, we could see the handsome old town of Warsaw, reaching down to the riverside in a cluster of coloured stately baroque. Then we gathered momentum and sped headlong eastwards across the plains, towards Russia. Our attendants were in a jovial mood and the nearer we came to the frontier, the happier they became. Both, like the others we had known over the previous few days, were big men, with the bulk, brawn more than fat, apparently typical of the Russian physique. Neither spoke a word of conversational English but were able to express their opinion of the Poles.

'You know hi-fi? In Poland they make,' one said to me scornfully. 'They think they are Japan!'

Out of the blue, with a fresh flower plucked from the vase in his cabin and planted between his teeth, lightly, with almost balletic agility, he skipped along the corridor, singing in an exuberant basso profondo:

Crossing the Vistula and departing Warsaw, Stalin's gift to the nation towering over the city centre.

'Istanbul was Constantinople
Now it's Istanbul, not Constantinople
Been a long time gone, Constantinople
Now it's Turkish delight on a moonlit night
So take me back to Constantinople
No, you can't go back to Constantinople
Been a long time gone, Constantinople
Why did Constantinople get the works?
That's nobody's business but the Turks!'

which, once it dawned on us exactly what we were witnessing, drew extravagant applause and presented me with my first insight into the quixotic nature of the Russian character.

According to the mythology of the time, all Soviet border crossings occurred under cover of darkness. Untrue, in fact, but true in our case. Our arrival at Terespol, on the Polish side of the frontier, coincided with the fading of the afternoon light. Through the window, we saw low wooden fences and neat little houses, the very picture of provincial life at the furthest reaches of eastern Europe. The pace of life there was slow, the pace of a postman's bicycle. I can say that there was a kind of flat charm about the place, which was reflected in the desultory examination of our passports by the Polish border guards, who afterwards stood chatting on the platform in the twilight, with the collars of their greatcoats high against the chill, before shouldering their rifles and ambling home. Only later, when I came to read more about this zone of shifting frontiers, did I come across this account by a local resident of her fate during the Second World War:

'In 1941, as the German Army made its way eastwards into Russia, the Gestapo arrested several women in Terespol, from where they were transported to Ravensbruck Concentration Camp. The survivors made statements before war crimes tribunals in 1946:

"At that time [1941] Mrs. Kiryłowa arrived from Terespol, having already been interrogated. In Terespol she was beaten for an entire week from morning until night, with breaks. She was a large person. She was terribly beaten, her beaten flesh began to fall off, the pus literally ran off her body in streams, the entire cell was filled with the stench of decomposing flesh. No one dressed the wounds. I took Mrs. K. to the toilet and I washed her wounds there under the shower. It was hard for the woman to get up from the bed, but it was good she went there [to the toilet], because the Gestapo officer would come into the cell and beat her with a stick where she was wounded. It was terrible torture for her to get up out of bed, and she would lie there the whole time bracing herself on her elbows and knees. Under these conditions, people would usually die from blood poisoning. Divine Providence watched over them, and it was probably thanks to this that she managed to make it to Lublin alive with such wounds.

"The woman who made the statement was to be the subject of medical experiments at Ravensbruck, involving the deliberate introduction of bacteria into wounds and the removal of bone and muscle tissue.

"In February 1943, I was taken to have an operation; experimental operations had begun in July 1942 – in most cases, it was minors who were taken. The *Aufseherka* took me to the *rewir*, where I was given a shot and immediately lost consciousness. I was taken on a cart. When I regained consciousness, I felt a terrible pain in my legs, and I couldn't move them. For a few days I had a fever of over 40° C. But the physical suffering was nothing compared to knowing that I was serving as the subject for experiments of my enemies. When we asked the doctor what kind of sentence ours was that they were torturing us so, we were told that we were bandits. We told them, 'We are only Poles.' Six other women with me had also been subject to the same kind of operation. I was in the bone operation group. My leg remained the same on the outside, except the scars from the stitches. Even now I react very strongly to changes in the weather. I tire easily, I can't walk for long periods, and I itch where the stitches were. I get a shock through my whole body if touched [there].

"Some of the women had operations done on their muscles. They cut out a piece of the muscle from their thighs or calves. Then there were septic operations on their muscles; they cultivated bacteria on undressed wounds.

This made the muscle decompose. Some were so crippled that they do not have calves anymore, their legs are completely deformed. There were also septic operations on bones. As a result, often even after the wounds healed, the person would get a fever and pieces of the bone would come away with the pus, as if the bone were rotting away. Very many people had operations five times in the same place, at 8-day intervals."'

It occurred to me, when I read this for the first time, that as I was standing in the corridor of our carriage awaiting the crossing into Russia, looking up at the faint fall of the first few flakes of evening snow, that poor woman perhaps still lived in Terespol. Or, if she no longer did, there were remnants of her family still there, and if not that then her life, for which she had suffered diabolical tortures, perhaps went entirely unrecollected. And the greatest tragedy, in a way, was that even at the moment of her agony, and that of numberless others, Stalin, dear old Uncle Joe, was plotting how to partition her country as war reparation and in doing so would, with the help of allies more scrupulous than he, wrap these inoffensive towns of Poland and all of Eastern Europe in a black winding sheet that would not be removed for almost fifty years. And now, expectant and apprehensive, we were approaching the frontier with the Union of Soviet Socialist Republics in squalls of snow.

The short journey across the frontier into the Byelorussian Soviet Socialist Republic was a drawn out and peculiarly mysterious affair. The train was by now cloaked in darkness unpricked by not even a glimmer of light. Even in this natural blackout the attendants felt duty bound to close the blinds and shield the motherland from our prying eyes. The Russians, despite their revolution, I was learning, were an obedient, paranoid people. The train rumbled and bumped along at a speed as near to walking pace as several tons of metal could manage, our slow progress punctuated by sudden checks and halts, which, even at that ponderous pace, meant that we lurched across our cabins, shedding cupsful of Polish vodka.

Just before the bridge over the River Bug, the train ground for several minutes to a complete stop. We dared to peep out from behind the blinds. What we saw was both familiar and quite startling; giant silhouettes of Soviet soldiers loomed headlong out of the dark from a blazing red horizon, charging towards us, rifle and bayonet at the ready, in an attitude of square-jawed aggression. I was reminded of childhood war comics – 'Take that, Fritz or Ivan or Tommy'. There was something so utterly, obnoxiously, fatuous about this pastiche of fervour, that I would have laughed were it not for an overwhelming sensation that was not fear precisely – because I knew that there was nothing to fear – but akin to the obscure unease that one feels in the presence of someone wearing a mask, or at behaviour that is not threatening in itself but which is obsessive or out of place. Here, I thought, at the border between two supposed allies locked together in an admittedly cold embrace, was a strange place for a display of belligerent propaganda. Considering where we were, it was surely superfluous! The message imparted was not 'welcome to the home of revolution' but 'keep out of it!' This theatricality, I was to discover, lay dormant at the heart of every stolid Russian. Russia, in its wintry, fickle way was every bit as fabulous as India, say, or distant Cathay.

We remained at rest before the bridge, awaiting the call. Flakes of snow, white as goosedown, drifted down from out of the black sky. Soon, tapping and scraping noises sounded from the roof, or from beneath the floor, echoing through the superstructure of the carriage. Men in blue overalls, bristling with torches and immense spanners, marched along the corridors from carriage to carriage, slamming the heavy doors behind them. One would enter our compartment, offer a peremptory good evening in Russian and wave his torch into the luggage stow above the doorway, before repeating the same manoeuvre next door and all along the carriage. We sat, intrigued. So far, everything was just at it should be.

Borders, with all their theatricality, are funny places and none stranger than this one. There is a presumption of rightness about a border. A river, for example, seems to represent the naturalness of boundaries. But a river can also be a convenience, an excuse for arbitrary redistribution of whole populations – east of the Bug is ours, west of the Bug is yours. The overnight journey ahead was to take us across what had for centuries been part of Poland. Individuals uprooted, families dismembered, scattered across the farthest reaches of the Soviet empire. As always, in the name of the people.

Finally, the train trundled hesitantly across the bridge. The flunkies in overalls were supplanted by a higher authority, a military man in uniform and a wide-brimmed cap, who drifted along the corridor, pausing at each doorway to scan the compartment's inmates with the supercilious eye of one who is untouchable. When the fancy took him, he would reach out for a passport, peruse it briefly and hand it back with a faint and knowing smile.

We drew up, at last, alongside the platform at Brest railway station. The clocks went forward two hours to Moscow time, as we were catapulted backwards to a different age. Every connection with what we knew had now been severed. We had entered a fortress, the drawbridge pulled up with a firm clang behind us.

All of this detail of the paraphernalia of entry into the USSR made a profound impression on me – even now, I see the blue eyes and the callow, earnest faces of the youthful guards in army uniform who streamed onto the train to collect all the passports – because of the resources that this vast and unwieldy country poured into the business of security. Nobody in their right mind dreamed of entering the USSR illegally, unless they were traitors to the country of their birth. In that place, the frontier between two allies, was manifest the great paradox; betterment of mankind had to be imposed on the unwilling majority because unless it came as a dictum from Vladimir Ilyich Lenin, we did not know what was good for us.

Framed in the doorway of our compartments, these lads in their spotless uniforms and highly polished black boots, torn between treating us with courtesy as guests and with disdain and suspicion as foreigners, opened our passports, then regarded us unflinchingly out of virginal eyes above wide, rosy cheeks. They were like farmers at their first country dance, hair combed, best suit donned, but awkward in manner, and merciless. With elaborate courtesy we were invited to stand in the corridor whilst a search was made of the compartment. I was asked back into the compartment and told to unpack. Books, magazines and maps were regarded with deep suspicion – it would have been easier to have imported a machine gun than a good map – and when I placed a map on the bunk, a map of the Soviet Union that had been hanging around the office in London, it was seized on with satisfaction until I pointed to a small line of Cyrillic script in one corner, which translated as 'Printed in the USSR', enough to elicit an approving nod. Able, now, to look at it with impunity he unfolded the tatty sheet and misty eyed simply said, *'Moshny. Sovetsky Soyuz moshchnym.'*

They left, and there was nothing but nocturnal silence. I watched the snow fall onto the platform. Then, the calm, the calm of order and procedure and bureaucracy at work, was shattered by a line from a Hollywood film.

'They've taken our boys, they've taken our boys!' screeched Slim, a stocky American veteran of the war in Vietnam. He had the pugnacious build of an ageing boxer and, clutching a tin of beer as if it were a grenade, he ran from carriage to carriage, screaming the same refrain. It transpired that one of the party had eluded our attendants and stepped out for a little exploration before the officials had given their permission, with the result that he had been escorted to the waiting room until the formalities were completed. Guppy was unnaturally tall, with a saturnine countenance and a habit of faux generosity at table that took the form of insisting that others take the last mouthful, whilst eyeing it greedily for himself. His cussedness was in the quiet English style and he was thus a natural ally to Slim, according to whom only dupes believed that Guppy was sitting in the waiting room – rather, the poor sap had been abducted by the KGB and was even now undergoing interrogation. Had I ordered Slim at that moment to undertake a commando rescue mission I believe he would have given a spring-loaded salute, bellowed, 'Yessir!' and dived through the window into the darkness.

Yes, that frontier was a curiosity. The darkness deepened its faintly sinister aspect, of course, and then there was our fatigue. Tension is tiring; ideology, given free reign, is a terrifying tool. At this border it was expressed in a long series of intimidating procedures punctuated by even longer periods of muffled silence. It gave rise to a kind of restlessness that infected even our stolid attendants, who seated in their own compartment drinking tea, wordlessly imparted to us a sense of unease that was an unhappy blend of patriotic pride and impatience with the whole business. They reminded me of school children apprehensive before their teacher. We knew that the border performance was a farrago; for all the detailed scrutiny given our visas (each consisting of three pages of print, our portrait photograph and various stamps and signatures issued by the Soviet Embassy in London), the inspector had missed the amendment I had been forced to make with a black ballpoint pen and whitener to one where the number on the visa and passport did not tally. Though we understood this was theatre, repeated endlessly for the many passengers passing that frontier every day, yet we were beset by a certain anxiety, which simply grew out of nothing and which we could not suppress. That is the Russian way.

Anyway, it so happened that one couple – I forget which one – was asked to leave the train with their luggage for customs inspection and according to the logic that prevailed in the USSR – one guilty, all guilty – it followed that everyone else in the party had to do the same. Certainly it was tiresome to have to take down all the cases and trudge with them through the snow to the customs room, but the inspection was nothing. Even I could see that it was just routine, at worst the consequence of some minor spat between East and West, with our group of hapless tourists at the very farthest end of a diminishing series of diplomatic ripples. It was of little comfort to those who preferred to wallow in their prejudices to hear from me that we could easily be put to the same inconvenience at home and with far worse consequences; our own dear excise officers are truly sincere in their zeal and quite as likely to be driven by some peculiar strain of ideological rectitude. On the other hand, the Russians who sorted through our belongings at Brest with an almost tender deliberation (for fear of accusations of casual vandalism), holding up the occasional item questioningly, nodding with shy smiles at the explanation, were probably merely curious. Once in a while a magazine or book would be discovered that was considered anti-Soviet or counter-revolutionary. With expressions of helpless regret, and a hint of disapproval, it would be removed and exchanged for a receipt that entitled the owner to reclaim the offending article on departure from the USSR, always assuming that it would be by train on the same route. In that capacious station there must have been somewhere a room overflowing and piled high with harmless pieces of literature, yellowing away or providing reading practise for local students of foreign language.

As we returned to our compartments, I was ambushed. An Austrian woman in the party, with the brittle beauty of the ageing aristocrat, invited me with glacial courtesy into her compartment, where she sat beside her silent, but no less chilly husband. It was obvious that both were brimming with indignation. She did not ask me to sit. You must remember that I was young; my hair was rather long and I was dressed in jeans and a casual shirt. But I was presentable.

Her full name was something akin to Princess Karolina zu Holstein-Linz-Sankt Veit an der Glan. A fine title! That she was a woman of impeccable pedigree was made manifest to me through the traditional method of polite, lofty disdain. In her flawless, porcelain English she accused me of being a liability because of the way I was dressed. Had I been more presentable, then she, in her pearls and neat wool suit, would not have had her world, neatly folded in her suitcase, unwrapped under the eyes of a low Communist. My jeans and open-necked shirt were not the petty bonuses that came with freedom but the cause of all our woes, not only of this party of tourists, but of the degenerating Western world. Now that I am older, my tailoring has not changed so much and yet the world still turns. What she despised in me was my lack of deference, not to the Russians, but to her version of civilisation.

'You are English, are you not?' she asked, as the interview drew to a close.

'Up to a point.'

'I see. In Austria we have magnificent cured sausage. We make it in our *schloss.*' Then, condescending to my English lack of sophistication, 'I will send you some for you to try.'

As it turned out, her attitude towards me was a struggle for dignity in the face of tragedy. Much later in the journey, as we sat stupefied before the immense Siberian landscape, in a moment of frankness she confessed in passing – there was something of the unwilling confessor in her speech – that her daughter had committed suicide. Her husband said nothing but looked sadly out through the stained window at the great forest, slipping by. I offered muttered words of condolence – frankly, what does one say in such circumstances – but I knew even then that I had failed to find the right expression to satisfy her sense of the correct form. I felt it; the right words, the right clothes, that code that some live by, I could not break it. As she sat in a Soviet train, powdered, vulnerable and intransigent, east and west and past and present seemed to collide in an incoherent heap of uncertainty and recrimination.

The train then moved away from the station into the shed, where the ceremony of changing the bogies took place, the gauge of the Soviet empire's railway tracks being wider than those of almost everywhere else in continental Europe. It is a small point but an interesting reflection of the Russian outlook on the world when you realise that the difference in gauge dates back to well before the era of Stalin. Then again, it is also true that there was no accepted standard gauge at the time; anyway, those that remained on the train throughout the procedure told me after that the scene inside the shed was like a Socialist Realism painting, all men in overalls wielding hammers and spanners, while the technique of changing the wheels by jacking up the carriage and then using a crane to hoist and replace each set of wheels, seemed to have been directly inspired by Heath Robinson.

I, meanwhile, was escorted from the train before it left for the shed. A representative from Intourist, the state travel agency, had introduced himself and invited me to accompany him into the station building. He had the same fledgling earnestness as the soldiers I had seen earlier, the same smooth cheeks and ethereal blue eyes. I followed him into the cavernous waiting room which reminded me of a church with its arches, its high ceilings and metal chandeliers and its rows of empty wooden pews. He sat me down and told me no more about his country than I already knew, which was little enough, with a touching confidence in its unique achievements, but at the end his parting words, before leaving me to exchange sterling for roubles with the solitary bank teller, a woman of extreme taciturnity, were uttered with extraordinary urgency. 'Please tell your people that in the Soviet Union we value peace. Please remember.' There was in this young man – how can I put this – a goodness that was arresting. It seemed to come from another age. He could have been a medieval priest, or some kind of seer.

There was plenty of time before the newly shod train returned to the platform and he pointed me to the bare, malodorous stairs that led to the Intourist office, where in stifling heat I found two women watching television. One, older, plumper and guarded, and with no English, sat behind an empty desk and was clearly in charge. The younger of the two, at a signal from her senior, brought me a glass of tea and we sat and watched what turned out to be a Polish programme. The girl, who spoke impeccable English in that warm, sweet Russian tone, which always reminds me of melted brown sugar mixed with cream (have you ever listened to a Russian women's choir?), told me with a perfectly straight face and without the slightest trace of irony, that Polish was much better than Soviet television. The ambition to produce hi-fis was contemptible but at least their television was watchable. She had perched on the arm of the ancient chair where I was seated, quite absorbed in the programme, whilst her matronly boss looked on with what I took to be disapproval, either of the programme we were watching or of the peculiar intimacy of the situation. Any remark made in my presence – in Russian or English – was addressed first to the boss, who seemed to perform the duty of a chaperone, dictating proprieties. I was struck, even at that early stage in my acquaintance with the Soviet Union, by the great Russian contradiction between patriotic pride and the desire to escape its stultifying embrace.

This girl, whose name was Natasha – yes, I know, but it is a common name in Russia – was exquisite. I had never seen beauty quite like hers. It was the sort you want to touch but dare not for fear less of causing offence exactly than of breaking a spell. Her dress, with its ruched smock top, complemented her balletic figure, whilst her auburn hair was coiled in a pile above a face of solemn, child-like frankness. If I say to you that she exuded a purity that was akin to love itself you will think me comically infatuated and possibly unhinged, but that was how it seemed to me at that moment. No doubt it says something about me more than it does her but at that time, in that warm run-down office, in the borderlands, I felt I could have stayed for ever.

Soon, with the sound of a loud whistle signalling the return of the train, Natasha escorted me down to the dark platform, which, even with a handful of uniformed men standing guard alongside the carriages under the lightly falling snow, was dead quiet. I remember the sulphurous smell of coal that fired the samovars and the Soviet hammer and sickle on the carriages and the bold red star on the locomotive and that, in an impulse, I turned to give Natasha a kiss, at which she gripped me hard by the arm with an expression of mute alarm and an urgent shake of the head. It was true; I was carried away by some idiotic notion, naively unaware of the consequences. Looking up, I caught a glimpse of her boss staring down at us from the office window above. Friendship and peaceful coexistence with westerners were strictly political abstractions.

Everyone was asleep and all the compartment doors closed. Before I could join them, there was one other duty to perform. The train now had gained a Russian restaurant car; after the packed evening meal provided by the hotel in Warsaw, everyone would be looking forward to a good breakfast when they awoke. I walked along the train and once at the restaurant car banged on its armour-like flanks to rouse the staff. At first no amount of shouting and slapping the door with the flat of my hand had any effect. Persistence eventually led to the unlocking of the door, around which appeared an irascible, tousled head.

'*Shto?*' it demanded, with the kind of glare that Clint Eastwood would have been proud of.

'*Dobra vecer. Ya anglichana. Y mna gruppa.*' I explained in very basic Russian that we were foreigners. Thereupon, the ice thawed a little; more so when it became evident that I was responsible for a '*gruppa*', a word that in the USSR had a certain magic attached to it. With that I was ushered with crude decorum to the restaurant chief's table, covered in spiked receipts and, inevitably and charmingly, a fresh flower in a vase. A glass of vodka was placed before each of us. Even in the dowdy surroundings of a restaurant car at midnight, it was important to observe certain formalities.

The most important item in a Soviet restaurant car was the abacus. In the USSR, which competed with the USA for the title of superpower, the abacus remained standard issue. As decisions were made, the restaurant chief would lunge at it and rattle the beads hither and thither at a fabulous speed, before committing the relevant figures to paper.

Deciding on the menu for breakfast was not simple – it was not a discussion but a negotiation. Negotiations were necessary because in the USSR simple matters were not allowed to be straightforward. Decisions that in the west were made without hesitation could not here be allowed to pass without a preamble. The banality of everyday existence in Russia partly accounted for this – to whip up a drama out of nothing made life more interesting. Decisions were always made by somebody further up the hierarchy; even the menu, in the tradition of the Soviet economic plan, appeared to have been designed by a committee. So whilst, on a given day, it might be possible to have a dish which included fried eggs, fried eggs on their own would be out of the question. Sometimes, I realised, there were other motives at work; the quixotic attitude of the restaurant chiefs or their relationship with the black market. The ultimate aim was to manoeuvre us into eating as much as possible, for all Westerners were rouble-millionaires. What the average Russian did not know, of course, was that the exchange rate between the rouble and so-called 'convertible' currencies was artificially fixed in favour of the rouble, so that eating a basic breakfast could be alarmingly expensive.

We sat facing each other across the table and, in the traditions of Cold War negotiations down the years, strove for a compromise. The Russian restaurant chiefs that I met over the weeks that followed maintained a peasant's view of the world. Although they probably could have quoted tracts of Pushkin's poetry and argued cogently on behalf of Karl Marx, when it came to money they resorted to cunning. Thus, caviar might be mentioned in passing, or, between doomed attempts by the government to curb alcohol consumption by forbidding its sale on trains, vodka or Soviet '*shampanska*'. A little vodka and caviar at the start of the Soviet day would have suited me and, I suspected, several members of the '*gruppa*'; for the others, adapting to the Russian way of life could go only so far.

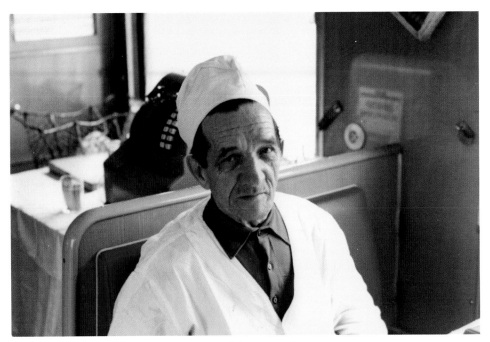

The restaurant car administrator, master of all he surveyed.

Language posed a significant obstacle to progress. The restaurant chief could certainly speak no English and I no Russian. The menu, not unreasonably, was in Russian and written in Cyrillic script. It was well past midnight: we had both consumed more alcohol than was consistent with concise thought. Although we were by now getting on very well, our relationship was one of mutual incomprehension. Slowly, almost by accident, we stumbled towards a solution. I knew the Russian for tea ('*chai*'), so that was easy enough. Coffee turned out to be a similar word in Russian ('*koffye*') and so, surprisingly, did jam ('*gem*'). With jam, it was clear we wanted bread and butter. There remained only the matter of eggs. My imagination failed me. All I could do was to flap my arms and make farmyard noises. The chief laughed, and gave a nod of recognition.

'*Da, da. Nye probliema, kharashow*' and he wrote it down, both of us sure now that we had understood each other perfectly. At breakfast, in addition to the eggs, we were each presented with justifiable pride by a vast plate of chicken, tinned peas and mashed potatoes.

Business concluded, there was more vodka. The other staff members joined us. There we sat, raising our glasses to Churchill and Lenin and chucking down the national liquor as the train rollicked through the night. As the bottle emptied I thought to myself that I rather liked these people. We are all just human beings after all! What is all this Cold War stuff, anyway? For as long as there was a language barrier and the peace-pipe that was vodka, all would be well.

A Soviet Railways steam loco driver regarding us with frank curiosity.

We slept as best we could - the five-foot gauge of the tracks made the train pitch like a boat – and awoke to grey skies and a steady sleeting drizzle that left the landscape smeared with smudges of blackening snow. The morning brought the first glimpse of the immensity of Russia. A view from a train is both precise and imprecise. It is a moving television image in the frame of the compartment window, an insight, at once intimate and distant, that drifts by to be replaced by another image or another perspective. Beneath grey skies, against unbroken rolling green plains, neglected churches, their brickwork exposed in patches beneath their plaster skins, battered in sleeting winds, disintegrated on forlorn hillocks. Just occasionally, a gilded cupola gleamed brassily through sheens of damp. Trains of tanks and guns trundled by with relentless regularity, guards in long grey coats and Cossack hats adorned with a red star, rifle in hand, framed in the wagons' open doors. I felt as if we were travelling away from a battlefront; the railway line hummed with mobilisation across a bedraggled country, as if put to waste by a retreating invader. Yet, there was something affecting in the scale of it all that was stubbornly magnificent.

We had to acquire a sailor's gait as we made our way along the corridors to the dining car. For some, it was all too much – an obese member of the party, having squeezed breathlessly along the corridors and wedged herself into a place at a table in the restaurant car, lunged for the flower vase, snatched at the flowers, and retched horribly into it, before going on to consume the massive breakfast that I had inadvertently ordered.

Soldiers everywhere, ever ready to deal with counter-revolutionary activity.

After trying the awful coffee, we sipped tea, mesmerised by Russia. When I saw an enormous obelisk rise up from out of the fields, the dining-car manager, who, partially obscured by his abacus, had been seated at the table that was his desk and office in silent contemplation of our every gesture, approached us and pointing towards it said 'Borodino … Napoleon,' before taking up a knife and drawing it meaningfully across his throat. We all have a notion of history; those scraps and dates and facts that provide us with a sketchy chronology of where we have come from and how it is that have arrived where we are. In some countries – at least, then – the past is also the present. For this man, there was no doubt. For him, Napoleon's retreat, which effectively began at Borodino in 1812, happened only the preceding day, as we were waiting at the border at Brest. The repulse of the Germans in the Second World War took place – for him – but a few hours before. These were the achievements that sustained him. We were all invaders, you see. Yet the original obelisk, dedicated in the presence of Tsar Nicholas I in July 1839, was destroyed by Uncle Joe in 1932, for who knows what motive. The Cathedral of Christ the Saviour in Moscow, built to commemorate the victory over Napoleon and where the *1812 Overture* by Tchaikovsky, itself a celebration of that victory, was first performed, was similarly demolished to make way for the Palace of the Soviets, which was never built of course, and instead became an open-air swimming pool. Now, I understand that one of the first things to happen when, finally, the Party lost its grip on power was the reconstruction of the cathedral. After sixty years or more of hell and millions of

A view from the train between Brest and Moscow, a stubborn survivor from before the Revolution on the skyline.

ruined lives, memories of what has been lost resurface in a determination to reclaim what was taken, from the people, in the name of the people.

Then, in the late morning, the countryside changed. The endless green horizon had contracted to woods of unexpected sweetness, of birch and of fir. Suburban stations – little more than single platforms of crumbling, low-grade concrete – began to appear, one after the other, with knots of passengers standing still and impassive, with monumental patience. These were not the unhappy, tired faces of Warsaw, or the fearful, cussed faces of East Berlin. On these faces there was inscribed strength and pride and they drifted by, inanimate, as the train trundled through the outer Moscow suburbs of identical concrete tower blocks amid groves of thin woodland threaded by networks of muddy paths.

And, finally, there was the embattled skyline of Moscow itself; we clattered through vast goods yards into a giant gothic citadel, with its seven goblin towers silhouetted against the sky, before coming to rest at the terminal that served the western regions, Byelorusskaia. Nothing could ever quite match the thrill of emerging from a train, as if from a subterranean passage, into the heart of the capital of all the Russias.

I have dwelt rather a lot on that first entry into Russia, but it was really only when we all left the train, and stood wearily on a Moscow platform surrounded by our suitcases, that we understood the foreignness of our situation. Even now, I cannot quite define what it was about Russia that imparted to us the quality of separateness, but even at that moment of arrival in a railway station at the periphery of the city, whereas I had been haunted by Berlin, and uneasy in Warsaw, I did not experience the same sense of dread in Moscow. In fact, it seemed rather homely. Slowly it came to me; everyone around us was completely indifferent to our presence, as if in conferring upon us the privilege of entry no further formalities were required. We stood shivering in the morning sunshine uncertain what to do next until after, what seemed a long time, an elderly porter shambled towards us, pursued by a woman in her late twenties dressed in a shapeless skirt, a thick down coat and a fur hat. Her cheeks were like pouches filled with walnuts – a European complexion stretched across Asiatic bones. Much to the disgust of some in our party, she welcomed us with a wide and natural smile and her name, Svieta. The porter wordlessly started to pile our luggage onto a two-wheeled upright barrow that was quite inadequate to the task and from which one case would fall as another was added until somehow he made them all stay on, lashed then together and wheeled them away. It is futile to expound the details of what we were taken to see those days in Moscow. The Kremlin, of course, with its officious policemen swinging their truncheons with careful nonchalance and blowing their whistles at transgressions of decorum (stepping off the pavement was one, I remember); Red Square; the Tretyakov Gallery; St. Basil's Cathedral with its coloured domes, as if made of marzipan and coloured sugar; the usual stuff. Well, I cannot deny that it was all, in its peculiarly toy-town way, impressive. In fact, were it not for the imitation American limousines

Lenin, Marx and Engels warmly welcome you to the USSR.

conveying who knows which universally unelected representative of the people that would occasionally thunder out across the cobbles from one of the massive fairy-tale gates, at which point the world came to a standstill in its honour, it was standard tourist fare. But it was the detail that made an impression on me. In particular, I remember, that first afternoon, the red stars that glittered on the points of the Kremlin towers. Even as symbols of Soviet power, they were rather beautiful, ruby red with seams of gold, turning in the breeze. And at night they glowed as if within each there was a blazing furnace. Stalin's work, of course. They replaced the imperial two-headed eagles that for decades before had reared up like hydra over the city. They are illuminated from within by incandescent lamps and refractors consisting of prismatic glass plates provide a uniform distribution of light; each lamp generates so much heat that each tower has two ventilators. In replacing the original stars, which were of copper adorned with a hammer and sickle studded with semi-precious stones and constructed in 1935, with glass stars in 1946, the challenge was how to allow them to retain their ruby-red hue in daylight, when red glass illuminated from the outside appears to be almost black. These challenges were met by the power and genius of the state, which, unfortunately, simultaneously fell short of perfection in other spheres; most notably in preventing the death of untold numbers of Soviet citizens by starvation, the result of Uncle Joe's misguided agricultural policies. There are people, even now, who refuse to believe that the same state that produced those glittering stars in the name of Socialism was, to be indulgent, capable of such tragic

Wintry Red Square, with Kremlin ruby star atop one of the Kremlin towers.

incompetence. I have no way of verifying it. Yet I believe it to be true because of what I came to understood Russia to be.

Each day we were collected from the hotel in a bus that can be thought of as 'design free'. It had the characteristic of many facets of Soviet life; that is to say, the thought process seemed to go along the lines of, 'Well, we need coaches to herd the proletariat from home to work and back and sometimes for transportation for it when on holidays of an improving nature in fraternal Socialist countries; and also for foreign tourists, who quite naturally will travel in large groups. And so, we had better find an engine and sling a body with seats on it, oh and a place for a microphone.' And so they did, the result being a charabanc best described as lumpen, with the added attraction of a heating system that seemed to be connected directly to the exhaust.

Our hotel was the most modern in the city. Standing on the ironically named Prospect Mira, or Peace Boulevard, in the inner suburbs, the journey along it from the city centre provided an opportunity to understand one of the most telling differences between Moscow and most other major cities – the almost complete absence of advertising. A single giant hoarding stood proud at the summit of a tall apartment block, emblazoned across it the name of the national airline 'Aeroflot', a superfluous reminder given that there was no other airline available and that, anyway, travel opportunities for the average Russian were, shall we say, somewhat limited. Again, one could not but wonder how it was that that lone item of publicity contrived

Moscow skyline, with St Basil's (left), the Kremlin walls, and Goblin Tower on the horizon.

to be there. What branch of what committee made it its business to come up with the project? Which factory produced it? A factory specialising in what exactly?

What was most remarkable about our hotel was not its vastness, nor the design, which was of its time, but the fact that it seemed to run itself. Apart from when we checked in, forming a long line to present our passports, which were confiscated for the duration of our stay much to the consternation of the nervous and the sceptical among us, we saw not a single administrative member of staff. The hotel was a creation of wish fulfilment, where a tape recorder had been left on to play the same variation on a traditional Russian tune, over and over again, as if this would satisfy all the bourgeois requirements of foreign guests. In fact, we were guests only in the most notional sense. There was a production line for food. There were several bars where the choice of alcohol was determined not by the laws of supply and demand but by the law of Soviet supply, so that beer and good dry Moldavian *shampanska* were invariably unobtainable, or obtainable like smugglers booty only in brief furtive unexplained spasms. Soviet citizens were forbidden entry to the hotel, unless they happened to be wreathed in perfume, or were local gangsters, who, after a whispered negotiation with the doorman, would slip swiftly through the only unbolted door in the entire building. On each floor, we emerged from the lift to be confronted by the *dzurnaya*, a formidable woman charged with keeping a weather eye on our comings and goings. These burly women took their work very seriously; when Archie pointed out to one of them that the emergency exits were all padlocked, she retorted, 'Please, don't worry. If there is a fire, I know where to find the key,' before adding, 'and by the way, if it should happen at night, please be sure to wake me.'

This was our hotel in Moscow, a kind of ersatz luxury created for we soft westerners and our filthy foreign money; an island of padded compromise at the heart of the revolution. It was a horrible place, artificial and suburban, exclusive in the direst possible way. Only a couple of the bars, dark, filled with smoke, which silently and perversely repelled foreigners, filled as they were with Russian men and their molls, were of interest to me, if not to the others in the party, who feared the primeval Russian nature that lurked there.

Whilst I don't believe there was anyone travelling with me that was anything more than curious about Soviet life, there were others in the world at large convinced that Western criticism of the USSR was so much malicious propaganda. It so happened that during our stay a party flew into Moscow that included a Famous Playwright, a man of the Left, and his family. Although passage through Moscow airport was a very long and nerve-wracking business, when finally they reached the hotel late in the evening, they were requested to go directly to the restaurant for dinner. Taken in by the hotel's plastic glamour, and objecting to being part of a herd, they instead went to their rooms to relax before entering the restaurant at their own pace. By the time they arrived, it was no longer possible, given the way the tables had been set, for them to sit together and so they simply sat at another table expecting that the staff would serve them there. But they had not bargained for Soviet methods. The

Rocket – Monument to the Conquerors of Space. Prospect Mira below and the Ostankino Tower beyond.

waiters simply ignored them, leaving their food at the tables where they should have taken their places. When everyone else had eaten, the staff left, turning out the lights behind them. Somehow it fell to me to explain to them that they would be hungry that night. They digested this news only with great difficulty, utterly confounded by the facts of Soviet life.

And yet, in front of the hotel was a monument of ethereal beauty. Some creations have a grace and suggestiveness that is immediate and this was one. The Monument to the Conquerors of Space seemed to me to encapsulate everything that was perverse and marvellous in Soviet Russia – the dreamer, the fantasist, the escapist, the potentate, the scientist and the artist all combined in a titanium-clad rocket powering almost vertically heavenwards on a sheaf of metallic exhaust plumes. There was in this reaching for the stars a balletic grace and delicacy that was astonishing – when the sun went down, its rays caught the silvery rocket's tail and it burned, burnished and brilliant.

At first I saw nothing but another Soviet extravagance. Yet the more I saw of the Russians, the more I saw in them a profound devotion to the numinous. It seemed to me that the rocket was an Icon, beyond mortality. That, I thought, explained the casual brutality of Russian life, a misplaced asceticism in its disregard for human suffering.

What amused me though, were the rocket's predecessors, which stood on the far side of the road in front of the hotel, beyond a garden threaded by avenues lined with unkempt bushes and lopsided benches. Here, on a gigantic pedestal, had been erected a different kind of icon. Here was a monstrous version in three dimensions of the cut-out soldiers at the border, some eighty feet high, 'socialist realism' at its most grotesquely bombastic. Now, the soldiers had mutated into the perfect Soviet worker and ideal peasant woman, their weapons, the hammer and sickle, held aloft like flaming torches, marching in purposeful harmony towards the hitherto elusive utopia. Even this was imbued not with the spirit of joy of the downtrodden freed from servitude, but with that martial fervour so beloved of Uncle Joe. In the short time I had spent in the USSR, taking shape around me was an ironclad dreadnought bristling with cannon. Everything spoke of Power, which, whether political, electrical or military, seemed to me to have become an end in itself. This spectacular, triumphalist piece of plastic demagoguery, the Worker and Kolkhoz Woman, had crowned first the Soviet pavilion at the *Exposition Internationale des Arts et Techniques dans la Vie Moderne* of 1937 in Paris, when the world was still in thrall to the Soviet achievement – remember the starving millions on the collectivised farms across the country – before being placed here as a symbol of the victory of the common man.

This pair of model citizens were the guardians of the Exhibition of Economic Achievements. As it turned out, I came to love this place. Not, as one might imagine because the name was a contradiction in terms, given that for all its aspirations, all

The Exhibition of Economic Achievements, at once fanciful and touchingly optimistic.

its successes in war, in space, in political jiggery-pokery, and, we were told, in the science of optometry, the USSR could never claim any substantive success in the field of economics. Naturally, when Svieta's announcement of the visit came it elicited a chorus of groans from Archie, Guppy and Co, accompanied by guffaws of disbelief from all but a few, above all the French contingent, who in that spirit of generosity towards our hosts that can so easily be mistaken for a Gallic caprice, jeered at the 'Anglo-Saxons' for their shopkeeperish ways. I must admit that I didn't relish the prospect of what sounded like an afternoon of unabashed propaganda, but once we passed beneath the grand portals and entered the precincts of an enormous park (the former domain, it goes without saying, of a noble family), I was enchanted.

A grandiose title, and a very optimistic one; 'The Exhibition of Economic Achievements'. How to describe this place of wonders? Well, it was like a film set; superficial, insubstantial, vacuous – anything you like, but as an exhibition not much of an achievement. Most of the pavilions were closed and, as we walked along the wide boulevards, asking now and then if we might have a look inside one or two of the more intriguing examples, Svieta, in a matter-of fact way that brooked no argument, with a disarming smile, would explain in her flawless English that they were under repair. They were, I was sure, under everlasting repair. Only the space pavilion, that area of technology in which the USSR indisputably excelled, was open, enough to impress those among us interested in such things, or to silence briefly those who said that the Russians could not organise the proverbial piss-up … but overall, the whole enterprise became just another of Stalin's overweening, self-defeating projects. I mean, if I were running a country like the USSR in the 1930s, in the aftermath of a violent revolution, in a world in turmoil, given the impossibility of a fruitful realisation of a scientific utopia, I, too, might be tempted to concentrate my energies in the meretricious – the *panem et circenses* technique, though, in the case of the USSR of that era, all too often without the panem. But this was a project too far. It was approved in 1935 as, irony of ironies, the All-Union Agricultural Exhibition, just as the great collectivised farms across the country were turning out not to be as fruitful as Stalin had envisaged. The architect, one Vyacheslav Oltarzhevsky, who had the temerity to raise his head above the parapet by virtue of his profession, was immediately implicated in one or other of the Great Purges of the era, but escaping execution – unlike many of his colleagues, including the Commissar for Agriculture, who was shot in 1938, quickly followed by his daughter, no doubt for the counter-revolutionary, and scientifically based, crime of being a blood relation – was instead sent to the new town of Vorkuta, to become its architect. This place of profoundly long, numbing winters and fleeting, broiling summers, lies just inside the Arctic Circle, and owes its origins to the seams of coal on which it sits, which in turn led it to becoming one of the most infamous among Gulag forced-labour camps and eventually a kind of administrative centre for the entire Gulag system west of the Urals. The Exhibition was a monstrous ghost of big ideas and tragic failures.

Nonetheless, notwithstanding its condition of forlorn abandonment, of a failed idea one does not like to admit to, I liked it. The pavilions, each dedicated to a Soviet Socialist Republic, or an arm of industry, were, in the simplicity of their ideological aims, in their theatrical construction, rather beautiful. One might say they displayed a naïve charm when you consider that the Soviet system betrayed its sentimental and overwhelmingly Russian roots in wanting to celebrate the traditions of the multitude of nationalities that comprised the USSR, whilst simultaneously undermining everything that they stood for by eliminating their cultures and histories in daily life, preserving them only in the form of dance and costumes for vaudeville consumption. But more than that, what I liked was the sense of calm that prevailed, for it was a place of recreation, where Russians could console themselves for what was missing in their lives with the display of Soviet if not greatness, then at least of ambition. It was here that I saw for the first time the egregious Soviet capacity for bourgeois self-satisfaction, for in this park there was manifest a wholesome and to most Western eyes surprising, contentment. The families that strolled here in what was left of the snow, children swaddled in dense winter clothes and by the infinite attentions of doting mothers, reeked of pride. I understood this; the flesh had dried on the bones but while the skeleton remained, respects were to be paid in the mausoleum. We had only to look on the enormous fountains that lay in our path, still waterless at the very beginning of the Moscow spring, the gilt on their sculpted sheaves of corn beginning to peel through winter and neglect, for in their Soviet rococo way, they were impressive as props in a kind of fantasy-land. At the very least, even while wondering if the money might not have been better spent elsewhere, one could almost admire the effort that had gone into them.

Not every citizen was lost in admiration. A young man passed close by; then, observing my foreignness, looked about him with quick, furtive glances before swerving to approach me to speak of football – which has never interested me – in order, he told me, to practise his English. As we parted with a shake of hands he left in my palm a creased slip of lined paper with a telephone number scrawled across it in pencil. Then, at the approach of Svieta, who had released the others to wander the exhibition at will, he vanished. He recognised authority when he saw it; but her expression suggested less disapproval than concern and although I told her of his interest in football, she, without reference to hooliganism or any other of the various labels beloved of Soviet propaganda, merely counselled caution. He could have been anything – a black marketeer, gay, agent provocateur, dissident, or just desperate to discuss Liverpool's or Tottenham Hotspur's defensive formations. I would never know. Later, when I tried to call the number from my room, someone answered in Russian and on hearing a foreign language put down the phone immediately with what I took to be a curse.

But what I really liked about the Exhibition was the opportunity it gave me to talk directly to Svieta. A kind of intimacy with her was one of my few privileges in my role as 'group leader', for we were allies united against a common foe, she and

I – the intemperate tourist, forever quibbling with her every statement, or quizzing her about the fate of Gypsies and Solzhenitsyn, although not then of homosexuality, yet to become a subject raised in ordinary conversation. Naturally, I was curious, too, about the alleged iniquities perpetrated by the Soviet state, but it hardly seemed fair to interrogate her on matters over which she had no influence. In fact, if what her inquisitors said was true, then their endless prodding and poking and baiting were tantamount to bullying, for in a country where expression of personal opinion could be considered not merely counter-revolutionary but *lèse-majesté*, how could someone in her vulnerable position have been expected to compromise her job or her family through frankness? She could not be frank! And who could tell what suffering her parents, or grandparents might have endured when Uncle Joe was in charge? If she had thoughts that were in any way seditious, she did not admit to them, not even when I came to know her better over the following days. I admired her dignity. As far as I could see, there was no trace in her of envy or bitterness; her profound sense of patriotism – which, by the way, I discovered was an ubiquitous Russian characteristic – tempered any misgivings she might have had about her condition. Why, she had even been to London and Paris! She was glad of the experience, she told me, but it was as if the visits had been the realisation of a dream from which she had happily awoken to find herself in her motherland. She spoke of these places without wistfulness. They were like verses of poetry that she treasured. She had seen the birthplaces of Shakespeare and Balzac; she had been acquainted with the great world and it sufficed. The gulf in worldliness between Russia and Poland or East Germany was vast – in Russia, there was no sense of victimhood, only pride and disdain and occasional pessimism. I must admit that surprised me. I had not foreseen that. I had expected a more cowed people and what I found was stony-faced belligerence.

We walked the Exhibition grounds, Svieta and I. Although it was April, the cold bit as the afternoon darkened. The dying sunlight glanced briefly across the peeling gilt of a disused church. Svieta had just married, she explained, and now had to part from her husband in order to look after us for the next week as we headed east to Siberia, leaving her young children from her first marriage, to an alcoholic, in the care of her mother, who lived in a flat in the outer reaches of the city. She seemed to be philosophical about her life; in fact, she seemed to be happy. What was most striking about her in a way was her ordinariness. Why I should have expected anything more I do not know. She was clever, well-educated, had unlike most of her fellow citizens travelled to the Western world. But she laughed with us, was curious about us as individuals, if not about our politics or our money. There was a kind of enthusiasm, a sort of contentment that I could have found less easily in an English suburb. Except, of course, this was Russia. To the eye, and to the pre-programmed mind it was all a mess, this Russia, a nightmare of crumbling concrete, uniformity, brutishness, arrogance, extravagant, monolithic ideas and pettiness. Yet who was to say that this was not Utopia, that in this iron stronghold lay a kind of perfection? Or at least happiness of a kind and even the illusion of fulfilment?

One by one, as the evening snow began to fall, the others drifted to our rendezvous at one of the fountains. The more diffident used the opportunity to ask polite questions about this and that, while tiptoeing around what really bothered them, nodding without demurral at what they would later describe as 'Svieta's orthodox answers'; for a few, the wait for us all to congregate was an opportunity to air opinions with embarrassing bumptiousness, to openly accuse Svieta of lying and, in fact, to gang up on her like the more obnoxious children in a school playground. She smiled bravely throughout the interrogation, promising to discuss openly anything and everything as we made our way across the country on the train to Irkutsk. For all her composure and her skill in batting away in a language not her own the tacit abuse directed at her, I could see that she found this exhausting, even though she told me in due course that it was her duty to deal as best she could with such scenes; that it was natural for Westerners to be curious about Soviet life and that they were entitled to their opinions. When she said this to me, I resisted the temptation to point out that in this respect she was less privileged than we were and was glad to have done so when she added, with the merest trace of self-pity, that it was a shame that some people could not see that she was a human being just as they were; and that she dreaded the Trans-Siberian because once on the train she would be subjected for days at a time to a relentless inquisition from which there was no escape. 'Unless I defect,' she added with endearing irony.

That evening, after a copious, meaty dinner, when the others had either gone to bed or retired to the foreign-currency bar, with its high prices for imported beer and the juvenile atmosphere of a student-union common-room, Svieta suggested that we return to the Exhibition grounds; for, she said with a conspiratorial smile, a fresh fall of snow could mean some kind of entertainment taking place there.

The darkness, once we left the hotel precincts and passed beyond the space monument, gleaming faintly in the hotel's reflection, was absolute. At the exhibition gates was gathered a knot of people, from which came the sound of whispered talk and low laughter. One or two had bottles concealed under their coats. We joined them; soon the gate opened and we slipped inside to behold a sight that took me completely by surprise, a sight so utterly Russian but so completely un-Soviet, that I remember almost laughing at the wonder of it. There, among the snow-laden trees in the wooded fringe of the park, tossing their beautiful heads and snorting streams of warm breath in the frozen air was a troika of small grey horses, with red socks about their lower legs, tassels and ribbons about their studded harnesses, the middle one haloed with an intricately decorated raised collar. Behind them, a Russian sledge, like a perambulator on skis, with a man in a fur hat hunched over his bunched reins.

A queue formed, and the two at its head climbed wordlessly aboard behind the driver, covered their knees in a thick rug and then, with a movement of the whip, the troika slid away with a rasp like an intake of breath and disappeared into the night. We heard eruptions of laughter and a shout of joy, and saw their faces taut with cold and excitement when a few minutes later, vodka bottle in hand, they tumbled stiffly out and wandered unsteadily away. Soon it was our turn. We placed some roubles into a waiting hand. The freezing air scoured our cheeks, the hooves thudded firmly into the snow-packed earth and we scudded among the trees at what seemed like an enormous speed, the pony at the centre trotting hard like a racer, the two others at its flanks keeping company at a gentle canter. As we rounded the first tree into the woodland, we found the way illuminated by flaming torches planted at intervals beside the track – I noticed the icicles on the branches above them glistening in their light. The ride seemed to go on and on and I would have been delighted had it done so for, with the cold, the odour from the sweating horses, the silent driver and the swerving, gliding and skidding motion of the sledge among the birch and fir, the gales of laughter from Svieta, I have never known exhilaration quite like it.

It is a banal image but to me it seemed like a fairy tale. Whose were the horses and where did they keep them? Where did that sledge come from? But that was the USSR; from behind the stolid front, an eruption of exuberance, a sentimental love of the old ways, an equally sentimental vision of the present, all the trappings of a dream. This I began to learn was how Russia was, how the Soviet Union was – for, notwithstanding all the official protestations that this was not the case, the USSR was not really, except in the most amorphous way, the sum of its vast and far-flung republics, but was Russia and Russia alone.

Then there was Slavyansky Bazaar. Isn't that a name to conjure with? A collision between primeval, tribal Russia and the more savvy exoticism of the Orient. So you might imagine, were we not in Soviet Moscow. This particular Bazaar was – and probably remains – a restaurant, located in a side street in the city centre not far from Red Square. You have to remember that in Moscow, then the capital of a great empire that stretched from the frontier with Poland in the west to the Pacific in the east and from the Arctic Ocean in the north to the Black Sea in the south, there were approximately five restaurants that were even notionally worthy of the name. And each of these was run by the state. Of these I remember one, Kitai, was supposed to offer a taste of China. Another, I forget the name – it might have been 'Delhi', specialised in Indian food. Both were said to be appalling. Then there was Aragvi, the only one, apparently, where the food was of a genuinely high standard – because it specialised in Georgian cooking, the Soviet Republic of Georgia being almost the only part of the empire where good food and wine were plentiful. A wild and beautiful place, Georgia, the birthplace of Uncle Joe. Oh, and I understood – I think it was Svieta who let it slip – that Aragvi was much frequented by what was referred to darkly as a 'mafia'. I managed to get in there for a lunch one day when, due to some administrative circumstance common to the politics of the Cold War and unbeknown to the traveller in question, I had to go to the Mongolian Embassy to plead for an entry visa, after the successful conclusion of which a good lunch seemed only right and reasonable. If only obtaining a visa to Aragvi had been so easy! At first, with the profoundly implied threat that is almost unique to Russian brusqueness entry was denied me; that was until out of the shadow cast by the brute at the door there appeared a young woman, who proceeded to address me in Italian. The nature of coincidence being as it is, the possibility remains, perhaps, that coincidence is all it was. Yet – coincidentally – the evening before, quite unexpectedly, a woman had called me in my room, speaking to me in Italian and suggesting a possible rendezvous, not at Aragvi, but somewhere in the unlit precincts of the hotel. I had ignored this and now, I surmised, here she was. Contrary to my instinctive suspicions, and as a result of the lunch that followed, I do not believe there was anything very sinister at work. She was a girl that spoke Italian with contacts in the hotel who had alerted her to my marriageable presence. She was a girl that wanted to find a way out of the USSR. That she happened to be patrolling the Aragvi when I showed up was however, I am certain, pure chance. More important to me was the manner in which she verbally beat the doorman about the head, he in what I was to learn was typical of the Russian male, shrinking before a female onslaught like a hapless drunk. So we left the street and entered another world; it was as if I had left the gloom of Moscow above to descend to a convivial basement restaurant in Soho. All was colour. Crude visions of Georgia were daubed on the walls. Tables were occupied by big men in cheap suits and by their bleached molls, just as in the bar in Warsaw. We sat in a corner and soon our table was laden with innumerable dishes of unleavened breads and sauces to dip them in; cold meats; shashlik; country wines one could drink for ever; and, of course, vodka. We feasted and talked well into the afternoon. From her frequent carillons of laughter, and multitude of toasts, I learned little of the USSR other than she wanted to leave it and for that she needed a foreign husband. Amusing and very faintly flattering though this was, I declined the offer. As finally we made our way up the stairs from the cavern back onto the despondent, broken pavements above, overhung by columns of frosted spears of ice now refreezing as the evening cold began to grip, she said only, '*Ma Andiamo cosi bene insieme*,' as if a few hours of drunken revelry was sufficient for a life together in the sunny and unspecific world that was the West.

But I liked the sound of Slavyansky Bazaar and the evening before we left for Siberia, I determined to go there. As a foreigner – no, as a Westerner, which was to be a dishonourable honoured guest – I was expected to pay in advance in foreign currency. In so doing, they told me at the Intourist desk in the hotel lobby, I would be certain of a table; which suggested that a table in one of Moscow's few restaurants was guaranteed only to those infidels in possession of dollars. For some reason this annoyed me. Being a tourist was bad enough but to be officially categorised as one somewhere in the Soviet hierarchy of workers, peasants, *kulaks*, *nomenklatura* and *intelligentsia* seemed so contrary to the spirit of life itself, that I resolved to go to the restaurant not with an overpriced voucher testifying to my foreign status, but with a fistful of roubles and a few packets of foreign cigarettes, which, I had understood, acted as a kind of currency and which would at least have the virtue of disappearing into the pockets of a waiter or doormen rather than into the pit that was the Soviet treasury.

It worked and whereas with the troika ride I had inadvertently found myself in the world of the Russia of another era, in this restaurant I encountered the Russia of 1981, which was also the Russia of 1941, a kind of hybrid creature that harked back to an indeterminate period of war and siege. You have to remember that Moscow then was not as I believe it has since become, a slave to commerce. But you did not need to be in love with shopping to find it odd that there were almost no shops at all. There was nothing. Then, the city centre in the wintry early evening was dim and empty, quite beautiful in its solemnity, especially on this ornate street, *Nikolskaya*, where, close by to Slavyansky Bazaar, stood the Synod Printing House, on the site of which in 1564 Ivan Fedorov printed the first book in Russia, *The Acts of the Apostles* and where in 1703, the first Russian newspaper was printed. As I walked past the building, sliding through the slush, I noticed on its wall a lion and a unicorn, the symbol of the imperial printing press, and above it, in the apex of the eaves, the Soviet hammer and sickle, taking the place, I supposed, of the Tsarist eagle; a palimpsest of censorship. I remember thinking that in my brief experience of Russians – just a few days, remember – I had already sensed in them a profound ambivalence towards freedom. On the contrary, I thought I detected in them pride in the strength of the very institutions that denied them liberty. In fact, I began to imagine that in their heart of hearts they despised freedom of expression as wild, uncontrollable chaos; a shapeless snapping and chattering in the void. I concluded that there was no point in making easy comparisons between Russian and Western notions of freedom.

I would have said that the atmosphere inside Slavyansky Bazaar was akin to that of a London dance-hall during the Blitz. The tables were set in rows perpendicular to the dance floor, where a band played with surprising zest a selection of big-band classics in the Glenn Miller mould that had been fashionable in the West forty years before. The menu, though vast, was an exercise in optimism as most of the items on it were unavailable – permanently so, I sensed. What was available, though, was excellent – little pots of hot wild mushrooms; stacks of blinis and deep goblets of glistening black caviar; flasks of vodka and bottles of dense red Georgian wines. But more than anything I was riveted by the movement on the dance floor. Everything about the dancers was old-fashioned; not merely the frocks and bows of the women, or the men's rustic suits, or the soldiers and sailors in their uniforms, but even the intensity of the men's expressions on youthfully ruddy complexions, the blurring of innocent blue eyes yielding to the wine and vodka, the tight, sentimental embraces – the intense desire for unreachable romance, only to collapse into maudlin, petulant drunkenness. I could not help noticing that there were in Russia two builds of women: the slim and lithe, with the grace of ballerinas, who wore their plain clothes with becoming modesty and even a certain flair, like Natasha at the border; and the hefty, with bleached yellow hair, raspberry red lips and extravagant cleavage, who before fumbling advances affected a tottering daintiness that was the nearest thing to glamour that I encountered in that country. All in all, there was about this tableau a beguiling, primitive innocence that I would have found disarming were it not for its utter disregard for the world beyond. Always, in Russia, I felt that I had intruded into a limitless state under eternal siege. Even now, all these years later, I have the impression that the mentality of self–immurement remains.

Well after midnight, I stepped out of the restaurant into a snowstorm, a dense silent cascade onto the icy streets. The metro had shut down for the night. I walked in no particular direction in search of a taxi, as yet unaware of their rarity and of their temperamental attitude to their purpose when finally they did emerge. Eventually, I found myself at the meeting point of several roads beneath a gigantic building of such baleful aspect that I shivered more from its silent menace than from the glacial air that pinched my face. Perhaps I exaggerate a little but just by a little – this was Moscow, after all. The falling snow, the emptiness of this great space, the absolute blackness. A grey statue of a man in a full-length coat stood high on a pedestal at its centre, the snow beginning to pile in a comical pyramid on his head. On the pavement beneath this fortress of a building, I noticed a policeman heavily swaddled in his thick grey uniform twitching his baton. As I scanned the streets for any sign of a taxi, my attention was caught by a movement behind me and turning, I was confronted by a pair of men locked together in a kind of uncertain, awkward embrace, grinning fatuously. Both were stotious drunk, as well as appallingly underdressed for a freezing night. Contracting his mouth into a wicked smile, one whispered hoarsely, 'KGB,' pointing wide eyed at the monstrous edifice overlooking the square. 'KGB,' he repeated, aware even in his crapulous state, of my foreignness and throwing up his arms, made as if to approach me. In so doing he deprived his companion of a supporting brace, whereupon he fell like a plank of wood face forward into the snow. He remained where he was, motionless, silent, and, shortly, a thin stream of blood, purple in the dimness, emerged from beneath his face and seeped into the snow. The policeman watched on impassively. Just then, a car pulled up beside me. The driver was in full military uniform, collar up, wide peaked cap in the Soviet style. He beckoned me over and pointing to the back seat said to me, 'Taxi.' I managed to convey to him where I was staying and we agreed on a fare of ten roubles, the equivalent then of ten pounds sterling. Afraid to dabble in the black market – which was not as widespread in the USSR as in Poland – I had bought roubles at the official absurd rate, which meant that my ride home was to be expensive indeed. For a moment the events about me seemed, yet again, to be taking place in a benighted wonderland where the usual superficial conventions of human behaviour were observed in parallel with other darker ones buried deep in our psyche – here at midnight in the shadow of the headquarters of the world's most notorious secret police; with a policeman patrolling beneath it, a drunken couple who could have been performing in the theatre of the absurd and a ranking officer in the Soviet Army – the enemy! – moonlighting as a taxi driver. All of the participants in this comedy acted with perfect equanimity. Life was rough, tough, but it seemed that everyone knew how far to go. Only had I pissed against the walls of the KGB HQ would the full wrath of the Soviet state have fallen onto my head – open disrespect was a sin, that very bourgeois concept of ordinary decency.

Hydrofoil on the Moskva River together with Kremlin walls and the giant Rossiya Hotel.

Everything else was perfectly acceptable. I sat in the back of the car staring at the cap stuck firmly on his silent, motionless head and at the row of stars along his shoulders and realised that here was Russia, a country, according to our ideas of hierarchy and propriety, that was eccentric to say the least. Better to have frontiers secured by an iron government, even a cruel one, Russians seemed to believe, than the threat of individual freedom. Sometimes, I ascribed this attitude to simple laziness. It is a great temptation not to have to think for oneself.

When the general, or whatever he was, arrived at the hotel – parking in the shadows about 100 yards away from it to be exact – and after I had handed over the fare, he reached into his pocket and confidentially vouchsafed to me what seemed like a small photograph, muttering the words '*moi droog*', which, I later discovered, meant 'my friend'. I was unable to see clearly in the darkness and only when I was in my hotel room did I see that it was a grainy black and white portrait of Uncle Joe Stalin himself.

Chapter 4

The Siberian Line

The morning after my night at the Slavyansky Bazaar, I awoke with the first of the many pounding headaches that were to be an almost inescapable aspect of life not only in Russia, but throughout the journey all the way to Hong Kong. From that moment on I was in a permanent state of mild intoxication, with occasional outbreaks of Bacchanalian excess, which seemed perfectly natural given our peculiar isolation in this endless belt of stifled humanity. Vodka, with its watery clarity, its neutral addictive flavour, its evanescent nature, was irresistible – I came to fully understand the love that the peoples of eastern Europe had for it. It was not merely a comfort, it was a symbol, a totem, a cipher and a ritual.

That day, we were to leave Moscow along the Trans-Siberian Railway. We gathered in the lobby together with Svieta, whilst the infernal *Moscow Nights* tune played loudly and continuously over the loudspeakers. In George Orwell's *1984*, one of the things I most remember about the great novel was the banality of a song sung by a woman as she hung out her washing below the room where Winston and Julia had their illicit assignations:

'It was only an 'opeless fancy,
It passed like an Ipril dye,
But a look an' a word an' the dreams they stirred
They 'ave stolen my 'eart awye!'

Each time I heard the wretched *Moscow Nights*, that image from the account of a totalitarian dystopia unfailingly came to me.

Even that annoyingly unforgettable tune, it turned out, was not immune to the whims of Soviet politics. The song was originally named *Leningradskie Vechera* – 'Leningrad Nights' – but at the 'request' of the Soviet Ministry of Culture, became 'Подмосковные вечера', or *Podmoskovnye Vechera*, the strict translation of which would be 'Evenings in Moscow *Oblast*', an '*oblast*' being an administrative term for territory, and which, notwithstanding its ponderous Russian title, apparently was once certified as the song most frequently sung in the world, a fact to which I can testify with the utmost certainty.

There we were, looking forward with some anxiety to the Trans-Siberian Express, when I noticed that one of our number was missing. Len was one of the Australian contingent, a sixtyish man of the old school, whose persona was a blend of Australian brashness and of a dated conception of Englishness associated with what he would have referred to as 'the old country', a place partly to be despised, partly to be recalled with fond inaccuracy. A product of the Second World War, during which he had lost part of a finger, from the outset he wore without fail a blazer and tie but I noticed that from the moment we reached Moscow his mood had become unpredictable and his behaviour erratic. He took to barracking Svieta. The tie became looser, the blazer slightly soiled, the shaving irregular and the drinking less happy. He shrivelled up, as if overcome by an unbearable disappointment. Fortunately for him, and for the rest of us, a fellow Australian, Sandy, of the same generation and background, but in every respect more stable, took him under his wing.

That morning we looked for Len everywhere, to no avail. All our bags, including Len's, were in a pile in the hotel lobby awaiting collection. I had collected his passport ready to hand back to him. Only later did Sandy confide to me that on realising that Len had absconded, he had packed his bags for him. At first the general consensus was that he must have forgotten the time or something of the kind. Sandy, out of loyalty to his friend and comrade, concealed his concern as best he could, but I could see that there was resignation behind the sanguine demeanour. When he affected surprise at Len's absence, it immediately prompted Archie, Guppy and the Vietnam Vets, ludicrously, to accuse Svieta of complicity in a KGB abduction, which naturally gave rise to murmurings among all the other mostly sensible participants along the lines of 'shame they didn't abduct you lot'. As the time drew near for departure, I thought I understood what was going on. Len's deteriorating conduct, and now his disappearance at one of those crucial moments when idiosyncrasy was no longer attractive or amusing, together brought me to an ineluctable conclusion; Len did not want to continue the journey and this was his way of baling out from it. His abrasive manner was bravado, a sham; he was unable any longer to suppress all the bitterness that comes with disappointment and the encroachment of decrepitude. Perhaps he had expected to find fellowship among battle-hardened Soviet veterans. For someone like him, however, there was no consolation to be found in Russia, which was unsympathetic to weakness; where, of course, there was no old soldiers' club in which he could have exchanged stories of exploits and comradeship that were the inevitable mementoes of war, perhaps the peak of an existence. Apart from anything else, for Russians, the Second World War was the 'Great Patriotic War', a heroic battle to protect the Motherland, for which alliance with the West was merely a temporary expedient.

Against this background of indifference and loneliness, there festered in Len a profound sense of injustice; and the USSR, with its cold and unbridgeable insularity, was no place for coming to terms with it. Had we left without him, I don't believe he would have much cared and for a moment, I wondered if I might not be doing him a service to simply go. But – and in a way this is a failing – I tended to optimism. More to the point, I am not sure this would have been even feasible; it would have unleashed an uncontainable bureaucratic squall that could have put paid to the whole enterprise. A Western individual roaming the streets of Moscow would not have bothered the authorities unduly but an unmonitored splinter of a group was another matter, because the 'group', representing security and indivisible Russian togetherness, was a single entity that could function only when whole.

I decided to have one last look. I made my way across the gardens in front of the Exhibition of Economic Achievements and on a backless bench, surrounded by patches of ice and ridges of blackening snow, there he lay full-length, asleep as deeply as if it were the middle of the night, his hand grazing an open bottle of whisky on the ground beneath him, the knot of his tie level with his heart, and one side of his blazer flung open exposing a swollen belly to the freezing wind. I stood over him for a moment, watching the strain across his grey features and listening to his stertorous breathing, almost wanting to leave him be – but realising that this poor effort at evasion was too half-hearted to be sincere. Although I was to regret waking him, I did so, and after a brief altercation, avoiding as far as possible the argument he would have preferred, urged him across the garden onto the waiting bus.

We lumbered through the city towards Yaroslavsky Station, point of departure of the Trans-Siberian. Most among the party made no bones at their relief at our departure from Moscow, which, for all its undoubted fascinations, possessed the power to unsettle Western composure. As Mr. Stimpson remarked – we only ever knew him by his surname, for he resisted all attempts by the others to prise from him his forename – only I knew it was Jolyon; he knew that I knew and made me swear on

Yaroslavsky Station and Trans-Siberian carriages. The plate on the side reads 'Россия' or 'Russia'.

pain of complaint not to tell a soul – one left Moscow with a sour taste, dissatisfied, like an expensive meal badly cooked.

We drove one last time along Prospect Mira. There was a moment of excitement when Guppy, the Saturnine Englishman, espied a queue, the discovery of which he vouchsafed to Archie and the Vets, whom he knew would not be shy of bringing it to the attention of the beleaguered Svieta. For Westerners, at that epoch, the queue was the *sine qua non* of Soviet failure, for they commonly claimed, with some justification, that shortages were an endemic feature of Soviet life. So it was with a note of triumph that one of them bellowed, like an excited child, 'Queue, there's a queue, what are they queuing for?'

Svieta explained that yes, well spotted, it was a queue, for shoes, as it happened; and that yes, it was well known that there were shortages of such goods in the USSR and that although there was every chance that in this case only left-footed shoes would have been delivered, they were working on it. Her dignified straight-faced answer, without the expected attempt at concealment of the truth, had the satisfying effect of temporarily silencing the mob, to the vocal satisfaction of the French contingent, who to give them their due, were in some respects more sensitive to Svieta's dilemma than were some of the others. Svieta's boundless composure was marvellous to behold. The old rhyme

'Never been loved,
  Never been kissed,
  We are the girls from Intourist,'

referring to dragons that allegedly kept an eye on the every move of their charges, seemed either to belong to an earlier time when the legacy of Uncle Joe was apparent or to the delighted reception of a certain kind of masochist. Svieta, and all the other Intourist guides I met along the way, were almost invariably amusing and sophisticated, if ultimately in thrall to an inflexible bureaucracy.

As we drew up to the station we drifted across the shadow cast by one of those seven so-called skyscrapers that then dominated the Moscow skyline. Whether by accident or by design I cannot say – though I think the latter – these gloomy towers were so disposed to give the impression of a fortress, like a gigantic outer Kremlin. Their towering presence was oppressive and ubiquitous – they watched over us like so many 'Ministry of Truths'. It was obvious to me that they were loosely modelled on the Empire State Building in New York but whereas the Empire State had the grace of art-deco style and the energy of originality, these were clumsy, stern and distinctly intimidating. Intentionally so, I am sure. Of course they were Uncle Joe's work. 'We won the war ... foreigners will come to Moscow, walk around, and there's no skyscrapers. If they compare Moscow to capitalist cities, it's a moral blow to us.' So, he had them built as hotels, blocks of flats, a university building, a ministry, ensuring that they loomed like giant guardians across the capital of Communism.

With that revolutionary obsession with class, each commission was to tally with the status of the architect, adjudged, doubtless, according to some perversion of Marxist zeal, and then sorted into two groups, *first class* and *second class* towers. Given the parlous state of the Soviet economy for most of its existence, and the absence of comfortable living space for the average citizen, it is interesting to note that in 1949 Moscow built a total of 405,000 square metres of housing, whereas the skyscrapers project exceeded 500,000 square metres, with a great deal more scarce money being spent on each skyscraper metre than on each gimcrack apartment metre. And at least one of them was built on the labour of thousands of Gulag inmates. Yet, like all such vanity projects, it was all in vain.

The station hall was crammed with the masses. All the peoples of the Soviet Empire were there, Kazakhs and Kirghiz and Tajiks and Buryats, with their patterned headscarves and burnished Asiatic faces which followed us and creased into dazzling smiles when our gaze met theirs. Indifferent to the murals and ornaments around them, they seemed like pieces of art themselves, the portrait of another era. They sat with patient dignity, surrounded by heaps of suitcases, parcels and shopping bags, mystified by the big city, proud to have been but eager to be off, awaiting trains to take them home to their ancestral lands.

We made our way onto the platform. My recollection of that entire journey between London and Hong Kong forms itself in two ways: a broad, misty strip of moving film, and a series of still images, both accompanied by smells and sounds and colours. Our arrival onto the open-air platform of Yaroslavsky station I see as a single image. Our train was plum red, with the dust and mud of travel sprayed across the carriages' flanks. Smoke rose up from each carriage in a slow curl towards the great grey canopy above and the reek of sulphur hung in the freezing air. Beside our carriage stood an attendant, a woman in a stodgy grey uniform surmounted by a cap that perched on a pile of bleached blonde hair, who, once she realised that her charges were to be Westerners, stiffened as a shadow of concern passed across her features. We filed in and prepared for three days of incarceration.

You might ask why anyone would choose to spend some eighty hours in succession cooped up in a railway carriage, with no prospect of escape from its monotony. The motives are banal: a delusional idea of romance; confusion with the past and misplaced expectations of luxury; even boastfulness. After all, stories abounded, even then, of the terrible nature of travelling on Soviet trains – that the food ran out; that there were no lavatories; that radios spewed an unstoppable torrent of propaganda. None of this was the case, although I concede that it may have been true once, when the Soviet legend sprang out of the excesses of Uncle Joe. What was interesting to me was the nervous expectation of the very worst that prevailed among some, combined with the knowledge that the myths peddled over the years could not possibly have any foundation.

Svieta, fully aware of the fearfulness present in the minds of Westerners, made light of the facilities aboard. An observation she made as we drove to the station concerning hygiene elicited an exclamation from the back of the bus – 'Oh, my Gaad! You mean I can't go to the toilet for four days?'

There was really only one significant reason to tolerate the discomfort of the days to follow; it gave Westerners the opportunity to mix freely with Russians in a way that for the average visitor was otherwise all but impossible. For the train was a workhorse; among its passengers we were the only ones travelling on it through the luxury of choice. The Trans-Siberian followed the road to exile and Siberia loomed large in the Russian psyche. 'Mother Russia' was a term bandied about far too freely to have much meaning but it conveyed something that was more than the maternal embrace – it included jealousy and ambition and possessiveness and earthiness on a scale that was so vast and overpowering to be frightening and daunting to those of us brought up on the comforting traditions of constitutional democracy and the rule of law. And now we were to be taken to her bosom! We had strayed into a fairy story, where wolves and forests and palaces and smoking woodland cottages and, above all, giants and ogres ruled the world.

At the time, the presumption, not unfounded, that opinion contrary to the Party line was not tolerated in the USSR, was incontrovertible. For Westerners, Siberia was where you ended up if you stepped out of line. And yet, before we left Moscow, Svieta – the blessed Svieta! – had whispered to me that if I had the time I should go to the cinema as a new film about Siberia had just been released. Svieta, with her ineffably broad smile, assured me that even in the USSR the silent era was over, forgetting that the presence of a soundtrack would mean only that the story would be more impenetrable than ever. More than that, I was frankly – absurdly – of the opinion that a Soviet film of any description could not be of any interest to me. But then, as I thought it over, it occurred to me that here again was the opportunity to mix with Russians, even if in the dark!

So, one evening, I found the cinema on Gorky Street, opposite one of the surviving Orthodox churches from which, I was surprised to note, a flickering light glowed in the darkness. I had a little time and entered; a full service was taking place. The interior was brilliant with candle light, the air fragrant with incense. A congregation of elderly worshippers crowded the alter, where the bearded priest in black robes and *klobuk*, in a voice somewhere between a baritone and bass, sang the beautiful Orthodox litany of prayers, canticles and petitons. A cup was raised and lowered. The congregation stood enraptured, my presence entirely ignored. After a few minutes, I slipped out and crossed to the cinema.

The last thing I expected to see in the Soviet Union was a film that satirised the Soviet system – the food shortages; the injustices meted out to innocent citizen; the horrors of the Gulag – all in the guise of a gentle romance set in a railway station. I would go further and say that the most astonishing thing was the laughter of recognition that rippled through the spectators. Not anger, or protest, but laughter. That was a clever film, I see now, for it wrapped the iniquities of the system in cotton wool and made its victims feel that all would be well if just a few minor adjustments (the KGB, the Gulag, the food supply, all round injustice) could be fixed.

In urging me to see *Station For Two*, Svieta was acknowledging the Soviet Union's imperfections. She was also demonstrating a certain optimism for the future. It seemed to me that such a future was a distant prospect. At the time, many westerners presumed their hotel rooms would be bugged, their postcards censored, their every movement recorded; a possibility, given the Russian genius for extreme punctiliousness when it was a matter of state security, that nonetheless was more in keeping with the East German tradition. At the same time, examples of Russia's police apparatus did inexplicably arise from time to time. I had taken a stroll only the previous afternoon with Svieta into the anonymous neighbourhood of apartments out of which the hotel had sprouted like a gaudy weed, wandering into a local shop which, true to western propaganda, had nothing to sell apart from the end of a sausage that had seen fresher days and a singular abundance of tins of Vietnamese pineapple, cheaply adorned in tropical shades of blue and yellow. Here again was that odour that seemed to poison the air in Warsaw; the smell of cheap disinfectant, a miasma not dissimilar to the stink of meat that is beyond its best – not rotten exactly, but sufficiently nasty to discourage consumption. Around my neck was my camera, enough it seemed to attract from the wainscoting the local rats in the guise of a pair of plain-clothed policemen who planted themselves before us to address Svieta, who, in her woolly hat and with her oriental cheeks, was unmistakably Russian. Since consorting with Westerners was an unforgivable sin, she of course was mortified; yet with an impressive act of will convinced them that she had taken foreign nationality, and that her ID – her passport – was, therefore, in the hands of the *administratsia* at her hotel. This served only to provoke threats of a visit to the nearest police station (which in the USSR did not advertise their presence as beacons of justice but were located anonymously in various examples of overweening grimness) when she, with an expertise that astonished me, seized my camera, ripped out the film, and, throwing it to the floor, stamped on it with a show of petulance and with a thoroughness that filled me with admiration. After which one of the spooks bent slowly down to pocket it before murmuring to his sidekick and shuffling out, looking back with undisguised venom at Svieta, whom, although he was convinced she was a Soviet citizen, he hesitated to collar, given that I was clearly a foreigner and the resulting propaganda would not exactly be a coup for the Soviet way of life. I mention this incident merely to convey the trivial level of watchfulness and suspicion that utopia spawns.

So, there we were heading for Siberia. That journey! The endless lurching, rocking, pitching, scraping, I can feel it – hear it – above all smell it – even now. The doors between the carriages were like armoured gates. Overlapping steel plates were the bridge from one carriage to the other and sometimes, at an imperfect join, there were glimpses of the track below, from where a maelstrom of freezing air swirled about me. Slamming the door, I was catapulted into a sort of vestibule, just before the carriage

Heading for Siberia along the fully electrified Trans-Siberian Railway.

corridor, where smokers gathered, the air dense with the blue fog of opaque, shiftless fumes.

On the Trans-Siberian, you were immersed in the reek of Russia. If not the pungency of *papirossi* cigarettes, then all the other rank odours that characterised the motherland of the proletariat. The stale air of the train, composed of grime, sweat, garlic, carbolic, pickle, and vodka became our very oxygen. I rather liked this peculiar Russian perfume. To me it was Russia itself, good and bad together in an unstopped bottle that also contained a delicate scent of meadow flowers, birch sap and berries.

Our clock was the meal timetable. Food became the focal point of the day and although we became less and less hungry with every eastward kilometre, when the call for lunch or dinner came, we unfailingly took the roller coaster to the dining car, becoming more and more costive with the passing of each inactive day. Icebergs floated like clouds below us as we crossed great river after great river. The snow stayed with us for a day, then ceased, to reveal the steppeland's sodden landscape of dripping birch trees and boggy fleets beside lank, yellowing grass, before resuming, piling up in thick wads against wooden houses and sleeting against the train's muddy windows.

By the second day, proper sleep was no longer possible. The incessant jolting of the train, which had at first been a comfort, as the movement of a car for a baby, turned into an irritant. I became comatose, finding it impossible to resist in the afternoon the soporific effect of lunch, but failing to sleep deeply through the night, drifting in

Our view from the train – snow and sleet and silent Siberian villages.

and out of consciousness with the train's starts and stops at the fringes of station after station, temporarily parked in yards where lights as dazzling as daylight pierced our inadequate curtains, whilst loudspeakers broadcast strange, deafening conversations. It was profoundly unsettling, like a fever. War – all I could think of was war. It was the work and cacophony of war, a medieval war, for which smithies forged swords and shields night and day in a mindless patriotic fervour.

And then in the morning, when I regained consciousness, we were still moving and behind the lace, it seemed as if we had travelled in a circle, for outside it was just the same. Forest as far as the eye could see, an immensity of green beneath a coating of white glowing pinkly in the thin aurora sunlight. That was what struck me more forcibly than almost anything else on that train in that country – the vastness, the sheer, immeasurable size of it. Miles of beautiful nothing, with this one artery, the railway, pumping away, for ever pumping. There was no life outside the stations, no sign of it anyway, except for the smoke drifting from cottage chimneys into the chilled vodka air and the occasional creature of indeterminate gender swaddled in black, carrying a log. We looked out onto unfathomable stillness. Yet it was not as if we were alone on the line – every ten minutes, or so, a train would rattle by, which meant that ten minutes before us and ten minutes behind us, each hour of every day, there were other trains steadily jolting along the entire 5,772 miles between Moscow and Vladivostok. Remarkable! And yet on each side of the tracks of this spectacular achievement, there was immemorial poverty, all but untouched by the machinations in Moscow. The Russians travelling with us were not on a train, but in a cottage in the woods, in a dark Arcadia administered by Baba Yaga, in a landscape where timeless rituals persisted despite the Revolution and where Old Believers could find refuge. On their solemn faces, as they stood at the corridor window, glass of tea in hand, was a patriotic pride as vast as the landscape and just as imponderable.

At Kilometre 1777 (our distance from Moscow was marked by posts alongside the track) was the monument marking the frontier between Europe and Asia. An ambition of many who had waited patiently kilometre after kilometre, camera in hand, for the moment when we left Europe behind was thwarted as we sped by, the fleeting view excruciatingly obscured by a passing train.

The dining car, in the days when alcohol was sold on the train, was frequently the scene of magnificent parties. Just as with a lock-in in a pub, so the best of these came about unplanned, when there was a happy coincidence of willing landlord, or dining car *administrater*, and eager customers. After dinner, a few of us might linger and buy a bottle of Georgian wine, or Moldavian *'shampanska'*. A glass would be raised to the dining car staff. They, too, their work done, would sit down for a drink and a smoke. The men and women that worked on the train lived the unhealthiest of lives, and bore the pallor and exhausted look of those permanently denied fresh air. Sleeping badly in cramped conditions, they worked long hours all the way to Khabarovsk, had a short break and then made the same journey home. When they were working they appeared never to leave the train. They were like miners who couldn't find the energy to surface.

Entering Asia. Passing the obelisk in the Urals marking the Europe–Asia frontier.

The restaurant and kitchen staff were used to foreigners, regarding them with both suspicion and curiosity. The tedium of their lives gave them time to observe and so they came to see that foreigners were not all devils in disguise. From their lowly position they, unlike the soft-class Russians in their lofty ivory towers, could see that they were enslaved to their country, even more than miners, to whom was attached a certain revolutionary glory. They had been instructed to show foreign guests respect but not to be taken in by friendliness. Over time, however, such strictures became irrelevant; but the only means of communication they had with us was through festivity – everybody could understand a party – and by means of the strange signals that come about between people who want to communicate but who are divided by language, a sort of bacchanalian communion was achieved.

The restaurant administrator, moved by impending world peace, produced bottles of 'shampanska' from a hiding place beneath his seat as if he were Father Christmas handing out presents at a children's party. Mutually incomprehensible toasts, each more grandiloquent than the last, rang out across the dining car. There were songs, and clownish dancing, the administrator never moving from his throne, looking on like a benevolent Pan, as the train careered through the Siberian night. As I left, one of the younger members of the party was locked in a passionate embrace with a cook on the galley floor.

These were excessive, but happy occasions. Very much unhappier were drinkers who, like Len, were serious alcoholics. The idea of an almost infinite train journey appeals to the person whose life has been derailed. For those that have to share his or personal nightmare, however, the experience is bitter, as being together dawn to dusk is difficult enough even for those, like soldiers, who are trained to deal with it. For a group of tourists, of all ages, backgrounds and nationalities, the strain of spending weeks on end in each other's company is considerable, still more so when cooped up aboard trains in countries where comfort both physical and psychological is absent. In those conditions it takes but one seriously disruptive element to turn what should be a happy experience into a nightmare. The charm of an unhappy traveller can be beguiling to some at first, even captivating, until it turns to poison before the very people it enchanted.

Once we had hustled him aboard the Trans-Siberian, Len appeared to be chastened by his failed attempt to defect. Nonetheless, it was not long before he resumed a routine of heavy, solipsistic drinking. Until lunch he was cheerful, if a little distracted; from lunch onwards he developed into a bar-room bore. For as long as he was in his compartment with Sandy, he was tolerable, even if stray insults and scraps of ironic laughter made their way along the corridor to the ears of those he wanted to torment. But it was in the dining car, with everyone present, that he became most obnoxious.

Americans, for all their appearance of easy-going bonhomie, have a serious, almost biblical attitude to life; they sometimes find the deprecating, mocking humour that is characteristically English or Australian hard to comprehend. Anxious to please, they can be both suspicious and unsure of themselves, treating unfamiliar phrases and colloquialisms with a reverence or incomprehension that makes them appear unfairly stupid. Foreign words – even English words – may baffle them completely, a perfectly straightforward place name becoming an unpronounceable riddle. They presume, because it is foreign, that it is difficult; and in the process of wanting to get it right, and not to offend, get it completely wrong. It reflects their inward-looking nature but some find it infuriating.

'So, how is life down in Austria? Say, did you ever see the *Sound of Music*? I loved that movie!' said one to Len, after several weeks of travelling in his company.

At the beginning, some of the Americans had thought Len quite a card; only slowly did they realise that his quaint Australian humour was actually aimed at undermining their sober well-meaning politeness – they had become his cynosures. When they began to realise that his remarks were insults, they were shocked; when his remarks were reinforced with foul language, they were initially mortally offended, then almost relieved that he had become a boor, no longer interesting or entertaining. Like the rest of us, eventually they became bored by his endless cannonades. Len bored himself, too, which was part of his problem.

'You Yanks,' he would say, 'you think you rule the world. Especially you Yankee women. Jeez, I wouldn't want to be married to one of you lot. I'd never be allowed out!' He'd turn to Sandy. 'Fuckin' Yanks! How long did it take them to get into the bloody war, anyway?'

The Yankee women were no doubt thanking God they had not been born in Australia; and that if they had, and had by some terrible error married a Len, they would have let him out all he wanted.

Bert on the other hand, who, when drunk, had a tendency to speak in tongues, was quite the opposite of Len, for Bert was maudlin. Len was defiant where Bert was sly and conceited. The only thing they had in common, apart from an addiction to whiskey, was luck; for both had the good fortune to share a room with patient, compassionate individuals. Len shared with a comrade-in-arms, Sandy, whilst Bert shared with Leonard, who though elderly, was tall and broad, with thick, wavy white hair and always had about his person a photograph of his beloved dog and his equally beloved Corvette. He characterised an older, earthier America, before the good life had corrupted it. It was he who quietly disparaged those who whinged about the comfortless East or who panicked at the sight of a Soviet soldier, finding such reactions both funny and pathetic. He was kind to Bert, because he understood that Bert could not help himself. Whereas the others dismissed him as a loser, Leonard saw Bert as a tiresome but vulnerable human being. Bert's wife, Leonard later told me when we had left the Western world far behind us, presumably concerned that her husband was capable of causing an international incident, had called Leonard in London to warn him that her husband was 'unwell'. It was true. He was often insensible to circumstances and more often merely insensible.

Bert's real name was Berthold. Like Herman, he was of German origin and, I conjectured, had found himself in the USA in much the same way that Herman had found himself in Australia. There the similarities ended. Whereas Herman was still identifiably German in habit and accent, Bert had taken on the persona of an American redneck, with a southern drawl and the chequered shirts, blue jeans and leather boots of a cowboy. But when he drank, the charade fell away, his language degenerating into a kind of German-American babble and the good ol' boy bluster replaced by a wheedling sentimentality.

Even a tourist, sufficiently reckless, could in those days have been a political hazard. On the Trans-Siberian we had been briefly accompanied by a senior member of Intourist, which as an organ of the Soviet state was of a political significance beyond its official remit. Power, whether in the USA or in the USSR, is the same; Alexei, as a member of the *nomenclatura*, had the bearing of an American senator or of a member of European aristocracy. He was urbane and confident; he spoke excellent English; he was approachable and genial, yet patrician and impenetrable. Cornered daily by Bert on the Trans-Siberian, however, his diplomatic finesse was to be tested to the limit.

In his depressed state, Bert was subject to the usual delusions that haunt the bruised and beaten and bitter. He believed that only he understood the world's ills, which all could be remedied over a bottle.

'If we could just talk to each other,' he would say in his mawkish way, with his baby-faced grin. 'Then we would understand each other, right? We just need to get together. We are all just human beings, aren't we?'

'Yes, that is true,' Alexei would reply, with infinite Russian patience. 'But human beings … we are all the same and yet we are all different. Talk; yes we must talk; but it is out of our hands!' And he would shrug his shoulders and smile as if it were the same the world over. 'Governments! Politicians!' If only he and Bert were running the world.

Bert nodded shrewdly and helped himself to another glass.

Each day, captive as he was in the narrow confines of a train piercing the interminable, inescapable Siberian landscape, Alexei endured the ruminations of Bert. Soon, Alexei began to sleep late and to find work that he had to catch up on; but at lunch and in the afternoons there was no refuge and Bert, making himself comfortable across the table from Alexei, would plant a bottle between them. Alexei had a great capacity for drink but wisely abstained, allowing Bert, whose physical capacity for alcohol was great, but whose mental tolerance was minimal, to drink his fill. Before long, Bert's words would become slurred as he relapsed from broad Kentucky to the German that he grew up with. Soon, when he became sleepy, Alexei would gently suggest that he go to his compartment for an afternoon nap.

'It is tiring, Bert, to solve the world's problems. Have a rest. Maybe tomorrow, we continue, OK?'

Alexei understood Bert. He saw Russians like him every day of his life, at work, on the streets. Like Leonard, he treated Bert with tolerance because he recognised his weaknesses and realised that his 'Americaness' was a shallow creation. Watching Alexei was to see the consummate diplomat and to understand how it was that the

USSR, for all its failings, was a force that could not be denied. Russians understood human nature far better than did their enemies; they knew how to get under the skin, a talent for which they had centuries of experience. Alexei was not corrupted by religion or by greed. His was a very pure form of power.

There must have been times when Russians looked on Westerners and then at themselves and thought that life could not be so much better in the West. In Irkutsk one night, in the hotel on the banks of Lake Baikal, Alexei stumbled against Bert, supine on the floor of the hotel lobby, pressing the imaginary call button of a lift that did not exist. Alexei, who was a big man, lifted Bert from the floor, carried him upstairs, and deposited him on his bed. The next day, Bert had no recollection of this undignified moment, whilst Alexei was enough of a gentleman not to mention it to him.

It was easy to forget that America, unlike Russia, was still a young country and, sometimes, it seemed that Americans' sense of nationhood was a fragile thing. Russians admired America, even as they reviled it. America, which had become a refuge for so many dispossessed, did not return the compliment. Among us in my group there was an English, Russian and Chinese émigré to the US, each looking on their ancestral homelands with a mixture of contempt and longing. There was the Englishwoman who told us constantly and despairingly in the accent of her adopted country of how the English could ever only 'muddle through'; the woman of Russian parentage, terrified at being in the land of her forefathers, yet who found a warmth among her kinsmen that surprised and delighted her; and the Chinese woman that recoiled almost with physical disgust from the poor in China, as if poverty were a contagion. A sense of national identity is an intangible thing; for émigrés, still in touch with their past, these journeys were like pilgrimages to the family temple to make peace with the ancestors.

We were an odd number in the party, so that I shared a compartment with Svieta, which, as I am sure you will imagine, gave rise to all kinds of peculiar speculation from the predictably ribald to the weirdly political. Slim, one of the Vietnam Vets, put it about that I was clearly a spy, as he had thought from the start, a theory to which, I was taken aback to discover from the Famous Writer, some of the others gave some credence. I must admit that I was faintly surprised to be thrown into such intimacy with a Soviet woman. Svieta put on a brave face, but I could see that her forced bonhomie barely concealed a reticence that would be perfectly normal in any other country that did not expect its womankind to be the embodiments both of feminine modesty and of Socialist indifference to distinctions of sex.

The Famous Writer was not one to mix too freely with the rest of us. Much of his time was spent in his compartment (he or his publisher had paid for his own), from which he emerged from time to time to observe his fellow passengers for as long as he could bear their company – not very long – and for meals.

'I hear of a guy with a name like yours,' one said to him at lunch, as the inevitable soup slopped up and down the sides of the tin bowls in which it was served. 'Writer, or something like that. You know him?'

He tried to remain anonymous for as long as possible but vanity being what it is, word got out. Famous Writers command, or crave, attention and what he got was a little awe. He popped up here and there throughout the journey and his book did well; his characterisation of the others in the party was selective. As it happened, there were several who might comfortably have found a place in a Charles Dickens novel; others he could have left well alone.

One day, we just stopped, in the middle of nowhere – or everywhere, it was the same. There we stayed for an entire afternoon. It was odd how the lack of movement brought on a kind of anxiety and impatience among the party members – they fretted and repined, fearing, I suppose, that the halt presaged something more permanent. In our compartment, I poured glasses of vodka for the two of us (I kept the vodka cold by jamming the bottle – by some miracle it went undiscovered - in a crevice between the carriages) and after the second glass, there was a silence, interrupted only by the wind that blustered about the train, making the carriage twitch clumsily. Then Svieta said to me quietly, and with a hint of confessional embarrassment, that she had heard that the reason we were stopped was because there had been an accident further up the line; whilst someone else had whispered to her that there had been an act of sabotage. There was doubt scored deep into her features – doubt that such a thing could happen, doubt that it was true. But her doubt was not that of one who feared that an act of vandalism, even terrorism, could have been wrought by those marginalised or disenchanted but more that perhaps an invader had insinuated itself into the country with the aim of undermining the revolution.

The dead stillness of the interminable and hypnotic Siberian landscape.

As evening fell, the train at last gave its familiar lurch to heave itself towards the cruising speed that would take us through another night and several hundred more miles of Russia. Of the incident that had caused the delay, there was not the slightest sign. To have pursued the definition of sabotage in the USSR with Svieta seemed discourteous – even cruel – and I consoled myself with the consideration that we would never know the truth of it. It occurred to me, lying on my bunk, dozing in concert with the ragged movements of the train, that outside our carriage was not merely a great remoteness but, between the towns and cities where we stopped every few hours, yet which to us as foreigners were forbidden, was a great desolation. I don't mean in the strictly geographical sense. This was Siberia. The warmth of the train had insulated us from the realisation that we were passing though the fabled region of banishment. No doubt that explained the unease felt by the others when we halted without explanation for a whole half day. It was a name that conjured up a fearful emotion but which to most of us had no definition.

Siberia. Another name. What is it to most of us? Mammoths preserved in the ice? A white desert? Ineffable bleakness? There is a condition that some of us have, which means that names – days of the week for example – are thought of as colours. That was how I saw Siberia – a sheet of whiteness, an expanse of frost. Had you asked me, before I set out on that journey, to name a single Siberian town or river or lake, I could not have done so. Siberia is a figment. Yet it is almost eight tenths of the largest country in the world, and forms all of Northern Asia, with a population that for the most part gathers around the railway line, which runs like a warming filament through the great

Great rivers we had never heard of cluttered with spring ice.

emptiness. Once, before traders and Cossacks and armies from Russia colonised it in the sixteenth century, Siberia was a land of nomads and of khanates. By the mid-seventeenth century, the Russian empire extended to the Pacific and by the time Russia became the Soviet Union, it ruled a sixth of the world's land mass. Even then, Siberia formed more than half of the USSR – so vast that when great and mysterious literally earth-shattering geological events have taken place, often it is in Siberia, which by its immensity is vulnerable to any stray meteor caught up in the Earth's atmosphere.

So, a natural place of exile, the land of the 101st kilometre, the boundless Room 101. Even in 1981, only, as it was to turn out, eight years or so away from the USSR's weary prostration, we in our train were trundling close to invisible outposts of the infamous GULAG, the *Главное управление исправительно-трудовых лагерей и колоний* or Chief Administration of Corrective Labour Camps and Colonies. By the period under discussion, they were no longer so great in number, nor as harsh in nature as they had been during the reign of Uncle Joe, and in fact, it seems that their purpose at the time of my journey was merely as centres of containment of criminals and supporters of democracy. But between 1929 and 1953, the birth years, it so happens of my own parents and of me, more than fourteen million people, it is surmised, were incarcerated pretty much on a whim in unspeakable conditions for years on end.

I don't want to be boring on the subject of the excesses of Uncle Joe Stalin. If I am, I apologise, but the scale of this genocide of the soul is breath-taking in its callousness – its barbaric, infinite callousness. It is true that these were not death camps in the manner of Treblinka and Auschwitz; the specific aim of the camps was not extermination. Yet, they say, at least 2 and up to 10 million died in them; sometimes I think they represented an evil every bit as malevolent as the death camps, for the thousands of days of suffering they caused, without any prospect of a merciful, quick release.

Why did Uncle Joe inflict this on his own people, whom the Revolution had supposedly released from bondage? Conjecture being a specious pastime and conviction its unhinged sibling, I am unable to give a definitive answer. Revolution, it seems, is inadequate to expunge memory, or placate resentment. Perhaps it is the bitterness of this realisation that spawns atrocious remedies. The Bolsheviks' solution was Article 58 of the Russian SFSR Penal Code, which came into being on 25 February 1927 as a pretext for arresting those suspected of counter-revolutionary activities. In their perverted determination, if the revolution failed to inspire, then it was not because of inherent weakness in the revolution itself but the fault of counter-revolutionary elements. Naturally, the reasoning was all dressed up in pseudo-scientific political jargon and tub-thumping demagoguery – but how many among the people wanted revolution? Really wanted it? How many just wanted better rulers? We cannot know. But, in my experience, most people want to be left alone. They require little. Except protection from injustice and corruption. The revolutionaries despised the people for their limitations, for their sloth.

So they came up with Article 58. Here, for example, is the definition of counter-revolution:

'A counter-revolutionary action is any action aimed at overthrowing, undermining or weakening the power of workers' and peasants' Soviets ... and governments of the USSR and Soviet and autonomous republics, or at the undermining or weakening of the external security of the USSR and main economical, political and national achievements of the proletarian revolution.'

And there follows a list of sections and sub-sections, together with the punishments deemed appropriate to the crimes, most of which are variations on sabotage and betrayal. In this state of bliss, you might wonder at the level of hysteria that gave rise to a list of such devastating thoroughness, handing to the secret police a prepared charge-sheet for any eventuality. The more I came to know of these things, the more I wondered; what was the point of all of this?

One point was to obtain free labour, needed to colonise the vast Russian wildernesses and, to repeat the Bolshevik *shibboleth*, to 'industrialise'. It was a failed, jejune enterprise. A terrifying, almost forgotten example is the Nazino affair. Not far from the Trans-Siberian railway is the town of Tomsk, the capital of a region through which flows the River Ob, another mighty river unknown to the average Westerner, including, then, to me. About 500 miles to the north of Tomsk

Siberian vista with a distant, abandoned church.

– hardly more than a stone's throw in Siberian terms – on the banks of the river, is an outpost called Nazino Island. This desolate place, barely more than a flat swamp dotted with spinneys of skeletal birches, was the scene in 1933 of a typical Russian tragedy, which, even by the abysmal standards of Uncle Joe, inspires awe for its cynical contempt for human life. The problem for the Bolsheviks was the painful discovery that ideas forged in the comfortable salons of Moscow and St. Petersburg, or even in exile among hosts sympathetic to the cause, did not necessarily work in practice. In their mania to teach *kulaks* and any element classified as 'undesirable' a lesson in social justice, they chose to overlook the fundamentals of human nature. Forced collectivisation of the farms led to famine and a mass migration to the cities, which in turn led to the introduction of internal passports and then the idea of forcible colonisation of the great wastes east of the Ural Mountains. So, like watchful cats, the secret police haunted the streets of Moscow and what was then Leningrad, pouncing on anyone regarded as undesirable – anyone at all – to pack them into trains at the end of April, with a daily food ration of 300 grams of bread, for the ten-day journey to a transit camp in the city of Tomsk. From Tomsk, they were loaded below decks onto four logging river barges for the four-day river journey, with now only 200 grams of bread to sustain them each day, after which they were dumped, like a herd of sheep into a field, in that patch of swamp called Nazino. Fend for yourselves, they said, transform this barren land, and yourselves into Revolutionaries worthy of the name. And so they did.

On arrival, 322 nameless women and 4,556 nameless men were counted off the barges with the twenty-seven who had died during the voyage, if I may dignify such an ordeal with that word, from Tomsk. A further 1,200 deportees arrived a few days after, and others later still. At Nazino, there was nothing. For food, there was what remained of twenty tons of flour. But since there were no ovens, the deportees consumed the flour mixed with river water, and became ill with dysentery. By the beginning of June, up to 2,000 deportees had died at Nazino. Three months later it was estimated that of the original 6,700 deportees, there were 2,000 survivors, of which half were bedridden, and a mere 300 capable of work. Some fifty people were arrested for cannibalism.

No doubt, there were many such stunts pulled by the Revolutionaries. Can you imagine the condition to which those wretches were reduced that they resorted to ravening after their own kind, not out of the instinct present in some species as a way of natural preservation of order, but out of insatiable starvation? Even Hitler made sure he got some work out of his herds before ushering them to the gas chambers.

I hope that this is not true. I would like to believe such stories are the work of those with axes to grind; but I fear that these things did take place, over and over and over again. Certainly, there were camps and there were camps, some better than others. One might, being charitable, ascribe this chaos to a mixture of glacial arrogance, childish spite and incompetence. But all were camps, the product of a search, whatever the cost, for a panacea. Remember Poland? By the time Stalin turned on

Hitler, he had occupied eastern Poland, sent countless thousands of Poles to Siberia and Kazakhstan, where they too were reduced to the base existence of the meanest, mangy animals; he played with his new allies until he obtained what he wanted. Yes, the Russians fought well and bravely, but Stalin never once stopped thinking of how he might work matters to his advantage by the physical attrition of entire populations. I cannot explain this; how a people whose veins are run through with intelligence and beauty and imagination, can become so cruel and cavalier towards their fellow beings. Is it some distortion of the ethereal, a sense that without suffering there is no joy? That comprehension and clarity comes only at the moment of death?

So we bumped on, stopping here and there at cities – Sverdlovsk, Perm, Krasnoyarsk, Novosibirsk, then closed to foreigners – which we peered at from the platforms through the station entrance for views of smoking buses and avenues of apartment blocks engulfed in a wintry fug. Sometimes we might buy a pot of homemade jam from women swaddled in a thick carapace of coats and scarves, seated still as ice at a little table near the exit. Or we might pace up and down watching the hefty women employed by Soviet Railways heave from carriage to carriage the great hoses that supplied water to them.

My recollections of that journey across Siberia are made up of details, the banalities of Soviet life that hang in the mind like pictures in a gallery. Sometimes, at a station, if we should halt opposite another train, I might glance through the window to meet the impassive features of young men, lying on bunks in 'hard class', who would stare

At work at a station in Siberia.

back at me with frank, imperturbable curiosity, as if they were examining something through a microscope. Like the border guards we had met at Brest, they were hardly men – there was something provocatively adolescent in their gaze. For the most part soldiers on their way to or from the war in Afghanistan that then was being fought between the USSR and the Mujahideen, they radiated the self-confidence akin to a semi-intellectual smugness that I came to know as the hallmark of Russian patriotism. In the candour of their blue eyes, there was the appeal of infantile innocence combined with unpredictable rages. On one occasion, a drunken gang of them burst out of their quarters further along the train into our carriage; they hung in the compartment door frames, leering and talking at us in their beautiful, seductive language in a way that was a faintly intimidating mixture of threat and cajolery loaded with suppressed aggression. These were the descendants of the pillagers of Warsaw and Berlin. Their bravado was soon exposed for its callowness; our carriage attendant came bustling down the corridor to unleash a scolding of such ferocity that they visibly wilted, protesting feebly, before sloping unwillingly away back to their bunks. Russia, it seemed, was still an old-fashioned matriarchy, where mothers instilled a manliness into their sons that depended on female approval.

Finally we arrived in Irkutsk. We stood freezing on the platform in the darkness of the very early morning, the rocking motion of the train still in us. Outside on the deserted street, an ancient bus idled, belching a cloud of blue smoke. In the hotel across the river from the railway station, we slept like children to the sound

Irkutsk – the view across the icy Angara river in Irkutsk to the Hotel 'Intourist'.

of whistling locomotives and clashing rolling stock; when we awoke, we saw another Russia. This was a gentler place – down at heel, broken – but cheerful, even homely. Although the news-stand in the hotel lobby sold among its foreign newspapers only ancient copies of suitable publications like *Neues Deutschesland* and the *Morning Star*; that on every available space there were brochures about the notional achievements of the USSR, invariably in Spanish (there must have been a large print run in expectation of revolution in South America); it all felt half-hearted, no more than a habitual conformity, a nod to the presiding ethos. In fact, in Irkutsk, I detected a hint of proud defiance, for Moscow was far away, its dictatorial pulse weakened by distance, all 2,500 miles of it. People in Irkutsk regarded the interminable directives from the Moscow Kremlin for the most part as irrelevant to them in their enchanted corner. Outside the hotel flowed the Angara, carrying away the crystal waters of Lake Baikal, flecked with ice, to the Yenisei and on to the Arctic Ocean. Beyond the river lay streets lined with timber izbas, with all the simple organic charm and tactility of wood, their high windows cut and fretted in the Siberian style from larch and cedar and pine. Where there was colour it was the blue of the water and sky and the green of the endless forest.

I don't know what currents of resentment and bile simmered beneath their proud provincial exteriors, but there was a quiet warmth among the people of Irkutsk that I found profoundly attractive. I could have imagined living there! Perhaps this was because in its isolation there was a rump of civilisation that had not entirely bent before the chill Stalinist blast. It was tired, though, this so-called 'Paris of Siberia', clutching at fading memories of a time when there was life there, real life; when the tea caravans passed through on their way from China; when intellectual life came to Siberia through the aristocratic Decembrists, living there in genteel exile. It had been a vibrant place, a warming light in a great darkness. All that had ebbed away. But what could not be taken from them was their precious Lake, their Father Baikal. Unfortunately, that was not necessarily true. There were precedents. In another distant part of the empire, the Soviet state in its infinite quest for the primacy of human production over fickle Mother Nature already had reduced what had been the fourth largest lake in the world, the Aral Sea – I mention this merely to indicate the scale of the Soviet achievement – to a few giant puddles of poisoned water, just as if a plug had been pulled. This immense inland sea that straddled Soviet Uzbekistan and Soviet Kazakhstan, which once had sustained tens of thousands of lives, had been reduced to a desiccated wilderness, littered with abandoned hulks rusting in the salty air. Had they wished, I have no doubt the Kremlin could have justified tampering in the same way with Baikal, a lake that holds one fifth of the world's fresh water. But perhaps, just perhaps, what was suitable for the Uzbeks and Kazakhs was not suitable for Russians.

Lake Baikal is not far from the city of Irkutsk. We were taken there in the *raketa*, the *rocket*, a kind of hydrofoil, a pleasant enough journey between the snowy *taiga*-thicketed banks of the Angara. Brief though this voyage was, there was enough time

A 'rocket', our means of transport between Lake Baikal and Irkutsk.

for one of those minor incidents to occur that seemed, in its triteness, to embody not merely opposing 'ideologies' – I suppose I have to use that word, although it seems an altogether glib term for the haphazard philosophies devised by mankind – but wholly different temperaments. It was like this. There was on board our *raketa* a toilet, which, in the ordinary course of things, was unneeded. It so happened that one of the party, a middle-aged American woman, who had been noticeably on edge since crossing from West to East, had a stomach vulnerable to the condition of her nerves. Until this moment this condition had been masterfully concealed, as she had never been far from relief when it was needed; but on this crowded, narrow and possibly gimcrack vessel, scudding along the river in a diesel mist, she succumbed. An urgent request was relayed to Svieta for permission to use the toilet, which, predictably enough, was locked. She spoke to the captain, who shrugged his shoulders with the news that the key, if one existed, was apparently not on the *raketa*, but locked in a draw in an office in Irkutsk. The toilet was closed. The woman, on the point by now of a fit of hysteria, spoke urgently to her husband, who came to me to suggest that I keep everyone else away from the stern of the vessel so that his wife might sully the limpid waters of Baikal. He did not use those words of course, but at any event she sat at the back and hung her pale meaty posterior over the superstructure to deliver a little peace-offering to the Baikal gods. In itself, nothing – rather cold and embarrassing for her – but nothing. It was not as if one dark stain was the remotest threat to the delicate ecological balance of an entire lake. No, why this stays in my memory is partly because it is a matter of scatological amusement, but in this case more because it seemed to me that in its way there was summed up the gulf between east and west – stolid Russia with its disregard for human frailty and its unforgiving sense of decorum, neurotic America with its presumption of comfort. Simplistic, perhaps, but it became very clear to me that no Russian would have travelled on that rackety rocket expecting to be able to use a toilet. No American would have boarded it had they known that the toilet was unavailable.

We came to a stop at Listvyanka, the little port right at the point of departure from the lake of the Angara. God, it was cold! That year, the winter had been long; the lake waters were still glazed with ice, waves at the shoreline suspended in mid-curl in skeletons of dazzling white frost. But the air, the air was pure and clean, above a flawless intangible mirror under the powder-blue sky, and far away, towards Mongolia, mountains shone. The hotel, a recent confection of poor quality cement overlooking the lake, was visibly crumbling away, like a stale cake. For once, though, we were grateful for Soviet incompetence. Apart from us, there was no one. From the dining room, we gazed across the lake towards the distant mountains as we gorged gratefully on fish, honey and fresh juice from forest berries. And the hotel was warm – the Russians knew the importance of heat. The curtains in the rooms didn't meet, tiles fell off the bathroom walls as you showered – but who cared? Everyone was enchanted, even the die-hard anti-Soviet, anti-Communist, anti-Russians among us. We sat at our tables at the wide windows of the restaurant, just as if we were on the train, at peace, and still.

'A fifth of the world's fresh water – Father Baikal'.

Locals in front of the hotel at Listvyanka.

In Listvyanka, a place without history, there was nothing to do. Here was a kind of Soviet Elysium. We could even forget that there had been a handful of Gulag camps downriver near the big town. In that village there reigned a great silence. Spring was close, to be followed by the Siberian summer, a hot and brilliant shooting star, so Svieta said. In Listvyanka, I could imagine the profound joy that the sun would bring. I could see the local women luxuriating like flowers opening in the sun, after the long, still winter. I could see that earthy Russian responsiveness to the waking lake.

The village was a handful of comely Siberian houses, with rusting tin roofs, scattered across a spongy marsh traced with mercurial rivulets and a disorganised tangle of electrical wires and telegraph poles, all askew from the shifting snow. Beyond the houses, away from the lake at the edge of the forest, stood a small wooden church. I made my way up to it, like a pilgrim. Not that I was exactly religious but I was in the grip of youthful sentiment. It did not occur to me until I was upon it that it could be anything other than the local church, the parish church. Then I remembered that I was in Russia, where, so I had understood, the opium of the people had been banned by a grateful populace. I almost turned back, presuming that it would be closed, or turned into a museum gloating over the foolish ways of the pre-Revolutionary past. But I recalled the church in Moscow on Gorky Street and with little else to do, I carried on. There were three of us, an unusual trio now that I think of it – apart from me there was the evangelical John, an Irishman with the usual quota of bonhomie, devotion and artfulness; and Mary, a black American woman who hated me with a passion, largely, I think, because she identified me with the sniggering racism of the Russians. A professional singer, she blamed me for a dose of laryngitis, apparently my fault for placing her in a compartment on the Trans-Siberian with a draughty window, in her eyes tantamount to a racist slur. I will always remember her looking at me with ineffable scorn one freezing day, jabbing at me as she uttered the words, 'You – you are the one that gave me pneumonia!' I was afraid of her but I liked her spirit.

As we approached the wooden church, a woman in black emerged from within and hurried away like a spider through the snow. The door was open and we entered, tentatively. By now the day was faltering enough to need the light from the votive candles that were placed about the room, casting flickering shadows across the icons studded into the walls, which gazed down on us with undisguised pity. In the centre of the room lay an open casket and in this, swaddled in a scarf and long woollen skirts, a thin and ancient woman, her hands clasped around a wooden cross, a scene of shocking serenity and holiness. I stood frozen in horror (I had never before been in the presence of a corpse); John crossed himself and recited a silent prayer; Mary stood silent, apparently unmoved, then, she began to sing, so low at first I thought it was the wind, her voice swelling as the words of *Swing Low, Sweet Chariot* filled the room. I must admit to feelings of trepidation at the reactions of my two companions, unworthy, I realise now, the result, I suppose, of my agnostic upbringing but because, too, in the back of my mind there lingered the possibly unreasonable fear of sinister consequences. But Mary's voice unleashed, soared, and whilst I cannot give in to the clichés of the pain of African enslavement, I can tell you that the beauty of that moment will rest with me forever, if only because I understood in a moment of clarity that the strength of belief, no matter how illogical, is an essential strength; and that in that small church, in that small village in the heart of remoteness, in a country that had tried for sixty-four years to eliminate an invisible God from the hearth and mind, faith and frailty were exposed not as opposites but as mechanisms in the balance that is humanity.

Once the silence enveloped us again, we prepared to leave. As we stepped out into the twilight, John muttered an excuse and returned inside. I saw him withdraw from his coat pocket what looked like a book and leave it on a table beside the door. Only once we were in Hong Kong did I learn – how innocent I was – that the book was a Bible, written in Russian, one of several in the appropriate languages that John left in our wake in Russia, Mongolia and China.

Behind the hotel, a path curled up among the trees, many tied with ribbons and shavings of tin foil and scraps of coloured cloth, a tiny remnant of Buryat shamanism, to arrive at a rocky outcrop overlooking at the point from where the Angara flows out of it, the lake, which, in the evening light, stretched far away in a wintry blue haze to the snowy Ardaban Mountains, beyond which lay first Mongolia and then China. By the time we had retraced our steps to the hotel, darkness had descended and with it the full force of the Siberian night. The sky was clear, the stars shining with diamond

Shaman tree, decorated with ribbons and scraps of material, overlooking the Angara river.

brilliance above the lake, scintillating across its perfectly placid waters. A pale light flickered from an anonymous building set back a little behind the hotel. Peering in through the misted window, I could make out only the blur of movement. Then a hand swiped the steam away and a face appeared, laughing; beyond it there were dozens of bodies, all naked, in various attitudes at their ease in what turned out to be at huge communal steam bath. I was waved in; there I found Svieta and what seemed to be the whole village wading, talking, in a state of relaxation I had not encountered so far in Russia. 'Come on in,' Svieta said. 'Don't be shy. It is not an orgy!' And so I did and again was introduced to the secretive Russian way, where exuberance is an emotion to be shared with intimates in worlds that even when not exactly private, offer seclusion and safety.

The next morning, we gathered outside on the crumbling concrete porch ready to return to the city. I heard someone complain, 'This place stinks – why, last night I couldn't flush the john!'

An earthy Australian voice growled, 'Aw, shut up and go and shit in the woods.'

That was it, we were almost done with Russia. We returned to Irkutsk in time to see at the tomb of an unknown soldier the changing of the guard by the Young Communist League, with their rosy, serious faces, the same faces that looked us over at the border with Poland all those thousands of miles away. They strutted with adolescent imprecision as they exchanged arms, drawing from some exclamations of disgust, as if this bellicose display differed from in the USA the right to carry

Young Communists at the Tomb of the Unknown Soldier.

arms; or in Britain the existence of the Territorial Army. In truth, I think there was a difference, for these young people were being taught to conflate peace with military might in a manner that smacked of religious exultation.

The thought of that ceremony, regarded as an honour by the participants, brings to mind something else from our journey across Siberia. A group of Russian students on their way to Novosibirsk or Sverdlovsk, or somewhere that was out of bounds to foreigners, had heard of our presence aboard the train. One evening, after asking Svieta's permission, who in turn asked ours, they approached us with an engaging mixture of curiosity and shyness to share a drink and to find out more about us. We were talking – well, hardly a discussion, a few words of English from them, our Russian being confined to Ваше здоровье! as we drank – when one of them brought out a creased photograph, black and white, the image grainy, of a massive truck bearing the weight of an even more massive missile. On the back, a single word written across it in pencil, 'Мир' – 'peace'! To me, that was a very odd gesture. There was no irony in it that I could see. The young man that gave it me was sincere – there was that ardent light shining from his eyes. He offered me the picture as if it were a pact, a bond between us, and this was the seal. For him, peace was power. He dreamed and he would go on dreaming. I cannot but wonder what he makes of Russia now.

The next morning, we left early for Mongolia. It was dark as we departed the hotel and trundled across to the other side of Angara to sit in the overheated bus awaiting the Moscow–Ulan Bator train; watching the diesel fumes rise slowly in the freezing air to enfold us in a stinking cloud, through which we caught glimpses as the day dawned greyly of local commuters squeezing into ancient, lopsided trolley-buses. There was no sorrow at our quitting Russia among the party members, only relief, a relief, I might add, that was palpable even among those inclined to overlook the USSR's egregious failings. For myself? Inexplicably, I felt a peculiar melancholy; now, looking back, I think I was seduced, like many before me, by the earthiness of the place; the flashes of suffocating warmth from the people, with their beautiful granite faces brimming with concealed emotion, and all their unpredictable contrary ways and their great gifts; the songs and music, the fairy tales, the magnificent, resonant voices and the rich, rich language. Russia – the sheer immensity! It was its own world. In the end, though, I did not fall for its temptations. For every instance of beauty and of gentleness, of ironic self-knowledge, there were too many more of brutishness and wanton cruelty, from which all the other joys were merely refuges. All big, powerful countries, the USA included, intimidate when they are deaf to the opinions of others. The Americans among us, who had entered the country beset by anxiety, left it with a feeling of superiority. 'The country is a mess!' they crowed. But it was the mess that was dangerous.

Of course, I was sad to be leaving Svieta. Not that there had been between us anything other than a bond of friendship but I had been affected by her fatalism that was, in its way, a kind of bliss. There were some in the party, most notably those who had given her the hardest time, who insisted on giving her a tip in American dollars,

'Intourist' dream team, guides, driver and bus.

less as an act of generosity than as a way of assuaging the very slight guilt they felt at their behaviour and as a proof that, for all her protestations, Svieta was in it for the money. Under sufferance, as I didn't think she would accept them, not least because it was a criminal offence to do so, I was deputed to perform this task. I had no choice; after a long discussion, she finally took the envelope. I would never know whether she kept it or whether she threw it guiltily into the Angara. In a way I, too, was guilty, through naïveté, of the same kind of imposition, for I presented her with my copy of *The Code of the Woosters*, a book, I now realise, which was probably hopelessly incompatible with Soviet values and probably, in its humour, impenetrable even to a sophisticate like Svieta. When she waved us off, some presumed that she was jealous of our freedom to travel beyond the Soviet frontier. I don't believe that was the case at all. No, she was glad her work with us was finished. She would have taken a plane to Moscow that afternoon and forgotten us; returned to the nucleus of the atom, like a nest at the heart of the great, dark Russian forest.

Our train had come all the way from Moscow, its final destination Ulan Bator, the capital of the Mongolian People's Republic, where we would arrive at nine o'clock the following morning. As we stood on the platform surrounded by luggage, watching the long line of smudged green metal caskets grind to a screeching, clattering halt, one in the party turned to me with an expression of frank puzzlement, saying, 'Why don't we fly? It's so much faster!' as if, after the thousands of miles we had put behind us and the thousands to come, the realisation that there were aeroplanes even there had only then dawned on him. I would never know whether this was a serious question or an example of recondite American humour.

On time – it was astonishing how train after train adhered to the timetable across these vast distances – we left Irkutsk. We picked up speed to reach that trundling Soviet Railway rhythm to which our bodies had become accustomed and very soon we were back at Lake Baikal, the southern shores of which we skirted over the best part of the day before striking south for Mongolia.

Railway history is a minefield of esoterica and trivial facts. But as a feat of will, the construction of the Trans-Siberian railway – and of course we were still following the course of the line at this point - between 1891 and 1916 (before the revolution, note it well!) ranks highly in any conceivable lexicon of human ingenuity and of all the sections along its entire 5,900-mile length, the most challenging of all was the section around Lake Baikal. The section immediately west of Baikal was the Mid-Siberian; to the east, the Transbaikal. Until 1904, the two were linked by ferries, which steamed across the lake from Port Baikal on its western shore (just across the mouth of the Angara from Listvyanka), to Mysovaya on the eastern shore. A pair of ships, the *Baikal* and the *Angara*, designed to break ice up to four feet thick and equipped with rails for transporting railway carriages, were built in England – in Newcastle – for the purpose. They arrived in parcels in 1897 to Listvyanka, where marine engineers reconstructed them before launching them to ply twice daily between the missing sections of the railway. Then the revolution came and the *Angara* was supplied with cannons to stand guard at Listvyanka, against which faction I do not know; the railway was completed but the *Angara* continued in service of one kind or another until 1962. Eventually it came to rest in the reservoir in Irkutsk, where I remember seeing it partially submerged. In fact, during its life it was swamped several times; in the 1920s, when it ran across rocks near the Ushkany Islands and then twice while it rotted where it lay. Whilst we were being shown around the city, as I stood gaping at the wreck, a local man engaged me in English, saying with Russian lugubriousness, 'It might be able to get into the *Guinness Book of World Records* as "the icebreaker that has descended to the sea bottom the most times".' His awareness of that book's existence had taken me by surprise, for I would guess he had never seen a copy. What he had was the singular Russian trait of intellectual superiority. He did not need to see it or read it or possess it.

In 1901, work began on the *Circumbaikal* line in order to put an end to the delays provoked by winter ice and summer storms, resulting in hundreds of disgruntled passengers trapped in the wilderness at the lake's edge. Between Port Baikal and Kultuk, a series of cliffs rise from the lake waters, necessitating the construction of hundreds of bridges, tunnels, scaffolds and trestles. At certain points, the labourers, working in all seasons, could reach the line only by boat; yet in only three years, the new link was completed, although not in time to prevent a disaster that came about as a result of an attack in February 1904 by the Japanese on the Russian navy anchored at Port Arthur. Reinforcements coming from the west found the *Baikal* and the *Angara*

The last resting place of the *Angara* once the missing link between two sections of the Trans-Siberian.

ice bound. A decision was made to lay a twenty-eight-mile section of track across the frozen lake to transport the troops. No sooner had the first train made steam than the ice cracked with a thunderous report and split asunder, the locomotive sliding, hissing and boiling, into the glacial waters. In the 1950s, a more direct link was added between Irkutsk and Kultuk, and so Port Baikal was mothballed. What is history if not the detritus and jetsam of decisions made elsewhere? When I claimed that Listvyanka was a place without history, that was so. But for a brief moment it was touched by the great events of the world and it cared little for them. Now, trains climb into the hills from Irkutsk, rumbling through the Taiga, fording innumerable streams, straining up to the junction with the old line from Port Baikal, before the spectacular descent to Baikal itself, which we saw yet again shimmering in the low matutinal sun.

Shortly after Myusova, at the foot of the Ardaban range, the snowy mountains sometimes visible from Listvyanka, we turned east again and finally, at Ulan Ude, capital of the Buryat Autonomous Soviet Socialist Republic (the Buryats being a once nomadic people indigenous to the Baikal region and not dissimilar physically and culturally from Mongolians; and who, naturally, were a suitable target of Uncle Joe's lethal embrace – he hugged several thousand to their death), we finally left the Trans-Siberian Railway and headed south towards Mongolia and China.

Chapter 5

The Mongolia Line

Mongolia, in my mind, was a wilderness, whilst there was nothing we did not know about China, a country that seemed to feature in the news every other day; a country that seemed to have taken over the manufacturing capacity of the entire world.

Sometimes, it seems to me, memory is life itself. The journey occupied one brief moment in time but the memory of it expands infinitely. There was something in the history of those countries – their recent history, we should not forget – that was a vision of mankind at its terrifying worst. That is why the memories are so forcibly, ineradicably imprinted on me. At the time, everything I saw, everything that happened, fascinated me. Only later, on reflection, did I look at those places with a more thoughtful eye, transformed as they had been by great and terrible events.

We trundled through a wilderness towards the Mongolian People's Republic. The train, composed of exhausted Soviet rolling stock strong with the smell peculiar to ancient carriages of greasy metal and calcified dust and a single brand-new carriage belonging to Mongolian Railways, was all but empty, one of those branch line services that exist to service the outer reaches of the empire. Just as we had entered the USSR on a dark and snowy evening, so now we were leaving it in the gloom of a blustery, stormy night; and as the frontier approached – at midnight again! – the landscape turned marshy and flat, beneath a turbulent racing sky fractured by lightning forks. Really, that was exactly how it was, the stuff of fairy stories:

'A savage place! as holy and enchanted
As e'er beneath a waning moon was haunted
By woman wailing for her demon-lover!'

Nor did it end there, because when finally we stopped at the bleak and benighted border town of Naushki, which might truly said to be in the middle of nowhere, the Russian guards took a dislike to the passports belonging to two Australians in the party. It happened that these passports were brand new, their photographs sealed beneath a plastic window, at the time a new idea, designed to discourage tampering. Naturally for zealous border guards ever watchful for spooks at an outpost to which news travelled slowly, such precautions were tantamount to an invitation. After requesting, with icy courtesy, the two citizens in question to follow them at gun point with their luggage through the driving rain into the station, in the search for microdots they proceeded to insert a knife beneath the plastic and photographs, thereby vandalising and invalidating the passports. I ask you! Microdots! Even then I

A stormy evening on the approach to the Soviet-Mongolian border.

had thought that the stuff of James Bond. There ensued the predictable uproar among the more volatile members of the party when the train appeared to be departing, leaving the unfortunate Australians behind; at which point I began to consider some kind of intervention, before discretion set in, which was fortunate as the train was merely moving to another platform, awaiting the decision concerning the alleged Australian spy ring.

I mention this partly because of the drama of the moment. There we were at midnight, at the border of Russia and Mongolia, at the height of the Cold War, amid a raging storm, with two frightened and bewildered tourists, tired and probably in an advanced state of intoxication, investigated as possible spies; whilst the rest of the party sat about in consternation, doubtless convinced that we had reached journey's end and holding me responsible for the whole debacle. Except the resolution was in the end predictably banal, as eventually the pair were returned to the train no worse for the experience, at which point the train resumed its journey south, approximately an hour behind schedule. But the thing that struck me was that we were not done with Russia as we had thought on leaving Irkutsk (and, indeed, in some ways were not done with Russia for a long time hence); and that the Russians, in their endless paranoia and enslavement to convention, simply did not care that they had rendered useless a pair of passports, which, had they been presented to the very same guards on entering the country, would have been firmly rejected. That was a revelation, the discovery of the inconsistency of ideology.

In the end, I concluded that the USSR was not quite the terrifying behemoth so beloved of the Western press. Certainly it was profoundly undemocratic, except in the most casuistic sense. There was well-concealed corruption and there was frustration and boredom and paranoia and acts of unconscionable cruelty, which sometimes were deliberate, but which mostly occurred through the haphazard application of flawed ideology-based justice. By 1981, the USSR was no longer a Stalinist hell but rather a bloated bureaucracy to which there was no appeal available for the dissatisfied or the wronged.

The physical gap between the two allies, Mongolia and the USSR, was vast. Just as with Poland, at the other end of the empire, the buffer was constructed to protect the mother country, so it was at this end; it must have taken an hour to get to Sükhbaatar, the Mongolian border town. I suppose that somewhere in that hour we must have crossed that line that is the official partition between nations but if it existed at all it was a formality, a token agreement between master and slave, a kind of conditional freedom.

I had barely given Mongolia a thought. I had read nothing; as far as I knew there was nothing to read. Mongolia – I speak frankly, with shame – was to me a sort of joke. In my mind it had no identity except as an amorphous expanse of territory, somewhere in Asia. In fact, I am not sure that I knew, with any certainty, that it was in Asia! For the record, it is, apparently – possibly – in Central Asia, itself a nebulous region without exact borders but which encompasses that tract of mountain and desert and steppe that was at the heart of the old Silk Road and which comprises the ancestral lands of its tribes of nomadic peoples. As children, we all knew of Outer Mongolia as a byword for remoteness without having the least idea where it was and that was still my position as I eventually entered it.

Its status as an amusing land of fable was enhanced by the border guards, who, small and bandy legged, in uniforms that seemed ill-suited to their stature, wandered along the corridor like excited children, looking into our compartments with undisguised curiosity and artless covetousness. They stood talking in their whispering, conspiratorial language; inspected our passports and visas without interest, even those invalidated not long before in Naushki; and opened bags, helping themselves to those magazines that took their fancy and trying to bargain for cameras and any device that could legitimately be seized under the pretext of material for spying but which, more to the point, was unobtainable in any shop for many thousands of miles in any direction.

Once all the formalities were over, a couple of them returned, sidling shyly into our compartments. 'Dollar! Dollars!' they would whisper urgently. I saw straight away that these were not a people with the almost preternatural purity of intellect, a kind of piety, that against the odds still prevailed among the average Russian but a people acting the roles that the Russians had created for them. Well, I say that I saw this but that is hindsight talking, as at the time we were once again somewhat in awe of events; or, should I say, most of us were. There were those, like Guppy and Archie, who, in finding common cause in their scorn for the enemies of Capital, spoke with such contempt of little yellow monkeys that I immediately felt myself a natural ally of the Mongolian people.

None of this lasted long and very soon the train swung back into action and we drifted into sleep, as we rocked our steady way across the invisible landscape; the single line, the Trans–Mongolian, the same gauge as the Russian, bisecting the country from north to south. Although we could see nothing, we sensed that we were travelling across a wilderness: there were no lights, no windy blast from passing trains; no shouts or whistles at the stations (and no stations). Just the creaking and jolting of our train and the occasional, hollow shriek from its klaxon.

In the morning we awoke to a scene of singular beauty. A delicate film of snow was laid across a rocky landscape of ancient high hills, streaked in mineral reds and indigos that sat changeless beneath a pale blue crystalline sky, which like a polished sapphire, seemed all the more magnificent for its tiny flaws, the smears of white cloud that hung high and immobile there. Through the window, we watched the carriages in front of us describing long curls and ellipses around the hills – sometimes the locomotive seemed on the point of turning back on itself. The land was empty; then we would slide over some crossing or other and there would be a single ruddy-faced horseman in high collar and felt hat on a sturdy little pony, solemnly raising a flag to signal safe passage. Sometimes in the distance, there was a plume of dust kicked up

Gers dotted across the Mongolian landscape, the nomadic way of life still much in evidence in 1981.

A yak, useful for meat, milk, hair and as a beast of burden among the cattle.

by a solitary motorcycle; and round white tents planted on the grassland like fat little cakes.

The train seemed to be making a long gradual descent, as if we were gingerly making our way down from a high plateau. The motorcycles spurting and surfing across the grasslands grew in number and then we travelled one final long bend to see the capital of Mongolia, Ulan Bator, cradled in a valley, dominated by a tall red and white chimney, which belched out a stream of thick white smoke. After the virginal countryside we had passed through, the sight of brute industrial power was a shock. The train whistled its arrival, we trundled through the detritus of yards and depots and came to a halt at the railway station, a Russian confection with tall concrete pillars and a few curlicues painted on the walls, a patronising nod to Mongolian culture.

And then the scene on the platform; the sun shone through the clear, cool air onto the crowd awaiting with palpable excitement the arrival of the train, an event, it turned out, that occurred only a couple of times a week. If anything, the scene reminded me of a gathering of worshippers after church, or a local market, an excuse to run into acquaintances and pass the time of day. There prevailed among the throng an atmosphere of quiet joy, expressed in the whispering language I had heard the night before – a murmuration of Mongolians. Flat, burnished faces hidden behind glinting dark-glasses, beneath felt fedoras, rose elegantly from wiry bodies bedizened in long, gorgeous gowns tied with dazzling sashes above black leather boots. Men and women and tiny, swaddled children stumping around in miniature boots with upturned toes,

Heading for Ulan Bator along the Trans-Mongolian.

milled about to no particular purpose and seemed shocked into delight if they were joined by the passenger they had come to meet. I was bewitched. I knew then that this was not a rustic Ruritania but a country of proud and independent people. We descended wearily from the carriage with our cases and stood amid the crowd, awaiting collection. The Famous Writer, casting a contemptuous glance over the scene, remarked, 'This is a colonial place, isn't it? This is a Soviet colony.' Of course, he was right, that was how it was. There was that ambiguity about the place, a blend of pseudo-sophistication and unasked for civilisation, of a kind. I thought of Africa or South America or India and of

A miniature Mongolian.

our own colonial past. This was how it must have felt once in Kampala or Khartoum or Lima. Here, we seemed far away from everywhere, in perfect isolation.

We stood for a long time in the cold before a representative of the state tourist agency, *Zhuulchin*, emerged from the station. She said, with the throaty quality of her native tone but in perfectly articulated English, that her name was Serena. Her cheeks were pouches beneath her wide spaced eyes, the shape of which reminded me more than anything of the twin symbols for Yin and Yang; whilst her skin had a chalky quality, as if mixed with copper. Her black hair was piled into a mound held up by a gilded clasp in the form of a dragon. But what was most striking was her sense of style – not for her the dowdy, dated skirts and blouses of Moscow, but instead proper jeans and a simple, classically tailored green coat. She was, now I think about it, no great beauty but somehow, in that empty land hemmed in by friend and foe, she had made herself chic. All of which is trivial, except that to me it demonstrated immediately a rather attractive defiance. For, if I have not already made this clear, the Mongolian People's Republic was a totalitarian Communist state closely allied to – or better, subject to – the Soviet Union.

Serena led us to a ramshackle bus and we drove the brief distance to our hotel. The Bayangol, or the Ulan Bator 'B', as it was known (in deference to the Ulan Bator 'A', a grander affair reserved for visiting dignitaries, hunters and other bearers of foreign and convertible currency) not very affectionately, resembled any other tower block to be seen across the communist world or, indeed, in any Western inner city. As we approached it we passed a tall black statue on a plinth, which I took to be of Lenin, in that ubiquitous hectoring posture of his, until I realised that the pose was more avuncular, and the moustache more suited to a Latin American brigand. That icon, which went unnoticed by everyone else, by then inured to the point of indifference to Soviet statuary, was of Stalin. I must admit to a moment of delirium. Surely not Uncle Joe, here: I put it down to fatigue and, in the general chaos of checking into the hotel, forgot all about it. Only later, taking an exploratory stroll, did I discover that my eyes were not deceiving me, for there he was, hand modestly tucked into his tunic, for all the world a benign Mongolian hero, a latter-day Genghis Khan. At first it seemed perverse to find him there, now that his reputation throughout the civilised world, even in the USSR, had undergone a significant reappraisal. I liked to think that it was a case of simple indifference on the part of the Mongolian people to past events, or even a positive acceptance of an undeniable fact of history, no matter how uncongenial; but I think that even then there lurked in the upper reaches of the Mongolian hierarchy a covert admiration for his methods.

The Ulan Bator 'B' was an idiosyncratic edifice of shambolic charm. In the lobby, a television, watched intently by a small group of local men, crackled noisily; the receptionist, a taciturn middle-aged woman with a bright, charming smile and bovine haunches who collected our passports, wore a pair of spectacles with blue lenses above a white Elizabethan complexion and there was a lingering, ubiquitous odour of something faintly rancid that I later discovered had a strong connection

The rooftops of the Mongolian capital from the Ulan Bator 'B'.

with sheep. The lift, of Russian construction, was given to anarchic unpredictability; and on every floor – for we would stop at each on our way to our rooms – we would see groups of whispering, bescarved women on their knees surrounded by buckets of putty for filling in the many holes in the plasterwork. But the old sheets were crisp and the water, heated by the monstrous powerhouse we had seen as we arrived, and which I could see from my room, was plentiful and scalding. Sleep in Mongolia was deep and long.

There had been no restaurant car in the train and so we had a late breakfast in the enormous, empty dining room. If you like yoghurt, go to Mongolia; even now I can taste the creaminess of it, see its buttery hues filling the glass goblet, and inhale the faintest hint of ovine hair, sweetened by the crust of sugar that sat invitingly at the top.

When I tell you that the highlights of a visit to Ulan Bator were yoghurt and a quixotic hotel, you might well look askance. Yet, in a way, that was true because what held my interest there were not the conventional sights – of which, anyway, there were few – but the atmosphere of confusion, by which I mean a kind of dislocation between past and present, the battle between old habits and the imposition of new ones. Looking across the rooftops, the city, cradled in a green valley surrounded by hills, filled with grandiose public buildings that served no discernible purpose and which seemed, largely, to be permanently closed, was laid out in an unnatural

View towards Ulan Bator from the Soviet Monument with its reminders of the power of revolution.

pattern of order, as if an enthusiast had deliberated on a typical civic scene for a model railway. Constructed in the style known as Soviet neo-classicism, with the addition of a few Mongolian motifs, they had been rendered in baroque blues, reds and greens. I was reminded of childhood wooden building blocks.

Here and there the horizontal nature of the skyline was broken by the upturned eaves of a building in the Chinese style, its turmeric-coloured roof tiles gleaming in the sunlight. Overlooking it all from one of the hills that encircled the city was the inevitable concrete gift (I had by now learnt to expect these tokens of subjugation) from the 'Soviet people', a monumental expression of lopsided friendship, surrounded, thankfully, if inexplicably, by an encampment of Mongolian *gers*. The city prospect was not an unattractive one and yet a peculiar listlessness prevailed, with all native gregariousness, seemingly, corralled into the forum of the station platform.

There was activity – worn-out Russian buses crammed to bursting, expressionless faces pressed against filthy windows struggled dirtily along the streets; a horse and cart cantered among them; single horsemen sat bolt upright on their ponies, which trotted rapidly along the uneven pavements; buzzards perched attentively on concrete posts; at the perimeter of Ulan Bator, where the roads seemed to peter out at the last apartment blocks, spirals of dust whipped by the wind spun across the rutted landscape – but there seemed to be no purpose to it. Occasionally we caught glimpses of long suburbs made up of *ger*, which, we had been warned in the hotel, were out

The edge of Ulan Bator looking across the untidy suburbs.

of bounds and not under any circumstances to be photographed. The government had forced on its own people shame for their nomadic traditions; Mongolia, the government insisted, was an emancipated modern state, open to the world. Except, of course, it was not and could not be so, for as long as Moscow dictated the terms of their alliance. Ulan Bator, however, was a city the origins of which were dependant on the very mobility of traditional nomadic tents, for in the pre-Revolutionary past it had been only one of several temporary administrative centres.

Later that day we were back on the ancient bus for a tour of the city. In the main square, under that clear blue and endless sky, was the tomb containing the founder of the Mongolian People's Republic, Sukhe Bator, a simulacrum of the mausoleum in Red Square in Moscow in which were displayed the doughy remains of Lenin. At the centre of the square, an unnecessary space in a country of infinite spaces, dominated by the Hural Government building, Sukhe Bator sat calmly on a rearing pony, pointing portentously towards a better future, a Mongolian version of Vladimir Ilyich. The current president, Tsedenbal, had been in power for decades and his portrait, together with those of the Soviet leader, Brezhnev, and Marx, Engels and the rest, overlooked us, it seemed, wherever we went.

Although there was little enough to discover from the confines of a bus (had Ulan Bator remained Urga, a city of temples and felt tents, then what a magnificent place it might have been) there were, in fact, two museums of genuine interest – the State Central Museum and the Winter Palace of the Bogd Khaan. Like most of the city's

Forbidden Ulan Bator – *ger* suburbs.

public buildings, they were underused and the truth may well have been that they were opened only when there were dollar-paying foreigners in town, so that visiting them was akin to opening up dusty, forgotten tombs. In the State Central Museum were examples of the vast array of flora and fauna to be seen throughout Mongolia, together with a remarkable collection of dinosaur skeletons, bones and even dinosaur eggs and droppings, discovered in the Gobi Desert, which backed up my instinct that Mongolia was the birthplace of the world.

The second museum was a mixture of monastery and palatial residence of the last Mongolian king, Jebtzun Damba Hutagt VIII, who was also Mongolia's Eighth Living Buddha. Most of the guides provided by Zhuulchin, the state tourist agency, spoke limited English and knew even less about the history of their country. This was perfectly fair. In part, their ignorance reflected Communist-inspired flexibility with the truth but it was also the case that Mongolia's history was so fragmentary and inchoate that it would have taken a talented story teller to have made sense of it. As for the last Bogd Khan, his story is remarkably similar to that of many early twentieth century rulers of helpless countries, strategically important to their neighbours, tossed about in the revolutionary tides of the time. His rather charmingly unpretentious palace contained his eccentric collection of gifts and possessions, including a gorgeous ceremonial *ger* and a stuffed giraffe, the neck of which had been filleted so that it could stand beneath the low ceiling.,

Of all the places we visited on that journey, I think I loved Mongolia the most. That was something I was not prepared for. Of course, it is easy to be sentimental! And magnificent scenery can have a poetic effect on one's sensibilities; whilst the enticing simplicity of primitive living is, as we all know, a chimera. And still: still, after all that, there was something deeply loveable about Mongolia, a poignancy that seemed to go to the heart of human existence. Old ways versus new ways. The misfortune for the Mongolians was that the resolution of what was an inevitable clash was at the behest of and under the auspices of the Soviet Union; and the Soviet recipe was not, you will not be astonished to hear, one of gentle encouragement.

After Russia, what was to become the Mongolian People's Republic was the second state to succumb to the Communist Revolution. A country with the thinnest population density on Earth. A land of herders and nomads and priests. A country, one might imagine, well suited to being left to its own devices. To describe Mongolia, whose peoples had once conquered much of the known world, as 'timeless', could be regarded as patronising, as if change was neither desirable nor feasible; but if change was to come, I am quite sure that industrialisation on the Soviet model was not the appropriate method. That was like throwing a hand-grenade into a chicken coop to pluck feathers.

Mongolia was unfortunate. To its north, Russia. To its south, China. At their most powerful, the Mongols had subjugated both the Chinese (the thirteenth century Chinese Yuan dynasty was Mongol) and the Russians, and others besides. But that was many centuries before. In the meantime, their territory had shrunk and their tribal rivalries faded away. The Golden Horde (what an evocative name!) and the other Khanates created to assert Mongol rule were absorbed into the Russian empire, surviving here and there even into the nineteenth century as corrupt petty princedoms; Buddhism became the Mongol religion; whilst from the seventeenth century, the Mongolian heartlands came under the suzerainty of the last Chinese dynasty, the Qing. The Qing dynasty rulers of China throughout the final three centuries of imperial rule were not Chinese but Manchu, a people of Jurchen origin, and therefore kin of the Mongols, whom they generally left in peace, if only to discourage expansion by the Han Chinese (by Han I mean the original non-Manchu population). Naturally, I simplify, for when you unravel the threads of the history of Central Asia over the centuries, it is quite easy to lose one's way, if not one's sanity, amid the multitude of names and customs and similarities and shifting allegiances and tribal migrations and splinterings; yet all, in my mind, have their origins on the plains and steppelands and deserts to the north of China and all are linked by a common ancestral tie. The Mongols and Kazakhs and Kirghiz now have their own states, but their *gers* and *yurts* and their ponies and their traditions are much the same. Mongolia itself, in the end, became a land-locked backwater, protected by the Altai Mountains in the west, the Gobi Desert in the south and Siberia in the north, where Mongols existed much as they had always done, living in the same felt-lined tents and riding the same rugged little ponies, herding their sheep, ever vigilant against wolves.

But the Manchu, just as I was, were wrong to have underestimated the Mongolians. It was true that by some criteria, the country could have been considered backward. Certainly, in a country where lamas had as much influence as tribal nobles, there was stasis and stagnation; but at least the Manchu had respected Mongolian cultural independence. As it happened, that had been in the Manchu's interest, as they, too, endeavoured to maintain their own separateness from the Han Chinese, whose country, China, they ruled. But, as with all conquerors of China, they eventually succumbed to the stubborn habits of millennia of continuous civilisation and when, in a desperate effort to prevent the revolution that would bring an end to imperial rule, and wary of the territorial ambitions of the Russian Tsar, the Manchu introduced a plan to plant Chinese farmers in what was then called Outer Mongolia, the Mongolian people, who had tolerated their fate with resigned equanimity, rose up. Their way of life was sacred; a petition from the noble families of Mongolia was presented to the Qing Government the essence of which was a plea – 'Consequently, we all desire that we be allowed to live according to our ancient ways.' The canny Mongolians, aware that the Tsar was anxious about the growing instability in China, asked the Russians for assistance. At this point, Russia had no intention of annexing Mongolia, preferring it as an independent but stable ally. The Qing Government held back from imposing the new reforms and the Mongolians, conscious of impending revolution in China, saw their chance and declared independence. A compromise was reached. Russia and China recognised Outer Mongolia's autonomy but as part of Chinese territory. This was an imperfect resolution, but at last there was a Mongol nation once more.

Regretfully, the euphoria was brief. Just as with those countries in Eastern Europe that finally had won their independence following the First World War, only to see it taken away again as if it had all been a tease, so it was with Mongolia. What happened? That wretched revolution in Russia. The new Chinese republic, established in 1911, chafing a little at having lost Outer Mongolia (they still ran Inner Mongolia, which had always been more closely integrated into Qing China, just to add to the complications), watching events in Russia with, presumably, mixed emotions, took back Mongolia – Outer Mongolia – in 1919. Meanwhile, the civil war in Russia continued. Don't forget that the First World War, in which the Russians were still involved, notwithstanding the revolution, continued to drag on. The country dissolved into factional fighting, essentially Reds (the Bolsheviks) against the Whites, composed of a loose alliance of imperial loyalists, democrats and an assortment of hotheads and nutcases, or eccentrics if you want to be generous. Among the latter was the Baron Roman von Ungern-Sternberg, another of those pathologically disordered visionary Russians (though of Austrian blood). An officer in the Imperial Army, whose posting to Transbaikalia had intoxicated him with the customs of the nomadic Mongols and with the Chinese occupation of Mongolia in front of him and the Bolsheviks gaining ground behind him, he saw the solution to the problems of the world; a pan-Asiatic monarchy in the manner of Genghis Khan, of whom the Baron, possibly, imagined himself the reincarnation. He and his followers marched into Mongolia to reinstall the Bogd Khan, the theocratic head of state from 1911, who had been removed by the Chinese.

The ramifications of this were far-reaching. Japan, concerned at events in Russia and in China and gradually developing its own philosophy of militarism, was involved with all of this, too, offering tacit support here, withdrawing it there, biding its time. That is another story but you can see the nature of the stew.

So, in he goes, this White Baron. He takes Ulan Bator – let's face it, there was not much else to take in that country of scattered nomads – by defeating the remnants of the occupying Chinese, who dug into a series of trenches around the city to no avail. A man whose ideas, whatever their value, were as usual in such cases, perverted by personal weaknesses (just like Uncle Joe) and so he resorted to killing those he did not like (just like Uncle Joe), impatiently and indiscriminately, an endearing habit that served only to open the door to the Bolsheviks who, together with their genuine Mongolian counterpart, Sukhe Bator, marched in and eventually defeated him. In his place (for the Baron, needless to say, fared badly at the hands of the People's Court), the Bogd Khan was reinstalled. The Baron was like a madder, badder version of Brigadier Ben Ritchie-Hook in *Sword of Honour*. Yet, he was no better or worse than what followed. He believed that western decadence could be redeemed through Asiatic, Buddhist wisdom, rather spoiling this intellectual vision of peace and harmony with a simultaneous belief in the sublime nature of war.

And for the average Mongol, out on the steppe, life went on as before, undisturbed by little beyond the rumours of what was to come. After the death of Bogd Khan, a Tibetan who had been pronounced as the reincarnation of the Jebtsundamba Khutuktu, the third most important person in the Tibetan Buddhism hierarchy, below only the Dalai and Panchen Lamas, and the spiritual leader of Mongolia, the Revolution took full hold. The Mongolian Revolutionary Government declared that no more reincarnations were to be found. But the habits of centuries have that annoying tendency to persist, even in the face of scientifically grounded 'Revolution'. With rumours circulating of the reincarnation of the ninth Jebtsundamba Khutuktu, the Great Hural of the Mongolian People's Republic responded with a decree that searches for reincarnations of the Bogd Khan were henceforth outlawed. Interestingly, the next reincarnation was discovered in Tibet, in 1936. The Tibetans, being wiser in matters of state than we in the west, concealed this discovery, aware that a public proclamation would inevitably lead to yet more persecution of Buddhists by the Mongolian – Soviet – Government. There you have it. The Mongols - constantly harried by greedy Chinese or by unstable White Russians – were compelled to take the only route left to them, the meretricious Soviet road to a socialist utopia.

Nightlife in Ulan Bator was, to be generous, limited in scope. In fact, there was nothing to do. The streets were empty of all but one or two knots of intoxicated young local men. The hotel bar did not open according to the advertised timetable – the padlock across its doors remained locked our first night – but, apparently, at the whim of the barman. On the second night it was open and, after dinner, I sat there with a beer and a book. Whilst this had nothing really to do with what followed, it was nonetheless faintly ironic that I happened to be reading at the time *Tinker, Tailor, Soldier, Spy*, a book that I am certain was unavailable in the book stores in either Moscow or Ulan Bator and which, too, would surely have been confiscated at any of the preceding borders had it been noticed. Anyway, I took my place, after asking the barman for tokens to play the jukebox, of the type once found in our pubs, listening to a succession of surprisingly recent hits from Britain and America; something that was unexpected, but that reflected the very loose hold that Communist ideology had over the Mongolian population. Thinking back, I suppose that it was strange to find a juke box there, but at the time it seemed to perfectly fit in with the eccentric nature of the country. The room was lit as if it were dusk. Cut into the ceiling was something very charming and beautifully Mongolian, a constellation of little illuminated stars, an interior reflection of the boundlessly crystalline skies outside.

A few locals, who were not permitted to enter through the hotel's main entrance, drifted in through the back door. Most of them were not purely Mongolian but, it turned out, had Russian blood, or some Russian connection, which, ironically, given that in Russia itself Russians were not permitted to mingle with foreigners in hotels, entitled them to use the bar in the Ulan Bator 'B'. So there I was relaxing with my book, when I felt that barely perceptible but nonetheless nagging sensation of being watched. Looking up, framed in the doorway I saw a young man in uniform, scrutinising me with intense, and clearly unfriendly, attentiveness. He was very smartly turned out, boots shining, blond hair neatly cut, cleanly shaven, subaltern's build, blue eyes unblinking, even when I met his gaze. But at that moment, a gleefully contemptuous smile broke his features and he advanced into the bar, which I fancy was out of bounds to even an officer in the Russian Army, with the swagger of someone keenly confident of his discovery. Standing before my table, surveying me still, after a few seconds silence, he proceeded to speak to me using the coaxing tones peculiar to the Russian language that, I had learned from experience, contained the seed of prohibition. When I shrugged and replied to him in English that I could not understand what he was saying, his smile broadened as he leaned down to look at the cover of my book, which happened to feature a family of matryoshka dolls, nodding slowly, knowingly, as if to say that he had discovered whatever it was that I was up to. I could feel his vodka tinctured breath, which quickened a little as he realised that the words were in a language he did not understand. He stared with a hint of puzzlement at my room key. Behind me, the boisterous roistering of the local drinkers had ceased. My new companion, aware of the sudden silence, looked up and scowled at them in a way that had the effect of a challenge. One of them approached my table.

This man was young with a colouring and with features that suggested mixed Mongolian and European blood. He addressed the soldier in Russian with quiet courtesy – a heretical courtesy, I would say, but that was how things were. When the officer responded, the other turned to me and with a perfectly straight face explained in English – rather good English – that the officer wanted to arrest me, as I was clearly a deserter from the Soviet Army. This was so preposterous in so many ways that I remember smiling at the officer with the misplaced confidence of the fool who believes himself immune to the absurd games of international politics (as indeed I was) and certain that he, too, would surely and finally see the absurdity of the accusation. There followed a dialogue courtesy of the local man during which it was pointed out that I did not understand Russian, so I was an unlikely candidate for the Soviet Army; that I was reading a foreign book; that since it was impossible to reside in the Ulan Bator 'B' without a passport, the presence of a room key confirmed my status as a foreign national. What I remember most vividly was that none of this impeccable logic made any impression on the Russian whatsoever, for in his determination to find threats where none existed, in his zeal to expose betrayal, he could not bear to be confounded by the evidence of his own eyes. In the tradition of his forbears, he presumed that treachery was ever present even among the ranks of the Soviet Army. He just rocked on his toes, maintaining his suspicious stare, before backing out into the lobby beyond the bar, at which point my rescuer returned to his companions. It was their explosion of laughter that brought the Russian back; and once again he stood before the table, convinced that he had caught a renegade and that he could cajole the truth out of me. Then, a most remarkable event took place. My rescuer stood up and bellowed across the room at the Russian, who in an instant became white with fury – I had never seen a transformation so swift, except once when an early employer, literally frothing at the mouth with anger, tried to throw me downstairs; but that is another story – and stood stock still. Quite, quite still. Everything stopped. A muffled snigger came from behind the bar. And then the bar erupted into … what? Well, what I can only describe as gales and waves of laughter, strong enough to eject, finally, my persecutor into the dusty street outside, where I watched him lurk unhappily among the rusting swings and roundabouts of a long-neglected playground before he wandered away to his barracks.

The juke-box restarted with a click – I recall that it was, of all things, a song called *Mr Blue Sky* – and I was invited to join my new friends. Naturally, I was intrigued to know what had been said to the Russian soldier but Khunbish, my saviour, seemed reluctant to shed any light on it. I was worried that he might suffer some sort of consequence, but he batted away my concerns, preferring to ask me instead about England. To my surprise, there was not much I could add to his knowledge. His grasp of life in Britain, short on detail and in some respects confused with America, was robustly positive in the way of someone desperate for emancipation. Without knowing their exact nature, he sensed that in other parts of the world, thousands of miles away in every direction, there were complexities and subtleties and possibilities, all missing from his own shrunken existence in the confines of a small town masquerading as a capital city. He – they all – radiated a kind of sophistication that had been blunted by experience into the fraternal nihilism you might find among gangsters in an impoverished inner suburb. We are neither one thing or another, they told me. We are mixed blood. We are no longer Mongolian; we don't feel any more the need to tread the grass and inhale the smell of sheep and horse, to move with the seasons. We have lost that. The Mongolians still have that choice, they can decide which is better – new ways or old ways. It is difficult enough for them but for us, they told me, we who are more Russian than we are Mongol, it is worse. The best we can aspire to is Moscow – and what is Moscow if not a giant Ulan Bator?

We drank together for several hours. When the beer ran out we drank vodka. The next morning, I awoke on the floor of a flat in a filthy tower block on the edge of the city, encircled by the whole slumbering lot of them. Khunbish took me downstairs and pointed me in the direction of the hotel for the walk through windy streets of snow crystals and concrete dust. Before I left, he gave me a rueful, haggard smile, retrieving a little painting from his pocket, which he pushed it into my hand. The simple painting on glass showed a Mongolian on horseback hunting, lance in hand, across the Mongolian hills. 'Do you know something?' he said. 'The Russians blame the Mongolians for their addiction to alcohol. They say we – we? they? – passed on the alcohol 'gene' during the centuries of what they are pleased to call the "tartar-mongol yoke". I have both genes. Lucky me.'

The following day, as you can imagine, was a long day for me but one which, fortunately, consisted of an 'excursion' to see the 'other' Mongolia. The trip into the countryside was made unnecessarily complicated by the way it was sold. There was a fixed fee, in American dollars, for the use of the bus. This fee appeared to have

Our Ulan Bator guide of unexpected sophistication.

no rationale, other than what westerners might conceivably pay. The more people participated the lower the fee, so that in the event of a full bus, the cost per head would have been reasonable. Not everyone was convinced of the excursion's value but since the fee never varied, with every person who chose not to go, the price rose accordingly. Those who wanted to go but could not afford it blamed those who did not want to go for making it more expensive.

'Why wasn't this included in the price of the whole trip, anyway?' someone asked.

'Because it was not possible to calculate beforehand a price based on the numbers in the party, when we don't know how many people will be in the party,' I replied.

'Why don't you negotiate with them?' someone else suggested, as if requesting a pow-wow with a tribal leader.

'Because this is Mongolia,' I said. 'It is a communist country. They don't do negotiation. It is a take it or leave it situation. The idea of negotiation doesn't figure in a planned economy.'

Ulan Bator was small and it was not long before we had passed through the suburbs: the decrepit blocks of flats; the haphazard puzzles of telegraph poles and trailing wires; the maze of wooden fences that were without purpose except as somebody's notion of urban living; the *ger* estates, seemingly so out of place in a city until I recalled that Ulan Bator had once, when it was known to westerners as Urga, been a city of tents, a meeting place for annual tribal pow-wows, where the only permanent building had been a temple. In fact, if you were drawn to the city for work or because your herd of sheep had been annihilated by disease or the cold, a *ger* was a most convenient way of taking up residence. You went to the edge of the outermost suburb, or simply located a gap, and set up home. No sanitation, but a roof, at least. Yet, I could not help feeling that something was wrong; out in the country, you could always move on. In the city, tendrils became roots, which soon stiffened into permanent binds. Once your tent became surrounded by neighbours you became a city dweller. Soon, you want a flushing toilet (even a Soviet one) and heating and a car.

It was not long before the asphalt ran out. That was one of the defining impressions of Ulan Bator for me at the time – a kind of caravan site, where nothing happened, surrounded by a wilderness at its most benign, convenient only for travel on horseback. Nonetheless our creaking bus, built for delivering commuters around Moscow rather than along a barely discernible country trail, jolted and shuddered into the uncorrupted valleys outside the city, beyond the reach of smokestack and generator. Before long from out of the thin grassland, piles of boulders and pleated outcrops of tawny rock rose up around us, the splinters and jetsam from the steep and stony hills beyond, crowned with a fringe of trees beneath which tumbled, here and there, like deep green waterfalls, cascades of woodland. I felt that I was in the oldest place on earth, from which all animate life sprang. Away from the trail, small encampments of *ger*, ponies tethered around them, stock still in the chill breeze, drifted tantalisingly by. We jerked across a rocky ford, where a herd of sheep lay inert

Locals at Terelj Tourist Camp, the nearest most westerners got to nomadic life.

in a woolly pile on its banks, and struggled up a rise to descend into a broad hull of a valley, flanked on either side by chains of verdant hills, with gentle, inviting slopes. There, in this gloriously unfettered space, was a fence. A fence that enclosed a few wooden chalets, a row of unnaturally pristine *ger* and a building that mirrored the Russian confections in Ulan Bator.

We were back in the USSR. Our immersion in the Mongolian countryside was to consist of the opportunity to sample traditional costume from the dressing up box located in one of the *ger* and a lunch – mutton, of course – in the building that turned out to be a hotel of an invigoratingly spartan nature. The place was a kind of holiday camp for the pupils of Lenin. As we wandered around aimlessly, psychologically confined behind the low wooden fence, a group of Uzbek girls emerged and holding hands as if they were in a school playground, ran in a line ululating with extravagant joy, before disappearing back into the warmth of their chalets. In the dining room, apart from us, there was a single bulky Russian couple, who sat in composed silence, wearing the dressing gowns issued to them after their morning sauna in a damp and glaucous treatment area and a small party of thin and miserable East Germans, with a cluster of patriotic badges sagging on their lapels, nursing glasses of beer. A portrait of the president of the Mongolian People's Republic looked down at us with porcine superciliousness.

I understood that this place was the Soviet empire in miniature, comforting in its way, offering protection from the temptations and threats of the world beyond its fence, a frontier not to be breached. Everything required for a bracing holiday in the limpid air of Mongolia was there in that corral. A little bit of tradition (the *ger*); a little bit of healthy physical conditioning (the sauna); a little bit of nature (the views across the valley). Above all, a good dose of safety (organised control). All far better than the unfenced, dangerously unconfined spaces of the Mongolian wilderness.

Now, I believe, in that valley there is a luxury hotel. I am not sure that it will be much of an improvement on its Soviet predecessor. Better food, I am sure; a shiny new gym no doubt, filled with treadmills and exercise bikes. Gates, probably, and a higher fence. A different type of captivity. Of the two I know which one I would choose, but I am not confident that either of them accurately express the will of the local people.

After lunch, Serena, who exhibited little enthusiasm for the camp – I mean, she gave us all the spiel about the rocks shaped like turtles and priests at prayer, but I could see that her heart was not in it – offered to take us for a short walk along the valley. A few stayed behind, Archie, Guppy and the Vietnam vets, seizing the moment to prove again to their satisfaction that the system did not work, as if proof were needed. A few others headed for the dressing-up box, but the rest of us went with Serena out into the open valley. We followed an icy stream of water faceted like a cold, hard gemstone, set between banks stiff and white with frost. Serena, who had dressed in a rather becoming *del* for the occasion, was transformed from a chic urbanite to a country girl, happily cupping the freezing water in her hands and drinking with

Mongolians on their rugged ponies, then still the preferred means of transport for many.

dainty relish. She told us that in the brief sunny summer, the hills and grassland were thick with meadow flowers – edelweiss, gentians and blue mist – and alive with crickets. It was not hard to imagine, even on that bitter day, because the landscape, though empty and windswept, had a gentle aspect that with sunshine and warmth could be transformed in an instant to a bejewelled wild garden.

We rounded a low hill and there, right before us, was a *ger*. A spiral of smoke rose steadily from a tin chimney poking through the felt roof. Serena seemed to hesitate, but then shouting out some greeting approached the painted wooden door, opened it without knocking and peered inside. There was a shout and then a man in a shabby *del* with a trilby perched firmly on his head, his skin the texture of old polished wood confronted us. He looked over Serena's head, staring in astonished incomprehension before his gaze returned to her at which his eyes contracted in recognition and his face collapsed into a delighted grin. It turned out that this old man – we discovered later that he was about eighty – was Serena's grandfather. I think the others all presumed that this moment was stage-managed, but Serena assured me after that the meeting was a coincidence. She, as a *de facto* if unwilling government representative, was charged with discouraging foreigners from associating with Mongolians in general but in particular those living in tents. But the one thing that foreigners wanted on a visit to Mongolia was somehow to experience the lives of the nomads. Up to a point they wanted that – but they didn't really want it. They wanted to be photographed with a nomad; they wanted to sit inside a *ger* (briefly, on account of the smell) but that, really, was it. The acid test of yearning for the simple life is – can you bear the stink?

Serena's grandfather – his name was Oktyabr – was unsure how to deal with this circumstance. His welcoming nature – the etiquette of the steppes – naturally inclined to invite us into his house, but this was at odds with the Soviet orthodoxy that insisted on apartheid. I saw the perplexity expressed guilelessly in his open face and I saw that he looked with pathos to his grandaughter for guidance. She cared nothing for rules. Here, in old Mongolia, she was in her element.

We filed in and took our places, sitting about where we could in a kind of respectful disorder. The heat of the interior warmed up greasy surfaces into a fug of homely odours; marmot skins and drying strips of mutton were hung about the fringes; an assortment of gimcrack ornaments and antique photographs decorated items of highly-coloured furniture that fitted neatly like a jigsaw against the lower part of the *ger* to the point from where, supported by a wheel of red wooden ribs, the roof sloped up to its crown. I was reminded of a circus big-top, or a time-machine like a Mongolian Tardis, a place of perfect containment, a fabulous corner of the world.

Oktyabr offered us first a very salty, milky tea, followed by fermented mare's milk. Of course most of us, including me, were nervous drinking from grubby cups that we presumed at best to have been rinsed in cold water; we sipped politely. Photographs were taken with attempted discretion, although our host hid his face the moment he thought he detected a camera pointing in his direction. Before long the others pleaded fatigue and returned to the corral, leaving Serena, Oktyabr and me to our *airag*, to the charm of which with its mildly alcoholic tang, I had succumbed.

I was curious about our host's name. Pronounced 'akteeahber', there was something familiar about it. To me, it sounded more Russian than Mongolian. When Serena explained that it was indeed Russian and simply meant 'October', with reference to what Communists called, as if it were a holy festival, the Great October Socialist Revolution of 1917, I understood. But her grandfather was older than the revolution – surely, I asked Serena, he had another, Mongolian name? She sighed; her grandfather laughed a little uneasily it seemed to me as she translated the question. But for the wind buffeting against the felt, and the blowing from the pony outside, there was a silence.

Serena cleared her throat and drank noisily from her cup (I noticed that her manners had altered in keeping with her surroundings). Her grandfather, of course, had been given a good, sensible Mongolian name at the time of his birth. But when the revolution took hold, he had changed it, at first out of sympathy and then out of fear. The old man stared unhappily into his memories. Looking at me from rheumy eyes, as if to size me up, he leant forward, took my head in his hands and delivered a faint kiss on my forehead, speaking throatily to his granddaughter. He wants to know, Serena told me, whether I would mind hearing a little of his life. Of course, I was willing to indulge him, expecting to hear nothing more than the rigours and pleasures of the steppe-lands. What could he tell me at the end of an afternoon in that place that I could not see by casting an eye over the accumulation of paraphernalia within that *ger* – the blankets and rugs; the wooden saddle; the chests and cupboards? For the rest – the grasslands, the animals, the nature of seasonal movement – all that was outside and was not his alone. That spoke for itself.

But no, that was not it at all. It turned out that my question had stirred something in him. Nobody before had asked him about his name. Oktyabr had laughed softly and then he had begun.

In 1921 he had been nineteen. He had been born into a clan with an ancient lineage that claimed descent from the time of Genghis Khan. There were many such claims, the accuracy of which was impossible to verify but I found this automatic belief rather touching and, anyway, perfectly plausible. It was not as if daily life had changed that much in the intervening seven-odd centuries.

Oktyabr's first years had been spent much as they were when I met him, living the life of the nomad, herding sheep, milking mares, guarding stock against wolves, moving with the seasons, coping with the climate.

'The summer,' Oktyabr exclaimed, 'how we used to love the summer, but so brief our summer, so brief, that break between two winters, when we could ride our horses and be in the open air and feel the sun. Not just the sun, but the air, warmed up, passing beneath our clothes and touching our skin. So used were we to being wrapped up like babies that each summer made us a little reluctant to remove our clothes in case we caught cold. Winter was hard; when the *dzuud* came, very hard.' Oktyabr had explained to me that there were several *dzuuds* – among them the black, when the land is frozen, yet there is no snow and therefore no water; the white, when the snow falls thickly and the animals cannot feed and die of hunger; the cold *dzuud* when the temperature remains so low over many days that animals can think only of warmth and so do not graze; and the iron, which brings nothing but ice and renders the earth stiff and unyielding. 'And yet, all in all, we found ways of coping. We were free. This was our land. We knew its boundaries and contours and horizons. There was the sky, the land and there was us. These were our gods. Even when the Chinese were our masters, we carried on just as we always had.'

'Then everything started to change. The Chinese, who for a long time, for centuries, had not really interfered in our ways, seemed to be everywhere.' He asked me if I had heard about the wall that the Chinese had built to keep the Mongols out; that once, a long time ago, in the time of the great Genghis, they had broken through it, and beaten the Chinese and ruled their empire. '

'It became our empire. Now, it seemed, they wanted their revenge. Then the Chinese left. And they came back. The Chinese were fighting each other and we were like their toys. From the north came the Russians, first the Tsar's soldiers and then the others. It was a strange, unsettling time; some of us wanted to become part of China, others wanted to be protected from China, others still desired things I could not really understand. What we all really wanted was just to carry on as before.

'But we could not. Because the Chinese wanted to make us part of China, whether we desired it or not, we had to ask for help. We asked the Russians, not the Tsar's Russians but the others, who were making big changes in their own country and, we understood, helping people like us. At first, all was well. Then the Russians, too, began to try to change us, I think maybe because they were afraid of the Chinese. We had a socialist revolution. I thought that our lives would stay the same but would be better. I thought the revolution would protect us from disaster and ensure that we were free for ever. It was then I changed my name to Oktyabr.

'At first, not much happened. We had our Jebtsundamba Khutuktu as our spirit head, chosen by the Dalai Lama himself. We seemed to be safe. Then the Jebtsundamba Khutuktu left this life and none came to replace him. Rebirth takes time, but we knew that eventually the reincarnation would be discovered. That was our belief.

'It did not happen like that. Instead, new rules were made. In Urga, which changed its name to Ulan Bator, Red Hero – because of the revolution – we had a new type of government. In the past, there had always been a government, whether princes, lamas, or the Chinese; we were used to obedience, which had nonetheless always allowed us to continue living as we always had. That was the important thing. This was different. The changes they tried to make were too big, too quick. If the rulers in Ulan Bator considered that we had too many, our animals were taken from us, or were forced upon us if we had too few. But we knew our limits, we had always known them. This reorganisation failed – many, many animals died and some herders, too. We killed our own animals to prevent them being taken from us! The Russians wanted our milk and our meat. We became confused and unhappy and very poor. Our animals were no longer part of us but were like pieces of paper in a leather pouch.'

Later, I came across a 1979 publication called the *Soviet Encyclopaedia*, which described thus the events in Mongolia of which Oktyabr spoke:

'an anti-imperialist anti-feudal revolution carried out by toiling livestock raisers, or *arats*, under the leadership of the Mongolian People's Revolutionary Party. The victory of the Mongolian People's Revolution led to the establishment of a people's government in the country, opening the way to full national and social liberation and to socialism and communism, bypassing capitalism.'

Well, apart from the bluster and, let us be frank, utter bollocks expressed in that self-serving example of Soviet propaganda, it turns out now, with the Mongolian People's Republic no more, that capitalism has finally surfaced in Mongolia, with not altogether admirable consequences. If the Russians had made a better job of their occupation, been a little less obsessed with being boss, a little less smitten with a complex of intellectual superiority, some form of Communism might have worked in Mongolia. For a while. But, that was not the revolutionary road. For Stalin, and those who flattered him through imitation, the road to revolution was smeared with blood or it was no road at all.

'The leaders of this government,' Oktyabr told me, 'did not listen to us. It was a bad time, which finished for a while because of the Japanese. Apparently the Russians feared the Japanese, too, as much as they feared the Chinese. Why are these great countries so afraid of everybody? They are so powerful, yet so preoccupied. Perhaps they were right to be afraid in this case, because the Japanese at the time wanted to take China and perhaps take Mongolia, too. But we could have fought them and we would have beaten them. Anyway, at least the forced "collectivisation", which was failing in Russia, too, came to an end.

'But the Japanese did not retreat. For Russia, we Mongols became as important as the Great Wall to the Chinese. So, after a few more years, our leaders started to kill us, just as Stalin was doing in Russia. To justify this strategy, they devised a strange and ridiculous excuse. This was that many of us were helping the Japanese to take over Mongolia. Why would we want that? We have an independent spirit! But they followed this course because that was what Stalin was doing. If Stalin killed lots of his own people, then it was surely the right thing to do. Stalin, of course, understood that our leaders, out of fear and vanity, would imitate him, which gave him influence and strength, and an ally that was more like a slave. Many thousands of lamas and tribal princes were executed because they had done terrible things; but we were used to taking the good with the bad, so these people, in our opinion, were not executed but murdered. We are a big country with few people. I have been told that for every 100 Mongols, three were killed. Some say more. Almost every temple across our territory was destroyed. Now there is only one temple left in the whole of our land and that is at Ulan Bator. Sometimes I go there, don't I Serena? That is why I am here now in Terelj, heading for the temple to pray to Sakyamuni for a good future and for a strong Mongol nation.'

Oktyabr told me that he soon became disillusioned. 'Still,' he explained, 'I kept my name Oktyabr because it was safer that way. Eventually, the Japanese were defeated but the Russians stayed. There were some good things; we had hospitals and schools for our children and protection for our animals in the winter. But often no care was taken to look after these new places and they fell into disuse. And we seemed to have to send a lot of what we produced to Russia, which was unfair. The Russians should have been nomads, then they would have had a better life and they would have understood how to look after animals! Instead, they tried to make us do things we knew to be wrong, like forcing us to keep only one type of animal in our herds, which we knew would not work. You have to mix the sheep with the goats. They kept trying to change things, as if change in itself was a good thing. It is only good if it improves things. So those kinds of changes were of little use to us. We knew what was the right balance. We had lived here for a very long time! We wanted help and advice but not wrong orders. I think the Russians wanted us to give up being nomads completely. And those Mongol leaders, they prefer to get fat in the cities. Some young people, too, like the changes, but I think they are wrong. It makes them unhappy and unsettled. Except for the clever, lucky ones like Serena. But she is a country girl, really, aren't you Serena?' He had smiled respectfully at his granddaughter, who had nodded indulgently, whilst casting a conspiratorial glance towards me. 'She,' Oktyabr continued, 'rather enjoyed some aspects of life in the countryside, especially when some of the younger people had ridden off together during *otor*, to get away from us older people!'

'Now,' he said, 'life is not so bad. Sometimes I agree with what they tell us, sometimes I don't. I don't think that the Russians should be here and I think our government is still too close to them. It could be worse. But I wonder if things will continue like this. The young people like Serena don't want to go to Moscow, they want to go to Hong Kong.'

With that the old man had stood up to feed his patient horse tethered to a staff outside. In the chilled air Serena had embraced him briefly and as we turned to go, he took hold of my arm. Through Serena he asked what had brought me to Mongolia ... it had not occurred to me that he didn't know – after all, he had invited us all in without the slightest demurral. How was I to know that this was merely the etiquette of the steppes, by which none are refused hospitality? I tried to explain how it was that I was in his country, but he soon stopped me, nodding and smiling, his sinewy hand still wrapped affectionately about my arm. 'You, too, are a nomad,' he said. 'You know what it is to see the world.'

Of course, our worlds – our ideas of the world – were different and yet there was something in what he said. I had sought adventure, so I thought, for its own sake. Most people in England regarded that journey with a mixture of curiosity and indifference, as if I were passing through the pangs of an adolescent love affair. I, in turn, considered their attitude to it strangely dull. Now, I wonder if I was not in the grip of something beyond my control, as if I were answering some primitive call fundamental to our condition. Then again, it could have been a case of infantile escapism. I would not know. I know only this, 'We travel not for trafficking alone: by hotter winds our fiery hearts are fanned.' So said the poet and I think there is something in it.

On the way back to Ulan Bator the old bus gave out just as it was approaching the crown of a rise. The driver shook his head but otherwise remained quite unperturbed. And then out of the gloaming – it was quite late by now and we were supposed to go to the theatre that evening, not that most of the people in the party, apart from the French and a handful of others, would have found the omission too painful to bear, were it not for the fact that it had been paid for – there appeared from nowhere that I could see a couple of characters on horseback, who dismounted and proceeded to tinker with the engine, one snaking beneath the vehicle, his trilby falling off in the process, the other peering down from above, with barely a word uttered. Within minutes there was a shout to the driver and the exhausted engine kicked back reluctantly into life. There followed a brief discussion between the three of them, whilst a small bottle of what I took to be vodka was passed around, after which the two mechanics remounted and cantered away. Not once did they acknowledge our presence.

Nothing in this might seem very remarkable. But you have to remember that we were, for all intents and purposes, in a position of complete isolation. Ulan Bator was not far away, but it might just as well have been at the other end of the country. In 1981, there were no mobile phones; in Mongolia there were few reliable telephones of any description. When it had become clear that we were going no further, I had scanned the surrounding countryside in search of help, but I saw nothing – not a *ger*, not a horse, not a herder, not a herd, not so much as a single yak – nothing but grasslands and hills and boulders. And yet, like a pair of phantoms on call, those two had trotted up emerging from the dusk. I understand the temptation, to which my callow nature would certainly have succumbed in those days, of giving in too readily to the romance of psychic powers. The desire for the implausible can be overwhelming. Nor do I discount them out of hand even now, though I think that there are other explanations whilst not necessarily of the occult, are nonetheless in the invisible realm; is it intuition? A form of sympathetic fine-tuning? The so-called sixth sense? Perhaps it is possible that when a people do the same thing over and over across the centuries, they develop that sense to the point when it becomes like a sound, the absence of which, as with the sudden lapse of a motor, is like an explosion in the void.

Much to the disappointment of some, we made it back to Ulan Bator in time not only for our mutton dinner but also for the evening's entertainment, which turned out to be not so much theatre as circus. In the middle of this city of tents a vast blue big-top had been erected, with a banner across the upper ridge between two red flags, which read in the Cyrillic alphabet, 'The International Circus'. The performers came, without exception, from countries east of Berlin.

There are two things I particularly remember about the circus. One of the performers was a contortionist from Cambodia, a girl painted like a Japanese doll, who moved with the grace of a quicksilver fish in the shallows fanning rhythmically against the stream. Played out in perfect silence, the climax of her act was a moment of political revenge. She lay face-down and contrived to place a bow between her feet in such a way as to fire an arrow from it over her head into the smug, glabrous maw of Pol Pot, yet another genocidal maniac, who, in the name of egalitarianism and as leader of the Communist Khmer Rouge, had only a couple of years before the period of our journey, murdered some 25 per cent of the population of his country of Cambodia. There are some that dispute this. Let us be magnanimous and say, for the sake of balance, that it was only 20 per cent. At the time, it meant nothing to me; in fact, it meant nothing to most, in awe as we all were to the glamour of 'new' China and to the nagging threat of Russia and, even then, to our obsession with the beguiling madness of Hitler; whilst, all the while, a small country, almost as disregarded as Mongolia, was skinned, disembowelled and boiled alive. What passes through the mind of one that skewers a child? A literal, not a metaphorical act. Or of one, accusing a starving woman of stealing rice, tests her protestations of innocence by ripping open her empty stomach for inspection, then leaves her to die? My God. The horror!

How ironic that in a circus tent, amid the torpor of the declining years of Soviet rule, we watched that lissom contortionist, rigid with angry concentration, fire an arrow into the cold heart of utopia.

'As many eyes as a pineapple,' they whispered of Pol Pot and his henchmen, emerging with the setting sun like Nosferatu, sucking victims dry and slipping away into the night. Even that is to credit them with some kind of ghastly nobility. They proclaimed that we had arrived at the 'end of history' through the establishment of a permanent nightmare. Their trademark was brutality stretched to the limits of imagination. Their work became procedural, an unending series of administrative tasks to be fulfilled, recorded and filed. They were but poor ignoramuses, those executioners, themselves terrified by their masters into believing in the guilt of the bewildered individuals who, randomly plucked from the fields, accused of espionage and conspiracy, were blindfolded, removed, interrogated, tortured beyond endurance and killed. 'Smashed,' to use the perverted vocabulary of their so-called ideology. Another routine revolutionary task accomplished. Can you imagine leaving home for work where your first job of the day is to attach a pump to an emaciated prisoner in order to drain him of every last drop of blood? Just to see what happens? Or to remove a liver without the use of anaesthetic? Perhaps a few cases of the old favourite, the slow extraction of toe nails, one by one? A job that grants you the licence to visit all of our most basic existential fears. Then, at the end of a hard day, return home to eat and sleep and make love. Play with the children. Your own children, who have been guaranteed protection, unlike so many others, from being 'smashed' across the skull. Not that the guarantee is without its unwritten sub-clauses; one little slip-up and your children, too, might require 'smashing', infected as they will have been by counter-revolutionary thoughts. Are we to forgive these simpletons their crimes because of their willingness to belong to the cause? In our hearts we cannot. That is the tragedy. They, too, granted leave to give vent to their inner sadist were lickspittle victims of the 'brothers' that were sure not to besmirch their own soft hands but sat in offices or jungle hideaways dispensing their meticulous justice. We should forgive them but we cannot, not from the heart, only with an effort of supreme intellectual will. I do not know what their punishment should be. Execution spares them ignominy and guilt. That they should suffer as their victims did is merely to perpetuate their inhumanity. Freedom is unthinkable; to pardon them, impossible, and yet I fear we must. The only deterrent, if deterrent there is, is that of the magnanimity of the human spirit. And what of their masters, Brothers One, Two and all the other Brothers that dished out the orders? What, I wonder, should be their fates? How tempting to have them 'smashed'; or to subject them to a little vivisection! But a solemn execution might do: yet, where to stop? When does the master become a servant? Only later, when we had completed the journey and gone our separate ways, did we understand the significance of the action of that performer in that tent in Ulan Bator, an action that seemed almost comically theatrical but which was a true expression of anger and revulsion. The contrast with what I saw then and what I know now, is unbearable.

At the time, it was all quaint to me, to all of us, I suppose – the whole set up. That particular line of ugliness had been rendered almost invisible but it was present all right, running all the way through time's prism, from Berlin eastwards to beyond the China sea.

In between the contortionists and acrobats, the clowns and the horse opera, there was dance. A troupe of girls cantered into the ring and to the accompaniment of an orchestra of galloping two-stringed lutes became, with the adoption of the saddle posture I had seen on the steppe and on the streets of the capital, and with perfectly mimed equine strides, Mongol centaurs. It was no use pretending that this spectacle, with its spangles and silks, was but a distant relative of what had sprung up as a celebration among herders of the animal that was the source of their being, for this was a spectacle given the circus treatment, a choreography part *Ballet Russe*, part Cossack tumble. But there was a charge in their exuberance that permitted me a glance into the soul of a people stuck between two countries and two eras. It comes back to me with perfect clarity; in that giant tent in the centre of a toy city in the middle of a vast and empty country, was exposed the anger and joy of humanity that wants little more than to be left alone.

The hotel bar, too, that evening was filled with the sounds of the circus, but only the Polish contingent dared to mingle with us westerners. I spoke at length with one, the high-wire specialist, who in fluent English told me something remarkable. Well, two things, in fact, the first concerning the contortionist from Cambodia. Her anger, he had assured me was quite genuine. Not only had she lost her entire family to the Brothers – so that she had not a single relative remaining, not so much as a distant cousin – but her own survival had depended on her ability to dislocate her joints at will. Concealing from her torturers her profession (given their pineapple eyes, a feat in itself; had they discovered her deception their pleasure in testing the limits of joint manipulation would have known no bounds), she was thrown aside like a broken doll. Her torturers, convinced she could not walk, had provided the opportunity she needed; quickly pulling herself together, as it were, she had made her way into Vietnam, where she had remained until she could return. But it was something else he told me about Mongolia that I found most intriguing. It seems that this Pole – I forget his name but let us call him Stanislaw – came from a family of horse breeders, which, courtesy of the Nazis, the Russians and subsequent regimes, had lost everything in the tumultuous decades following the First World War. The hippomania, however, had survived, spurring him on to join the circus, where, naturally, he had expected to school their performing horses; this was to underestimate the perverse nature of the Party, which instead decreed that his physique was better suited to a career on the high wire. Still, the circus had allowed him to remain in touch with the animals he loved, as well as bringing him to Mongolia, which, Stanislaw had affirmed, was the country of the horse, like an open-air temple dedicated to its spirit. Over the preceding few years he had performed not only in Ulan Bator but, too, in the remoter settlements, where the audiences had consisted as much of Russian technicians and

Russian military personnel as it had Mongols. But the experience had given him the opportunity to ride out with local herders, among whom he had come to appreciate their profound respect for their animals, which amounted to something – these were his words – something 'bestial but in the noblest possible way,' a Mongol without a horse, as they say, being like a bird without wings. There had been an occasion when one of the herdsmen's ponies collapsed and lay inert, spent, clearly, as Stanislaw knew from experience, on the point of death. The herdsmen had discussed the matter with an urgency expressed solely through their stiffened posture and the intensity of their murmured exchanges. I found their concern, in its complete absence of histrionics, very moving, Stanislaw had explained. From his saddlebag, one of the number produced a musical instrument like the ones that had accompanied the dancers in the big-top earlier that evening: a kind of lute with just two strings and a long neck culminating in a carved horse's head, known as the

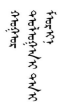

the *morin khuur*, the 'fiddle with the horse's head'. The bow strings are made of horse hair; so, too, the main strings, one of hairs from the tail of a stallion, the other from the tail of a mare. According to Stanislaw, the music produced was akin to an equine language. The player had crouched in the grass close to the sickening animal, beginning to saw rapidly the bow across the strings, using the same galloping rhythms, though rendered with less finesse, we had heard in the circus. 'It was a concerto of all the noises made by Mongol horses over the centuries, many discernible, perhaps, only to the senses of the herdsmen,' Stanislaw said. Finally, closing with the staccato sounds of a neighing horse, the musician had stopped, resting the *morin khuur* against his leg, watching the animal intently, biding his concerns, until it had revived with a tremor, shaking its shaggy mane, forcing itself onto its forelegs and struggling up and stamping its hooves to crank its sluggish heart. The cure, it seemed, was complete. Stanislaw's eyes shone with pleasure in the recounting of this episode; to one unfamiliar with horses, he said, this is nothing but hocus pocus or trickery. He understood it well, but never had he seen the bond between two creatures so simply and wonderfully expressed.

When I heard all this I was giddy on vodka and doing my best to attract the attention of a girl from East Berlin, whom I had noticed in the audience at the circus but who, since entering the bar had consistently rebuffed my advances and who, understandably, smiled with indulgent scepticism at my promises to visit her at home in that city of secret police and informers. He must have been annoyed at my wandering eyes, and I do not blame him, since the opportunity to speak with someone unafraid of careless talk was rare in that world at that time; but Stanislaw's account of the horse cured by music outlasted the fog of that evening and stays with me even now.

The British Embassy, Ulan Bator, a remote posting.

There was also the matter of the two vandalised Australian passports to be resolved. Western interests in Mongolia were represented by the French and the British, the only two west European nations with embassies in Ulan Bator. Given the infrequency of western visitors to Mongolia, one embassy would perhaps have sufficed; but, as I was told at the British embassy, 'Of course, we were here first, in 1963; naturally the French couldn't bear that and, voila, it wasn't long before they were here too.' It was gratifying to hear that the old rivalries and struggles for one–upmanship were still being played out in the fastness of Outer Mongolia. Still, each must surely have been grateful for the presence of the other, surrounded as they were by embassies almost all inimical to western interests. I gained the impression that east and west, diplomatically speaking, did not mix much, even here. Cocktail parties, if they took place, must have been strained, watchful affairs, not so very different to the inter-war world of Fitzroy Maclean and Eric Ambler.

The British and French embassies occupied adjacent plots at the eastern periphery of the city. The staff of the British embassy were informal, the few Britons passing through welcomed almost with gratitude. The ambassador's wife gave me tea and biscuits, while the ambassador himself did what he could to smooth our path eastwards. My immediate thought was that as diplomatic postings go, Ulan Bator must rank rather low on almost any imaginable scale. For the ambitious, thrusting young diplomat, I suppose it may have been a launching pad to greater things but, otherwise, it surely qualified as a hardship posting.

The problem was not that Mongolia was an uninteresting place to be – far from it – but that then, with the end of the Cold War yet unimaginable, the representatives of western countries were hemmed in by suspicion, their motives constantly questioned, their movements severely curtailed. If superficially it all seemed unnecessarily melodramatic and if the staff at the embassy laughed off Mongolian regulation as so much posturing and unwarranted hostility, a western diplomatic presence situated snugly between the two great Communist superpowers must have served some useful purpose. The Mongolians themselves were very cordial to foreigners with the exception of the Chinese, for whom they harboured a visceral loathing, whilst they endured a relationship of uncomfortable dependence on the Russians, whose paranoia had infected the Mongolian soul just as it had in each of its allies from East Germany to Cuba.

The British and French, therefore, simply had to accept their lot. They liked Mongolia and its people but as diplomats they were not permitted to travel more than a certain number of kilometres beyond the city limits; each time an embassy employee got into the Land Rover, I imagined a local minder tracking his movements on horseback.

The atmosphere in the embassy was cheerfully informal, as if the World, once you accepted its imperfections, was not such a bad place in which to pass the time. Phlegmatic, as tradition demanded, the staff made the best of unpromising

The last monastery in Mongolia, a defiant survivor.

circumstances. But my hosts at the embassy were remarkably sanguine; and no doubt they left Mongolia much improved, having read a great many books. The passport problem was treated as a mildly exciting interruption to routine – the Mongolian border authorities were informed; the Australian Embassy in Peking asked to prepare replacements and that was that.

In Ulan Bator, there was the one working monastery, the Gandantegchinien Khild, known as Gandan, situated in defiant isolation at the top of a rise in the north of the city. If the authorities had had their way, this, too would have been classified as a museum. Visiting the monastery turned out to be fraught with obstacles. There had been a great deal of mystery attached to it, with the hapless Serena acting as nuncio for both the abbot and for the state, each of whom, it seemed, made claims of obstructionism on the part of the other. It was closed. It was open, but not to visitors. It was under repair. The monastery elders were being difficult. There was a problem to do with money. The bus was not available. Then, for no apparent reason, all objections vanished, as if it had all been a silly misunderstanding.

The Gandan monastery was a survivor. It had survived Mongolia's revolution, the Russian occupation and the waves of purges that afflicted the country in dreadful imitation of Stalin. Its architecture was not especially distinguished – imposing and intricate in comparison with most other buildings in Ulan Bator, but a minor example of lamaist Buddhist vernacular that in Tibet would have passed as a parochial effort. Only the fact that it was there at all endowed it with a special quality, and once you

A child stirring pigeons at Gandan Monastery, Ulan Bator.

passed through the gates into the courtyard, you felt as if you had reached sanctuary. Even the guides, who in general bore the usual hallmarks of disaffected youth, were roused sufficiently from their apathy to do the Buddhist equivalent of making the sign of the cross.

The visit took place in the morning, when the air was at its clearest and freshest. A flock of pigeons had also taken refuge here, and small children, dressed in their *dels*, would stagger among them in their leather boots, delighting in making the birds rocket upwards all together to fan round the courtyard in a maelstrom of cooing and vibrating wings. Against one of the pavilions, a row of old men with faces buffed to a polished sheen sat meditatively in the sun. A shaven-headed priest in shining saffron would hurry past, shielding his face from prying cameras; whilst from the prayer hall emanated the sound of chorused humming and resonant chanting.

Gandan was the only place in the city where a sense of peace prevailed. Only there could the rituals of everyday life, religious or not, unfold without interference – all other rituals had been crushed or banned by the authorities. Consequently, our presence was resented by everyone and only borne because the continued existence of the single monastery left in Ulan Bator depended on the government being able to use it as a demonstration of religious tolerance.

I could usefully have made a few runs along the rows of prayer wheels at the monastery – the next day was to be one of the most frightening of the whole journey. The day following that, we were to take the train from the Mongolian People's

Worshippers at Gandan Monastery, Ulan Bator, a last refuge for the believers of Mongolia.

Republic to the People's Republic of China, between whom relations, being brittle, were gleefully exploited by the Union of Socialist Soviet Republics. The consequence, from our point of view, was the infrequent train service southwards from Ulan Bator; most rail traffic shuttled northwards, towards Russia. The so-called International Train ran once a week between Moscow and Peking and the later into the journey that you wished to board it, with very few passengers disembarking in Ulan Bator, the scarcer the chances of obtaining tickets. For foreigners, these were provided by the Mongolian state tourism organisation, to the offices of which I trekked following the temple visit.

My interview with the state tourism bureau representative, one of those convenient zealots thrown up by ideology, had been devastating; there were no train tickets for us. In London, having been warned of the capricious nature of the authorities in Mongolia, to smooth the path I had brought with me a bottle of whiskey, which I had duly offered to the man in question, who had duly placed it in his desk drawer, with a mute acknowledgement, before informing me of the appalling news. There was nothing to be done. As I pointed out repeatedly, perhaps hysterically, since visas were only issued to visitors on the condition they had the means of arrival and departure, there had surely been a clerical error. He merely shrugged, in the way that people who can afford to, do; and when I mentioned that all our train tickets and accommodation throughout China were now useless, he smiled the ineffable smile of one who secretly believes in nemesis. In those days, it was not as if there was a question of bolting down to the railway station and purchasing tickets directly. As foreigners, all transactions had to be in US dollars or any so-called convertible currency and only the palms of a select few were permitted contact with it. No phones, nobody to complain to. We were truly stuck.

This was an unhappy circumstance. I did not care about spending more time in Mongolia. On the contrary, I could happily have spent the days in the hotel lobby, watching the woman with the blue lenses selling postage stamps and my evenings in the starlit bar. But for the others, eager to reach China – this was purgatory. For some, it was hell itself; their curiosity assuaged, they needed to move on in order to feel assured of their liberty. These – the Vets, Guppy, Archie and their kind – existed in a constant state of nervous apprehension. But the authorities, except in so far as we might have dollars to spend, had no interest in detaining us any longer than was strictly necessary. No, at the root of our dilemma was something far more banal and that was state inertia. The arteries no longer pumped, the intestines were blocked solid. One error and everything ground to a halt. If you wanted to go to Mongolia in those days, you had to accept the consequences of its situation. As for me, had it not been for my position as group manager, I was secretly charmed at the frank nature of the Mongolians' approach. Our presence was not remotely problematic to them; in the face of human failure they simply ignored the terms of their own visa regulations. Our eventual departure was their responsibility but in the meantime, we were, in their eyes, part of the scenery.

But then, I wasn't paying for this journey, nor was I in the grip of Cold War neurosis. I suppose that I may have been naive in these matters; but it did not occur to me for a second that we would be in Mongolia for very much longer. Things would be sorted out – they always are. That is one of the advantages of inertia. What intrigues me now, looking back, is the reception that greeted the announcement. All that ensued sprang from that moment. So much depends on presentation! An infelicitous emphasis here, an awkward laugh there, that's all it takes. The reverberations don't die down – they become louder! Because of my seemingly flippant attitude, there were some who saw in me a fellow traveller, a sympathiser, a bit of a commie – a red! One of the Vets leant forward and hissed, 'American hater,' as if I had exhibited a particularly vile form of racialism. Archie, to my relief, merely gave a loud guffaw, and shook his head in mock despair. Yet the one I remember most clearly was the most silent. Guppy fixed his cold eyes on me, with the kind of mirthless half-smile that behind the plausible exterior conceals a mind working on a self-aggrandising project. As for the rest, there were questions, of course, and grumbling and protestations but, all things considered, a spirit of cooperation appeared to prevail. There were suggested remedies – when panic sets in, everything is an emergency and everyone knows best – but flights between Mongolia and China did not exist then and as for going overland, among many objections, the presence of the Gobi Desert, lying between Ulan Bator and the Chinese border, was perhaps the principal one. And there was the inevitable formation of a delegation to the British Embassy. Yet, once the shock wore off, the party dispersed in a cloud of sullen vexation. I, after several weeks of lionisation, found myself isolated. Whilst most accepted the unalterable nature of the circumstances, some could not bring themselves to forgive me for bringing them to this place, as if I were a prophet that, at the last minute, had laughed in the face of their gullibility. There we were in an annoying but by no means life-threatening position, which, one might have thought, called for patience and a resigned shrug; instead, there was a general sulk and the same herd-like mentality that bedevilled most of the benighted countries we were passing through.

Once the hullabaloo diminished, I conferred with Serena, who explained that I was not to worry; that we would, she was sure, be on the slow train that left in a few days' time for the Chinese border. I went to bed only slightly comforted by an assurance derived from sympathy more than from certitude, for the notion of urgency had not struck me as a Mongolian characteristic.

I lay awake for some time, fresh and warm in the stiffly laundered sheets, the shadow of the power-station smoke unfurling through the thin curtains and drifting across the ceiling. As I fell into sleep, there came the sound of voices in the corridor and of a turning key and when I awoke and dressed the following morning, the door of my room was locked.

Now, the immediate reaction to a locked door, when unexpected, is invariably one of panic, especially in the state of first-light fog. Surprise obliterates rational thought. Is it broken? Stuck? A joke? Then, a surge of relief on remembering that the key is on the bedside table, followed by the sense of puzzlement and fear when the key will not fit into the lock because there is another key on the outside preventing its entry.

I went to the window and looked down on the all but empty street below, before sitting philosophically at the edge of my bed. Had I overslept, the chamber maids already at work? I looked at my watch. No. Then there had to be another explanation. I looked for the telephone to call reception, before I remembered that there was no telephone. The corridor outside my room was soundless. No programme had been set for this first morning after the announcement of our becalming so there was every chance that I would not be missed. Then, I half-heartedly banged on the door to no avail and even called out, but I was oddly constrained from shouting by the peculiar sensation that I was missing an explanation so obvious that I was unable to locate it, as if my mind was operating in a separate dimension. Or was it just a plain old nightmare? Then it came to me – it was that Russian Army officer!

After a couple of hours, I heard whispering outside my door. Then an American voice cleared its throat and began to speak. 'We are holding you hostage,' it went, 'until you get us out of this hell-hole.' Of course, I recognised the voice. It belonged to Gail, one half of a couple that had, until this juncture, been all amiability in their dealings with me, although Gail's wife, whose face was a landscape of creases and furrows like a ploughed field in winter and whose occasional thin smile struck only at the most inopportune moments in the manner of a threat, was one who sat in silent command. The position was rendered clearer when I heard the voices of the Vets and of Guppy, each of whom, in their different ways, repeated Gail's opening remark.

My first reaction was one of relief that I was not a prisoner of the Soviet Army. The second was a batter of irritation and helplessness. At the distance of years all of this will sound laughably petty; and so it was. Why is it that inaction has such a bad name? There is no shame in judicious passivity. You cannot compare it to apathy. What did these people really imagine that I could do? Whisper in the ear of Party Secretary, Yumjaagiin Tsedenbal who, in a uniform laden with a magical array of medals and badges, stared down on his people from posters across the city with amiable blandness? No, but they did seem to think that it was within my power to have a few undeserving passengers give up their tickets in our favour. As the representatives of beacons of democracy, it was obvious who should take precedence. Why, they said to me, we paid for our trip months ago!

I lay on my bed, sipping at my vodka, awaiting developments. At lunchtime Serena, in a perturbed state, came to the door, accompanied by the same deputation of bounty hunters who in their deluded condition had convinced themselves that she, too, was in a position of power and influence sufficient to get us, or them, on that train. In they trooped, and took up a platoon formation in front of the door, which they took care with a precise drill to lock behind them. Serena came forward apologetically to present me with a plate of cold mutton and a glass of mineral water. 'Well?' said Gail. 'Have you come to your senses? We want out of here, and fast.' By now I had drunk a significant volume of vodka, which allowed me to listen to their ravings whilst exhibiting something akin to sincere interest.

I can see it all now. The tense little group shuffling at the door, before which spokesman Gail delivered their ultimatum in the deliberate manufactured style of an actor reciting lines, with all the wooden passion of John Wayne. Gail was a small, pale man with thin hair who thought that he had discovered his metier as the epitome of the American way. Had I not been notionally responsible for these people and, furthermore, not incarcerated in a hotel room in a place of political and geographical isolation, I would have burst out laughing. I wonder now if that might not have been the solution, but there was something a little intimidating in the intensity of their protest. Gail was sincerely in a state of panic, whilst the Vets, intoxicated as ever by an unceasing flow of weak beer, were prone to casual mercenary violence. Guppy, the Englishman, stood silent, tall and saturnine, his long face chipped by a mirthless smile.

I explained to them again that the circumstances were not of my making; that we were, as they themselves had pointed out tirelessly since arriving in East Berlin, in a totalitarian country where *diktats* were a way of life. But they believed that I was in charge of purchasing the tickets and that the failure to obtain them was all mine. Serena, who was unused to confronting rebellion, did her best to defend my position but through her own naïveté succeeded only in making matters worse. She suggested that we could go en masse to the station and purchase tickets on the spot. I pointed out that this was out of the question and did my best to explain why this was so. 'Well, if it is a question of dollars, then it is very simple ... everyone understands the American greenback,' Gail burst out triumphantly, eliciting a gruff chorus of 'damn right' from the Vets and a portentous nod from Guppy. I said to them that in that case they were very welcome to trot down to the station and while they were at it if they would buy a ticket for me, I would be grateful. 'Now, don't get smart,' Gail said, 'because we might just leave you here in this paradise, since you like it so much.' There was nothing to be done but let events take their course. Eventually they left, taking Serena with them, leaving me to my mutton and vodka.

That evening, they returned. They were accompanied by most of the other members of the party, who had only just been made aware of my imprisonment, or 'way of being made to see reason', as Gail had put it to them. They, to their credit, were mostly appalled at my circumstances and there soon followed a mild altercation between them and Gail's followers. Interestingly, among them there was a small caucus whose instincts, though sound, were also suspended for as long as they considered that a strong-arm technique might have some bearing on matters. In the end it took the intervention of a quiet American – Leonard, he of the Corvette and dog – to bring everyone to their senses. He was the obverse of Gail. He was like the John Wayne one might have met in person, rather than the persona that he assumed on film. 'This behaviour,' he growled, 'might in more respectable circles be regarded as a mutiny, if it were not for the absence of a meaningful motive, and, more pertinently, the absence of a ship to commandeer.' Then he had added, 'And with all due respect to our estimable captain,' – indicating me – 'he is in no position to navigate us from the storm, except by continuing to man the wheel. Now, I suggest that we all calm down, back off and let events take their course, as they surely will.'

Hysteria dissolves when confronted with plain speaking. Lionel commanded respect not through bluster or high-flown language, but through his honesty. The rest of them could not but collapse before it. Gail and his henchmen retaliated with a few muttered protests, and those who had been sitting on the fence were relieved to be able to dismount to the side they had believed was the right one from the start. Guppy merely looked disappointed. The Famous Writer, who had passed most of our stay on business of his own, reappeared, his slight irritation at the rescheduled timetable, which meant the postponement of a party in his honour at a foreigners' club in Peking, fulsomely compensated by a chance meeting on the street with a Finn who was an admirer of his work.

Thus, the mutiny fizzled out. I was welcomed back into the fold, as if nothing had happened, which was fortunate given that I held various documents and visas essential to our progress and there still lay several more weeks of travelling before us, during which time Gail was to sulk and keep company exclusively with his taciturn wife (whom I overheard him describe to one of his allies 'as the ugliest woman I ever knew'), the Vets and their disciple, Guppy. But the general atmosphere had changed for the time being from one of optimism to one of impatience and irritation. That was a pity but there it is.

There was in all this a magnificent irony. Until now, we had become accustomed to travelling in compartments that housed only two people, so that overnights on the various trains were like staying in uncomfortable, tiny rooms in mobile hotels. Over the coming weeks, from Ulan Bator onwards, in compliance with China's requirements for transportation for the masses, we were to be four per compartment. Compartments for two did not exist, which meant that even the Famous Writer was forced into a compartment with others. It was my job to decide who shared with whom; or, rather, I made it my job, as it was in my interest to do so. To have left the choices to the participants themselves could have resulted in havoc. So it was that I looked at the various tolerance levels; burgeoning friendships and enmities; and accordingly, accompanied by a misquote from Confucius (Confucius say: 'there is no such thing as a perfect rooming-list'), put a notice up in the lobby for people to learn their fates – *fait accompli*.

In truth, it was a relief to be getting out of Mongolia. We left the next day, after Serena confided to me that tickets were available for the border train. Gail, as was to be expected, took full credit for this turn of events, whereas I knew that the protests and deputations whether to me or to the British Embassy (the ambassador had apparently entertained the British and Irish contingent to tea, Garibaldi biscuits and sympathy) or to the French Embassy (where the ambassador had been unavailable due to a hunting commitment) were nothing more than ways of passing the time.

Our departure was inevitable; the Mongolians, for whom urgency and emergency were one and the same, did not regard our misfortune as comparable to the loss of a frozen herd of sheep, or to the murder of uncooperative counter-revolutionaries. Yes, I could have done with a little more information, but I came to admire their sense of proportion.

Our ancient, dilapidated bus made it to the railway station. As we disembarked a front tyre that had rolled up against the kerb when we stopped slowly deflated, with an exhausted hiss.

The scene on the platform for our departure resembled the one that had greeted us when we had arrived; the same congregation of burnished faces, the aimless, happy milling, the brilliant sunshine gleaming on sunglasses and sparkling on silken sashes. Our carriage – like all the rolling stock we had travelled on since Hoek van Holland, constructed in East Germany – was a surprise, highly polished and factory fresh, from the door of which there leaned the carriage attendant, dishevelled in his new ill-fitting uniform, waving energetically in our direction – specifically, it seemed, at me. We were not the only westerners trying to board, for there were two pairs of Europeans, one French, the other British, each, judging by their frantic expressions, as desperate to be away as were we. Serena pushed me through the crowd towards the attendant, who plucked our tickets from her hand and commenced bellowing at the throng seething impatiently on the platform at his feet. 'He is my cousin,' Serena whispered to me, 'don't worry,' and somehow we all clambered up the steep steps into the familiar landscape of a railway carriage. The others took their seats in evident relief, or stood leaning at the window regarding the scene below with stony disdain. I waved to Serena, who nodded before turning to an elderly man beside her. Oktyabr looked briefly up towards us before he too nodded and the two of them walked slowly into the station building and into the parking area beyond. I watched Oktyabr mount his pony, lean down to speak to his granddaughter and then wheel away to trot out to the road that led to the city centre. Serena looked after him a moment, then climbed into the bus beside the driver and they drove after him, overtaking Oktyabr in a puff of dust.

And then, we were away, tooting slowly through the suburbs of quixotic Ulan Bator, heading for China.

Chapter 6

The Peking Line

In leaving Mongolia I felt, if I may resort to hyperbole, that I was leaving life itself. Undeniably, there was some relief because of the nature of my circumstances and because of the faintly unnerving level of uncertainty that prevailed in the city; but that was nothing compared to the elemental struggle between progress, change, advance – call it what you will – and tradition, habit and what may be seen as fatalism or even sloth, but which I saw as a great human attainment, the windswept steppes, beneath the firmament the perfectly circular tents, warm and cool, that console in their rude beauty. I exaggerate, a little, because I am wistful for a life that I could never have tolerated. But for all its failings, there was a kind of perfection in it, that should by rights outlive all change, but which I fear cannot survive except as a 'lifestyle option', or whatever term is current. When it dies, as it surely will, with it goes a completeness and a satisfaction that will be lost for ever from our consciousness. We will no longer be human beings. We will have become something different and so be it. But I, for one, regret the passing of the sixth sense, the loss of empathy, of doing things for the

Mongolian landscape from the train, vast and much of it barely touched by mankind.

sake of love, or for the sake of continuity, of togetherness, of intangible enrichment; the simple habits that breed instinctual understanding. I look back on that country and I see a gimcrack citadel towering bleakly over an earthy Elysium, bisected by one railway line along which travelled the world looking out at it with benign curiosity.

We left Ulan Bator, chugging south towards China. At first, there developed an optimistic hum of conversation, as if better times lay ahead and China was close by. Because to be in China then, represented for many people the realisation of a dream. For most Americans it was a country seeing the light, abandoning Communism for democracy and free trade – a new friend; for many Europeans, a sentimental curiosity. There were those who had waited all their adult lives for the opportunity to visit the world's oldest civilisation. Had they been asked during that time, 'Which country would you like to see before you die, given the chance?' it would not have been India or Peru or Antarctica but China, with its fabulous history and mysterious present.

Soon after we had trundled across the shadow of the power station chimney, its endless pennant of steam unfurling above us, we were in the grasslands again; and they, in turn, before long, petered out and shrivelled way before the stony dry-as-dust plateau that is the Gobi. The air became warmer. Herds of Bactrian camels plucked at sparse vegetation. A herd of antelope scattered. Parked on the horizon, shimmering mirages in the haze, were squadrons of Soviet military aircraft. Our carriage formed the tail of the train – we could stand at the rear and watch the railway line unroll from beneath us across the bloodless landscape.

Green Gobi Desert with Bactrian camel, possibly wild, more likely domesticated.

We took our lunch because it was there, not for the quality of the fare – shrivelled shavings of meat on a bed of desiccated rice, preceded by a broth too tepid to cook the yolk that floated yellow and raw on its greasy surface.

Our attendant, Serena's cousin, was an amiable man with a great appreciation of vodka and *arkhi*, bottles of which he had secreted about his small cabin near the end of the carriage and which, as the afternoon wore on, he began to empty with accelerating rapidity, together with any gin or beer he could lay his hands on from among the party. Because of my connection with his cousin and apparently aware of the shenanigans that had taken place in the Ulan Bator 'B', he singled me out for friendship, ushering me forcefully into his cabin, and handling me tumblers of liquor. Unable to maintain anything like his rate of consumption, after a while I was grateful for the complete disintegration of his speech into incoherent babble, which he directed mostly towards the cabin wall.

Naturally, I would normally have devoted large portions of an afternoon like that one to talking to the people in the party and preparing them for what was to come, as far as I could; but I was simmering still at the ridiculous attempt to hold me to ransom, preferring instead to spend my time with the quartet of Europeans I had seen boarding with us. They, it transpired, were two French diplomats and two British diplomatic couriers, the Queen's Messengers, all four of whom had been compelled to take the slow train for reasons never disclosed, but which, as they said with a degree of affectionate exasperation, was typical of that quixotic country we were

The Trans-Mongolian crosses the Gobi Desert.

leaving. The two Britons, who were drinking pink gins, an absurdly endearing cliché of colonial Britishness, had their diplomatic pouches handcuffed to the little table bolted to the compartment window. Retired from other careers, and presumably of impeccable credentials, they seemed not to have noticed that, except possibly in Ulan Bator, the United Kingdom was a country of diminishing influence; they informed me with unconcealed pride that among all the embassies around the world, only the one in Ulan Bator, because of its peculiar location, was serviced by train. I could only wonder what there could possibly be in those pouches so valuable and confidential that it was left in the custody of two elderly men, as if in the clubbable diplomatic sphere; ungentlemanly behaviour was out of the question. Facing the pair across the table were junior members of staff from the French Embassy, two girls in their twenties, with that peculiarly translucent and delicately blue veined skin characteristic of high-born Frenchwomen, who treated the two Britons with affectionate disdain. They had opened a small bottle of Burgundy, which they consumed contentedly with bread and cheese and Russian pickles. They talked a little of their confined lives in Mongolia. One of the girls said to me wistfully, 'In the winter, we go skating *chez les British* – they make a very beautiful rink in their garden.' It was an image that I retained with relish; two uneasy allies wrapped in scarves and fur hats, slicing the ice in circles about an English garden in the frozen fastness of Outer Mongolia. I stood framed in the doorway of their compartment, looking down on this picture of diplomatic harmony, as we trundled at rocking-chair rhythm across the yellow Gobi. After the grim, sealed Soviet world, with its neuroses and interminable fantasy of persecution, there was something reassuring in the gentle conceits of West European superiority. Then, the world was still slow. Now, change gallops along at an inhuman pace and what I am speaking of must seem impossibly antique, like a scene from a black and white film; and yet, it is only yesterday.

When I left the diplomats, out of curiosity I wandered into the adjoining carriages. In most prevailed the blend of excited conversation and intangible relief that is part of taking one's place on a train. Only in one was the atmosphere eerily dissimilar. The door to it opened only by pushing hard against an item that scarcely yielded. Beyond it, the corridor was choked with household chattels, so that I could make progress only by vaulting over sacks and bags and sticks of furniture. The whole carriage seemed to have been turned into a travelling warehouse, until, among it all, crammed into the darkened compartments, I saw whom I presumed to be the owners, peering watchfully out at me from among the numberless piles of bags, plastic suitcases and parcels that filled every available space. The occupants had drawn all the curtains and sat mute and immobile in a faint twilight like distressed animals; a host of faces, apprehensive, resigned and impassive. From an old thermos flask, gaudily decorated with flowers, steam rose in languorous coils. As I clambered over one of the coarse jute sacks, a chute of flour spurted onto the floor and splattered onto a broken egg, creating a skiddy mess. The faces were eastern but not, I thought, from Mongolia – they lacked the ruddy, hide-like complexions of Mongolians. Their bodies were lithe and thin and even in their stillness I could sense a contained charge of energy. They were Chinese but not as I had foreseen. A resentful gloom hung over them, as if they were prisoners, or failed escapees; nothing otherwise accounted for their journey to China in that wretched condition. You have to remember that in those days, the citizens of the People's Republic of China, who were still very poor and beholden to the caprices of government control, could not leave their country on a whim. These unfortunates on the train were encumbered with not just the paraphernalia of travel but, it seemed, all their earthly goods; yet, there was no one to watch over them and no one I could find to explain their presence. I asked the French diplomats and the Queen's Messengers but they were as mystified as I was.

Only later, when I returned home, did I discover the truth in the form of a note from a friend working for a national newspaper on its foreign desk, to which from time to time reports of events in the obscurer recesses of the world chattered in on the telex. Most such stories were, of course, discarded in favour of bigger events; it was possible, too, that Mongolia in its isolation and remoteness, shunted into a forgotten siding where the grass grew through the tracks, was irrelevant to the self-importance of the great world. What I saw on that train was the result of one of those campaigns beloved of totalitarian states when a scapegoat is required for failure or inertia. In this case, the Chinese residents of Ulan Bator, expelled on some pretext or other, were the hapless victims. The report quoted the Soviet news agency, *Tass*, to the effect that the expulsion was being used only against 'individual Chinese citizens who systematically and maliciously violated' Mongolian law and who, like most Chinese in Mongolia, 'shirk socially useful work'. Before expulsion, they had been offered the chance to take part in agricultural projects in the north, where climatic conditions for farming were said to be favourable. Western reports that Mongolia had tried to resettle Chinese forcibly in desert areas were 'slanderous fabrications' because 'the question of Chinese citizens leaving Mongolia for their homeland is their personal matter. The Chinese citizens refusing to work in the People's Republic of Mongolia and expressing the wish to leave it are issued permits to leave solely on a voluntary basis.' A senior Chinese official said Chinese workers had been given fourteen days to report to two desolate state farms on the Soviet border. When they refused to leave their jobs, he said, they were 'forced to sign a "voluntary" pledge to leave the country.'

It was the same old story; a miserable, to all intents and purposes overlooked, now certainly forgotten episode in a remote corner of the world. Small tragedies, of little importance in the great scheme of things – except for each of those pawns, for that was what they were, shunted about to suit the political expediencies of the time, heading back towards the country from which some had, no doubt, already escaped in the hopeless quest for a better life. How ironic to read those words of the Chinese spokesman in Peking, considering what took place – what was still taking place – in China then.

We arrived at the border town in the late afternoon. We disembarked onto the platform and watched the sun set with blinding incandescence on the yellow stucco

A small station on the Trans-Mongolian Railway, the Russian influence much in evidence.

of the border station, which stood in isolation on a wide plain of stony sand. It was a long wait; several hours of unexplained indolence, during which, apart from when the door to the station building opened and shut from time to time to allow the passage of anonymous individuals that appeared from nowhere, there was no movement of any kind. As the sun slipped over the horizon a Mongolian nurse, in a uniform that with its winged headdress and long skirts would have not seemed out of place in the First World War, wandered among us, distributing forms on which we were to admit to any of the identifiable diseases listed, a peculiar procedure considering that we were about to leave the country. We returned to our carriage and waited, wrapped in blankets against the intense desert cold. The Famous Writer wandered up and down the platform, ear pressed to a short-wave radio to obtain the latest news from the outside world. In that wind-scoured place, even cataclysmic events – the Syrian Army's retaliatory arrest and execution of over 100 young men with connections to the Muslim Brotherhood – and Soviet politicking – Politburo members in Warsaw to lecture the Polish Government on its ability to contain the 'Solidarity Movement' – felt like irrelevant gossip. Even the news that an eminent Chinese author, Bai Hua, had been accused of 'bourgeois liberalism' and his career terminated by his government could not dampen the general air of enthusiasm current among us at the tantalising prospect of entering China.

Towards midnight, the commotion began. I went into the corridor and pulled back the curtains that my friend the carriage attendant had drawn shut on awaking from his coma. Outside, piles of sacks and plastic suitcases and broken furniture were being dumped under the gaze of a platoon of nervous Mongolian soldiers, marshalled by what I took to be a Russian officer. Groups of shivering Chinese of all ages from the neighbouring carriage, permitted to remove a single item from among their flimsy possessions, remonstrated hopelessly before being ushered brusquely back to the train. Finally, it was done and there was a buffeting and screeching as our carriage was attached to the train that would take us on; then there was a roar from the locomotive as it stuttered into action and we headed for the Chinese border. I remember looking down through my compartment window as we gathered speed to see the pale light from our lamp fall in passing on the frozen carcass of a wolf, stretched across the fence that ran alongside the track, its grey coat stiff with ice, its jaws agape, its paws steeped in a shallow drift of frozen slush.

The arrival in China was, for almost everybody in the party, like reaching Paradise, a moment of transfiguration after the journey through Purgatory. China was the Holy Grail. A tangible excitement ran along the corridor. It was now dark; the Chinese border station at Erlian was lit up like a fairground. As we drew slowly to a halt, my impression was of a red building framed in dazzling white bulbs, like a theatre dressing-room mirror. Immediately, a gaggle of officials piled onto the train in that way they have in China of unruly organisation, talking loudly among themselves, replying patiently to the chorus of '*ni hao*', the words of greeting that everyone had learnt before leaving home, and calling out the single word of English, 'leader',

We have friends all over the world – China opens the door to the West.

required for their work. For in China then, everything was done on a group basis, and for every group, just as there had been everywhere since Berlin, there was surely a 'leader'. That was me, the helmsman for a motley party of tourists, the man holding the list of their names on the group visa with the seal of approval from the embassy of the People's Republic of China in London. In Chinese eyes we were a delegation, representing the Western world. For all that it was merely a minor propaganda exercise; it was refreshing to feel welcome after weeks of resentment among the Russians and their allies.

In China the trains ran on the same gauge as in most of Europe. Once the formalities were dealt with, everyone disembarked as the train was shunted into a shed, where the wheel bogies were changed. I could not help observing that, whereas on the Soviet border with Poland the method of changing them was a cumbersome affair, involving winching the wheels from one track to another, the Chinese technique was far more sophisticated – they simply raised the carriages and rolled the wheels out from beneath, a difference of approach that reflected the practical nature of one people and the delight in drudgery of the other.

And in a siding, smoke drifting from its chimney across the spangled night sky, stood the embodiment of another contrast between the two; the restaurant car that was to be attached to our train was already open for business, even at this late hour. The rush for a table was unseemly but hardly unexpected. Rice and meat and vegetables, in the overheated and greasy train restaurant car, were delicious prospects. Together with Chinese beer, we ate our fill, and everybody was suddenly in good spirits. I rather think that many in the party believed that the remaining weeks were going to pass in a drama of good food, good fellowship and fabulous exotica. But as I ate, I saw through the restaurant car window the pathetic Chinese refugees from the neighbouring carriage, clutching their remaining possessions, being led away by soldiers into the station building.

We returned to our carriage. Our Mongolian attendant was nowhere to be seen. Only later, as we got underway and the carriage was quiet but for snores from the gluttons among us, did I find him, in the washroom next to his compartment, his arms wrapped around the toilet cistern, his features screwed up into an expression of alcoholic anguish. He spoke to me through clenched teeth, shaking my hand and vouchsafing to me what turned out to be a marmot skin, not so cured that the meaty tang of Mongolia was undetectable. I bade my friend farewell, for I did not expect to see him next morning, and as the train pelted across northern China, I too slept, to the smell of coal-scented steam as it drifted the length of the train, and to the sound of cinders rattling across the windows.

In the morning we awoke in China. During the night we had rattled through Inner Mongolia at enormous speed, accompanied by the owl-like screeches from the steam locomotive, to reach the province of Shanxi, and the town of Da Tong. Later, in recalling my first daylight glimpse of China, I was convinced that I had looked down from the train onto a row of shimmering willow trees beside a river, where a man

Paddi fields and water buffalo, the stereotypical image of China.

in a straw hat wielded a switch to drive on a pair of water buffalo: a vision of China printed on a million pieces of porcelain. There are no water buffalo in the north of China – water buffalo are found where there is water and Shanxi is an arid, desiccated province. What I saw was a fantasy. Yet, after all these years, part of me remains convinced of the truth of that image framed in the carriage window, an instant and perpetual stereotype and like most stereotypes, no more than a half-truth.

We were met on the station platform by the local guide and by another who introduced himself as a guide but who throughout our time in Da Tong remained strangely aloof. Of course, the usual suspects immediately presumed that he was a state minder. Even if true, I knew after our time in Russia that surveillance, if that was what it was, in dictatorial state had become a kind of tradition, a habit that was usually, as it were, not personal. After an uncomfortable night on the train, most in the party had thoughts only for a hotel room and a wash. But, no, we were whisked away on an absurdly plush and vast Japanese coach that whispered and sighed its way through the dusty, colourless streets of industrial Da Tong to the first of our scheduled visits. Protests were met by the guide, a plain woman, careworn despite her youthfulness, with a fixed smile and darting eyes, with relentless evasiveness; and so the pangs of the love affair with China among the more querulous individuals dissolved into the first signs of disenchantment.

Miss Wang was dressed in the conventional dress for the China of the time – dark blue baggy canvas trousers, from which peeped at their cuffs the luminescent pink of the inevitable long-johns, and matching jacket, and canvas shoes and, because it was early spring in the north of China, a heavy down-filled overcoat. She was typical of her era – young, but old enough to have had her life turned upside down by the Cultural Revolution. There was a greyness about her, in her skin and in her air of fatigue that mirrored the down-at-heel city that surrounded her like a shroud. She had not planned to become a tourist guide, or to live in Da Tong. The government had sent her there in the 1970s to share the lives of the peasants and workers and so now it was home. We stood warming our hands over the brazier in the ticket office as she spoke laconically about her life; she accepted her exile with good grace, because she had no control over her fate. In an explanation that I was to hear many times over the coming weeks, she said, 'The government wanted us to learn from the peasants. We had to obey. It was hard work but I learned many things.' Such sentiments were uttered with a heroic absence of bitterness, if without many signs of enthusiasm.

Da Tong was a filthy place. No, filthy is the wrong word, and in using it I do the place a disservice. It was dreary, drab, moribund. And cold. Had it been anywhere but 'exotic' China, this ancient town would have attracted nobody but salesmen and service engineers. The air was sulphuric – you could taste the coal dust on your tongue. I saw no birds, nor heard any song. Datong was threadbare; China was threadbare, in a state of acute impoverishment. I was reminded of a shrivelled autumn leaf. To the pneumatic sigh of well-engineered Japanese suspension, we looked down on gaping workers in their thin blue jackets as we bumped along a dried river bed below mountains of coal bricks and blackened smokestacks, until we reached the great caves of Yungang, filled with gigantic Buddhist statues carved some 1,500 years before out of the yellow loess; in the city itself we visited two venerable and creaking temples from the Jin and the Liao dynasties and the blistered Ming nine-dragon wall. They stood in pathetic isolation amid the factories and faceless blocks of flats and the handful of streets thankfully still flanked by simple broken-down houses with their pretty upturned eaves and rice paper windows, fortuitous relics of the ravenings of the Great Helmsman. The inadequacies of our guide only highlighted the poignancy of their survival. But the fault was not hers – for most of her life she had been poorly nourished on a diet of selective interpretations of Chinese history before 1949, with the emphasis on its failings. Now, there was a new government policy. Westerners, previously regarded with official suspicion, were welcome; and so our guide had been drafted in to learn a smattering of English and ordered to extol the achievements of the Communist Party and, furthermore, to impress foreigners with the vitality of ancient Chinese culture. But so little was left. We looked upon these wondrous creations, these isolated remnants of a great civilisation, in mystification.

That was partly because we did not know what China was. Before leaving England, I thought I had a clearer picture of China than of the other countries we were to pass through: if as a child you collected postage stamps, you knew of Mao Zedong; we had heard of chopsticks, even if we had never handled them; we had an idea, though a false

one, of Chinese food; we knew of mandarins, fireworks and gunpowder, the invention
of paper; and we would recognise Chinese script and Chinese paintings and Chinese
architecture (although we might confuse them all with Japan and possibly Korea).
We knew of poverty, hordes of bicycles, and had heard of the Cultural Revolution,
the Gang of Four and the Democracy Wall. We knew of Hong Kong. We knew 'Made
in Taiwan', even if we did not know exactly why there were two Chinas and which
was which. In all, we had a confused image of China composed of two sets of clichés:
an inscrutable Fu Manchu China; and the New China of Long Marches and brave,
if flawed, Revolutionary endeavour that had finally embraced the Western world.
We expected to see them both and both would be equally wonderful. Whatever our
misconceptions about China, there was for many one characteristic greatly in its
favour, for above all, China was not Russia.

Shortly before leaving London there had been an article in the colour section of a
serious newspaper that exalted the accomplishments of modern China, celebrating
in particular the miracle of the People's Communes as an example to the world,
especially to the self-regarding West, of what can be achieved when people work in
concert. The fascination with change in China blinded some to unpalatable facts,
most notably that the present daily life of the Chinese people, by tragic irony, had
not changed as much as all that since the heyday of imperial China. The effort since
1949 to obliterate history in order to create a pristine society uncontaminated by old
ways had failed; China had been a country of peasants before and so it remained. In
our ignorance of what China had been and what it had really become, we looked on
at China in 1981 in a state of charmed stupefaction, for it seemed to us that if Russia
was cold and slow, China was vibrant and mercurial.

What did it matter if Datong had been, centuries before, an imperial capital and
was now a sooty backwater? When I gazed on the urban wilderness that was Datong
and realised that this was China, I felt like one who stumbles across a polluted canal in
a down-at-heel suburb. You admire the achievements of another age, you kind of revel
in the romance of neglect and yet you yearn for the return of the vigour that inspired
it. The resilience of the Chinese was admirable, but one could not help but despair
of the suffering that inspired it. In that exhausted city all that was exquisite was in
the people, as they practised on the pavements before us their immemorial tasks and
trades: the dentist with ancient barber's chair and rusty drills, advertising his skills
by means of a sign painted with a set of grinning dentures; the shoemaker reduced
to working in plastic and rubber, hammering away at nails with the intense precision
of a master-craftsman; the wok mender and his tools that glowed in the white heat of
his furnace; all working with laser-like concentration, all endlessly talking, all then
stopping in wide-eyed synchronicity at the phenomenon of Westerners wandering
among them like ghosts. For the time being, at least, by government decree, foreigners
were to be treated as friends and even mentors. Around the rows of craftsmen, the
streets were always busy with weary cyclists and antiquated lorries packed with heaps
of coal over which, slumped like sacks, lay sleeping workers, oblivious to the rough

ride and din. Somewhere in all this, in spite of what had gone on before, there was detectable a fresh energy and an incipient optimism for the future.

We were in what had once been the capital of a Chinese dynasty. This was mentioned in passing, but it went over our heads, partly because of Miss Wang's strangled delivery, partly because it meant nothing to us, these titles that were not Ming, or Song or any of those Chinese names that were familiar to us. Yet Shanxi, an arid province large enough to be a country, resting in the shadow of the Great Wall at the frontier with the outer world, once an entrepot on the ancient caravan routes, had been the seedbed of the greatest of all Chinese dynasties, the Tang.

As I came to discover, everything in China was a mixture of exasperating punctiliousness that frequently turned to intransigence when a matter of rules and regulations and frustrating vagueness when it came to historical facts. Try as we might, it was almost impossible to glean any true understanding of Chinese history. At first, I presumed that the explanation for this was the absence of so much of its physical evidence. But later, I came to think that there was another, more subtle reason and that was custom. Chinese civilisation and even the run-down version of it that we were seeing, was based on centuries of habitual patterns of behaviour and thought, the origins of which had been all but forgotten. Dynasties came and went over millennia, but the essential routines of daily life barely altered. For Miss Wang it was all one and the same and she had no idea how to make what little she knew interesting to ignorant foreigners. And we had no idea what we were looking at or how to appreciate what we saw. The Yungang caves were physically spectacular and the remaining temples in the city clearly old, creaking and time-worn but of their significance, their origins, their place in time, we knew almost nothing.

In the past, Datong had another name. Names in China are laden with symbolism. They are a cipher for power. Shanxi was once known as Tang, and later, Jin. When Datong was called Pingcheng, during the Northern Wei Dynasty (386 to 534 AD), it was an Imperial Capital. The founders of that dynasty were the Tuoba, a clan of the Xianbei people, who were pastoralists and nomads related in some way to the Mongols but who, having seized for themselves tracts of northern China, succumbed, as with all invaders of China, to the peculiar order and intellectual strength of Chinese civilisation. Consequently, the name 'Tuoba' through an edict of Emperor Xiaowen, became (元) or 'Yuan'. Why 'Yuan'? When a new dynasty was established its founder would select a magniloquent title for it that implied a celestial mandate. Since 'yuan' has a variety of possible meanings, it must have carried some propitious weight. The same character, with the same pronunciation, can mean 'unit' (and in particular a unit of Chinese currency) and can also refer to the later Mongol dynasty, the one featuring Kublai Khan. It is also possible that the Chinese, unable to pronounce those barbarous steppe names, made them more palatable and in so doing the Tuoba themselves became more malleable and soon forgot their horses and their tents and were happy to be made into Chinese. I admit that is a long shot, just a hunch based on the way the Chinese have of turning threats to their advantage.

While we are on the subject, I may as well go further, for the same word, 'yuan', with the same pronunciation, but written with different characters, can also mean 'wall', 'garden', 'source' and 'cart shaft'. Then again, if you pronounce the same word with a flatter tone, it can mean something wholly unrelated, a 'deep pool' or 'profound'. The conundrum of China, I came to understand, and perhaps, too, the origin of the well-worn cliché of inscrutability, is its dual nature, by which I mean many aspects of Chinese life are simultaneously simple and perplexing. Is the language highly sophisticated because of the complete absence of grammar? Or does that make it primitive, as well as a convenient shield from nosey foreigners? Are the sayings of Confucius banal truisms or piercing insights? Is Chinese poetry an astute marriage of thought and image, or cryptic gibberish? Ultimately, it was the endless pursuit of a hopeless task, the constant uncertainty about the truth of anything that in China held us spellbound.

One of the problems of an unchanging civilisation is that the bad stays along with the good! At the time of these events, in the fifth century AD, China had been already united for 600 years. And as for the mighty Tang, I will discuss them in due course. In the meantime, remember this shabby city, Da Tong that was our introduction to the glories of China.

In the afternoon, we were taken to a factory, visits to factories and farms being essential elements of almost any itinerary, partly to make up for the fact that so much of beauty had been lost to political upheaval, partly to demonstrate China's commitment

Driving a steam locomotive in China , this one possibly made in the USA in the 1940s.

to economic progress. Admittedly, the Da Tong Number One Locomotive Factory was a factory quite unlike any other, for it was one of the last in the world, perhaps the only one, still manufacturing steam locomotives, an attractive proposition, indeed a temple, one might have thought, for a group of people travelling by train from the edge of Europe to the tip of Asia. But lovers of trains for their own sake form a separate breed, for they are obsessive collectors and when it came to railways at least, none of us were in that category. The romance, if that is the word, of the age of steam was lost on most of us. Only the British members waxed a little sentimental at the thought of this outpost of Victorian engineering, whilst the French contingent stood around impatiently, dragging on their cigarettes with expressions of disgust at Anglo-Saxon imbecility. We were led through a jumble of a workshop along a path littered with abandoned train trinkets where the workers, free of protective encumbrances against the clanging, banging hammers or the raging furnaces, worked in sedulous disorder. Finally, we stood outside in a weedy yard and awaited in anticipation for the emergence of a just completed loco, which, anthracite black, pierced the giant factory doors with the compacted power of a domesticated mammoth, onto which we then clambered like children in a playground before trundling 200 yards along a siding. 'March Forward' was the name of this genus of locomotive, a proud standard bearer of Communist Chinese advancement.

As I remember it, the front of the locomotive was emblazoned with a huge red star. But there I may be mistaken, for the era of overt Maoist propaganda in China had

Under full steam – steam locomotives were still built in China.

passed. Nonetheless, I discovered that even locomotives were subject to the moods and politics that prevailed at a given moment in the revolutionary spectrum. When it was first manufactured in 1956, based on a Russian predecessor at a period when China and Russia were still enjoying comradely relations, it was 'Heping' or 'Peace'. In the 1960s, during one of the Great Helmsman's periodic destructive campaigns, it became 'Fandi', or 'Anti-Imperialism'. Now, it was the 'March Forward' class, a title that also dated from Mao's final years but with its storybook echoes of a gallant engine straining to do its proud best, a less tendentious one. Although it seemed to me very peculiar to change the name of a glorified boiler on wheels to reflect the whims of dictators, I suppose that I should have learned after my experiences in Russia and Mongolia that revolutionary politics concerned itself ultimately only with trivia.

Then, there was the meeting. On the way in to the factory area we had passed at the entrance the inevitable statue of Mao beaming cordially, offering a friendly wave as a man of the very people he condemned in large numbers if not to death, at least to a life of unrewarded toil and false hopes. It was interesting to me to note the different standard poses adopted by the dictators whose images I had seen in abundance over the preceding weeks: Lenin in full heroic declamatory flow, scroll or worker's cap in hand, pointing prophet-like to a promised land; Stalin more akin to Napoleon, one arm inside his coat, avuncular and martial; and now the Great Helmsman, waving and smiling, modestly acknowledging the approbation from the adoring billions as

A 'brief introduction' Formalities had to be observed at any visit to a factory.

the herald of a bright future. All three in their heavy greatcoats, armour-like, ever ready to fight the good fight.

Then, upon entering the factory precincts, we passed beneath a banner inscribed with the words, 'Warmly Welcome to our British Friends'. We were ushered into a conference room with a long table and requested to 'take a rest'. Presently, a troupe of factory officials filed in to take seats opposite us, beneath the crimson and gold banners hung on the wall behind them, which, we learnt, bore witness to the fulfilment by the factory of various laudable achievements – production quotas, political education, safety records and the like; bowls of fruit dotted with drops of water as evidence of good hygiene rested untouched at intervals along the table; tea was served; and a verbal welcome by the deputy director extended to us through the offices of Miss Wang. We were then given what I soon came to know very well, 'the brief introduction' to the factory, its history and current position. We were not mere tourists but a Western 'delegation', as if we were on an inspection tour or a buying trip. Of course, the factory staff would know we were not there to appraise their work or to purchase locomotives. They would have charged a fee for hosting us and conferring the inflated status of delegates was a tacit acknowledgement of our contribution. Looking back, I believe that beneath the pious talk there stirred the first signs of the 'capitalism with Chinese characteristics' that later became government policy. In contrast with the Russians, who clung on with the zeal of prophets to a vision of a socialist future, the Chinese were pragmatic operators for whom the allure of wealth or a bit of a gamble was irresistible. No birch tree branch switches or ice cold baths for them.

Questions were invited. After a moment of silence, out of politeness someone cleared their throat and asked about future production of steam locomotives. When the predictably anodyne answer came, it seemed an appropriate moment for me to thank the factory for their hospitality and to leave. As I rose, Guppy, currying favour with his cronies, in his role as fearless defender of the Western world interrupted.

'Were you a Red Guard?' he asked of the deputy director referring to the early days of the Cultural Revolution. Miss Wang's translation was somewhat longer than the question merited. The deputy director nodded and laughed in embarrassment as she struggled to find a diplomatic way of putting the question.

'That was in the past,' he replied. 'Now, China is looking to the future!' adding, 'Thank you for your understanding,' another phrase I was to hear often when things looked as if they might go wrong, or when we were asked to put up with some inconvenience; at which he muttered something to an aide and closed the meeting, to a round of applause from the rest of us, which was returned by the exiting committee.

Afterwards, Guppy said to anyone who would listen, 'Didn't answer my question did he?' Then in reference to Mao Zedong, 'He didn't get to be deputy director by defying the Chairman, you can be sure of that!'

Just as it had been in Russia, it was easy to score cheap political points at the expense of those whose histories we did not and could not know. How could we know what kind of hell the deputy director might have lived through only a few years before our visit? That was how it was, then. At every school, every commune, every factory, we were invited to 'have a rest' and listen to a 'brief introduction'. We were clapped in by waiting committees and clapped out (so to speak), just because we were Westerners. Those decades of anti-Western propaganda were as nothing because the new policy insisted that we were now friends of the Chinese people. In fact, we were controlled not, as those like Guppy and the Vets liked to believe, through the curtailment of our freedom but through an excess of courtesy and constant appeals to our goodwill.

Now that all the Mao statues have been squirrelled away, and the bicycles exchanged for cars and Chinese investors are piling into every corner of the globe, these pictures of China's recent past can seem incredible. Nobody expected China to change as it has and so quickly, sleeping tiger or not. Then, we spent little time pondering the future; most were charmed by the unending smiles that it seemed to me, even in those first few days, were clearly not to be interpreted necessarily as indications of joy, contentment or even of amusement. They were a protective feature, switched on and off according to need. The smiles drew you in, as the eyes scanned and assessed you. And yet there were several in the party for whom a face without a smile, no matter how insincere, was the face of misery. They found the endless rows of teeth captivating; others less enchanted, were nonetheless moved to observe 'how happy everyone seemed, even though they are so poor'.

Finally, we went to our hotel. The staff greeted us on the steps and clapped us into the lobby, where a great show of enthusiastic chaos attended the checking-in process. Again, the contrast with stolid Russian ways was unmistakable. Everything was like that – the simplest task complicated by anxiety to do the right thing, with numbers of inept helpers all piling in with apologetic smiles – 'thank you for your understanding'. I found this both engaging and sinister, because it was obvious that all these displays of bonhomie and welcome could, if decreed from above, just stop. No more smiles, no more apologies. Everything was politics.

The hotel itself had been constructed in the 1950s for Russian 'experts', who in those far-off days were, politically speaking, regarded by the Chinese as experienced older brothers. Until 1961, when the Great Helmsman accused the Russians of Marxist Revisionism, they were there to pass on their skills in engineering, socialist economics and anything else that they could bring to the Communist table. Even in 1981, almost all the hotels that existed in China had been built to house Russians and I rather liked them, with their spacious rooms, their worn carpets, their deep armchairs and antimacassars, their rumbling plumbing and scalding radiators – like British country-house hotels less the hunting prints and well-stocked bar but with even greater class barriers, for although our hotel was built in the name of the Chinese 'People', its guest list had never included them. As in Mongolia, it bore all the hallmarks of colonialism, that is to say in this case, Russian construction with a few half-hearted acknowledgements to Chinese taste. In each room there was a large wooden writing desk, on top of which rested an empty ink bottle, rice notepaper and plastic dip pens, such as we learnt to use at kindergarten. To enter one of these rooms with its creaking beds and scratchy blankets was to inhabit another era, when ink from leaking pens left blue smudges ingrained into fingers and thumbs and there lingered the fragrance of pencil sharpener shavings and the crumbs of rubber erasers. A tin spittoon lay in wait in the corner.

At that time, Da Tong, if not wholly off the tourist map, was by no means a fixture on it. We were the only foreigners in town, apart from a handful of 'foreign experts', no longer Soviet but West European, Australasian or North American. The hotel was their home for months at a time – laconic Germans, sceptical Britons, visionary Americans – like modern incarnations of Lord Jim, they were even handed in their love and loathing of China and the Chinese. They were out in the field all day, returning in the evening for a solitary dinner accompanied by as many Chinese beers as they could down, before disappearing to their room to draw up a fresh set of plans for the next project. For those used to the solaces of bars, television and domestic comfort, life was dull in Da Tong.

Sometimes, as they waited on the hotel steps for their driver and interpreter, I would fall into conversation with them. Inevitably, the first topic was the question of China's future. Were these changes here to stay? Or would the hard liners get their way and throw the foreigners out? Opinions varied according to national psyches, from gloomy romanticism to effusive optimism.

'Great people, these! They learn fast!' the American engineers would say admiringly, blissfully certain that Communism had had its day in China, for democracy was an inevitability and wealth and the rule of law would surely follow. But in 1981, in that windswept, coal-blackened northern town, who could have been sure of anything? Even if Da Tong was a living testimony to the failure of the past forty years, to underestimate the autocratic tradition of 3,000 years would have been foolish. And yet, it did seem inconceivable that there could be a return to the suicidal politics of the preceding years, which had truly brought China to a level of degradation. But if I ventured that opinion, there were those who would shake their heads with a knowing smile. 'You think so, do you? I wouldn't be so sure,' without really say why they wouldn't, just as I could not have explained my own intuition. Then, Russia was still the USSR, controlling most of Eastern Europe and waging war in Afghanistan; Albania was a secretive, impenetrable oligarchy, as was North Korea, one of China's close allies. On that basis, things did not look too promising.

There was our introduction to China, an emaciated body on which ancient flesh hung thin and loose, but the lungs of which were beginning to fill again with clean, fresh air. Exhausted, poor and beaten though they were, the latent energy of the Chinese showed itself in a multitude of ways. It is no surprise to me that China has transformed itself into an economic power house. More astonishing is the pace of the transformation. For anyone unable to compare the China of then and the China of now, the scale of the change is unimaginable. This is not a case of organic change but of wholesale metamorphosis, like scenery shifted in the theatre; a revolution in reverse. Nor is it just a matter of the replacement of jerry-built low-grade concrete constructions with gleaming towers of glass and steel, even in cities, like Da Tong, on the fringes of the country. The greatest revolution is in the outlook of the people. The hints of cautious optimism discernible even among the poor, exhausted and beaten people of Da Tong has turned into nation-wide confident enthusiasm. That not everybody has gained is self-evident, but even the marginalised are no worse off than they were before. As for Miss Wang, I wonder what became of her; did she catch on to the spirit of the time, transfigured from a pale automaton in threadbare cotton into a sleek captain of industry or was she a mute beneficiary of better times?

That night we boarded the train again, a fully Chinese train now, with its own perfume of camphor and urine, heading for Peking in another night of high-speed rock and roll across the plains of northern China. As with all the rolling stock we had come to know since quitting the North Sea coast, across Germany, Poland, Russia and Mongolia, the carriages of the People's Railway were manufactured in East Germany. Although each had differed in small ways, reflecting each country's priorities and expectations and small vices (in Chinese trains there were always vegetables soaking ready for cooking in the washrooms or in a bowl in the corridor), it was astonishing to me that a single factory in the German Democratic Republic had succeeded in monopolising the supply of railway authorities right across the communist world. It was as if every car in the world, because its quality and value

The iron road to Peking. Passenger trains were still steam-hauled in northern China.

for money could not be bettered, was a Mercedes-Benz. I found that an impressive achievement. Striking, too, that with the exception of troublesome Poland, the colour scheme was the same, always green, not of grass or of leaves but the martial green of tanks and camouflage.

Our national guide, whom we had barely seen throughout our stay in Da Tong, had reappeared and was to accompany us throughout our tour of China. His role was to act as our custodian as we travelled between cities, but his knowledge of English was poor and, as far as I could tell, his allegiance to the status quo absolute. His tunic and trousers were of a better quality than that of the local guides, which led me to believe that he occupied the equivalent of a middle-management post in the provincial town that was his home. His manner was jovial, his presence innocuous. I think, far from being an official sent to keep an eye on us, he was on holiday. His capacity to doze without warning and under any circumstances earned him the soubriquet Sleeping Buddha.

I imagined that Peking would be a great city. Datong was a spent provincial town, but Peking, we felt certain, would be glorious. In a way, it was. We entered the city in the early morning. The line passed close to one of the old Ming city gates, its grey bricks beneath curling eaves emitting a waxy sheen in the pale pink sun. We crossed over a wide, straight avenue and watched a traffic policeman on a dais waving his baton mechanically at the lorries and trolleybuses that drifted ponderously amid shoals of bicycles. Then we pulled with a jolt into Peking Railway Station.

Peking railway station, with its nod to traditional Chinese architecture.

This station was a remarkable piece of architecture. The scale of it was not evident at first, as we were lead through an all but empty waiting room filled with armchairs and their antimacassars, the air heavy with the ubiquitous odour of camphor, solemn like a chapel of rest. A single patrician figure in a finely tailored version of the cotton fatigues that constituted the uniform of the masses was being served tea by a waitress in a red-star emblazoned cap. Then we descended into an underpass, into a tumult of passengers weighed under with bundles wrapped in plastic, or dangling pendulously from bamboo yokes, rushing not in flight from catastrophe but in desperation to obtain a seat on a train. We bumped our way through the torrent and emerged into the capital of China.

Outside, there was a hint of warmth. After the weeks of travel, we had arrived at the beginning of May. Peking's chill winter had thawed and in the air we could taste the dust blown in from the Gobi. I looked behind me at the great station building. By now, I was inured to the curious architecture of the Communist world with its gigantism and its overblown nods to tradition. Somebody asked the local guide – who, by the way, was a stripling in every way, thin as a rake and extremely young, yet with the poise of an ageing mandarin scholar – during which dynasty the station was built. The poor boy, notwithstanding orders to humour Westerners at all times except in matters relating to rules and to politics, was unable to conceal his amazement at the question. The station, it turned out, impressive in its way, but obviously a mongrel confection that in keeping with what I was to learn was a Chinese infatuation with the power of numbers, had been constructed in 1959 as one of the Ten Great Buildings to celebrate the first decade of the People's Republic of China and to show as part of the Great Leap Forward that Peking was a modern city like the great cities of the West.

These Ten Great Buildings were a motley collection: hotels (one for that category of Chinese known as Overseas Chinese, another to house the fifty-five minority nationalities now subsumed into China's revolutionary family); a Workers' Stadium; the Great Hall of the People, where lively political debate was never heard; two museums (the National Museum and the Chinese People's Revolutionary Military Museum); the Cultural Palace of Nationalities; and the State Guesthouse. And one other ... what was it? Oh, of course, the inevitable National Agriculture Exhibition Hall. There you have it in a way – all you needed to know about New China during the first three decades of its existence; a collection of ill-afforded grandiose buildings to celebrate the achievements of one man – Mao Zedong! Who, by the way, was lying in state only a short distance from the station in the very centre of the city, as he does even now. But I think that the most interesting of these was the Overseas Chinese Hotel – not the building itself, which was not architecturally distinguished and which anyway has, I believe, been demolished – but the notion of a special hotel for overseas brethren seemed to me at the time to be a peculiar one. From this I understood that Overseas Chinese were a special category of human being, who, being of the same blood as the citizens of the People's Republic of China, if misguided politically, were, through some contortion of the ideal of mutual cultural understanding, to be kept apart from we Westerners. This segregation seemed to serve several purposes; a natural clannishness that can seem like contempt for outsiders and simultaneously, control of anyone contaminated by western values.

As with Uncle Joe in the USSR, in the New China of 1959, as these Great Buildings were rising up to impress the masses, all was not well where it mattered, in the mouths and stomachs of the hundreds of millions of adoring subjects.

The Great Helmsman was a vain man. All such men – and until now, as far as I know, they have always been men – seek vainglory. It is not long before their righteous anger, if that is what impels them to set out along the revolutionary road, is superseded by a belief in their own superhuman abilities. Soon they cannot bear contradiction or to hear words of caution. Eventually they no longer see the evidence of their own eyes. They stop looking, they don't bother to listen. Finally, the realisation of failure blinds them to all sense of compassion, deafens them to wise counsel, for the fault is never theirs. All that counts is the scheme, the project, the five-year plan, or whatever dream haunts them and to hell with the consequences. An experiment it may be but, you never know, it might just work ... and if people die in the process, so be it, you can't make an omelette ... the cause, you see, must prevail ... so in 1958, the Great Helmsman unleashed the Great Leap Forward. Everything is 'great'. And a 'leap', no mean little 'step' for Mao. No chance of overtaking the Great Satan with the pitter-patter of progress. Only a leap would do.

It was all so easy! A simple case of turning an agrarian society into an industrialised one. Thus, the country is on the open road to full communism. Resistance would not be tolerated but hearts and minds were easily won over; 'struggle' sessions were conducted to ensure compliance. With its hint of rigorous democratic debate, it is an interesting euphemism when expressed in colloquial English for the literal translation from Chinese, which is the more pugnacious 'inciting the spirit of judgement and fighting'. If you were accused of being a 'capitalist roader' you were condemned. If you confessed with the intention of making amends – you were condemned. Under those circumstances, under which it is impossible to avoid incriminating oneself, it is safer always be the accuser, rather than the accused. Safety is never guaranteed, however, for sooner or later, the accuser will also be the accused.

The really clever bit was the introduction of mass-industrialisation. Money was poured into state-run steel works, which led to rapid urban expansion and so to problems with food distribution, solved by the clever notion of backyard steel furnaces. Because the Great Helmsman had decreed that China would overtake in industrial output first the United Kingdom and then the United States, peasants throughout the land were ordered to produce steel at home, from scrap metal. The countryside was ransacked for the fuel to fire the furnaces and all available metals, graciously contributed by the peasant themselves, were thrown into them. The result was at best pig-iron, discovered in China, almost 2,000 years before. But not steel. Certainly not steel. Production targets may have been met – who knows – but figures, mere figures, that was all the targets were. No steel. Certainly no steel.

But there were benefits. The Great Helmsman had learnt his political craft at the feet of the master. Stalin, remember, loved nothing more than schemes and plans that would improve the lot of his people, schemes and plans that were executed with no regard at all to facts. The great advantage to what one might call the draconian approach to reform is that you need not bother listening to tedious nay-sayers; suffering is an obstacle but a temporary one. We must all die anyway, in the end. And so, as with Uncle Joe, so with the Great Helmsman. The Great Leap became a plunge into the abyss. We will never know the facts in detail, but the numbers of people who died of starvation as a result of his leap run into the tens of millions. The leap became a famine. That is as certain as pig-iron is not steel.

That is not the end of it. There is more! Great Helmsmen don't give up at the first sign of failure. They weather the storm and navigate to calmer waters, tie up and gather their strength. But we were in Peking, one of the great cities of the world and what did we see? We saw vanity. We saw the bleak spoils of conceit. A once fabulous city so reduced by wrong-headedness is hard to take. And yet we were fascinated, just as we had been in Da Tong, by what had vanished as much as we were by what remained.

Some might say that these tyrants were the product of their histories, of their epochs, of the societies that vomited them into existence. That in some way they could not help themselves. That they were popular. I am not so sure, because there were people, and plenty of them, who in their hearts understood that the deliberate

Peking street leading to Tian An Men Square – traffic free.

fomentation of chaos in the name of order was not just wrong-headed but inhuman; they just lacked the means to fight back. The ancestors of these scientists of disorder, the Emperors and Tsars, who had built in their own image the Kremlin and the Forbidden City, claimed their acts of cruelty were sanctioned by God or by Heaven. Their successors had no such excuse. And to think it was all in the cause of improving the lot of Mankind.

Since we had arrived in Peking in the early morning, we were taken to a restaurant for the usual breakfast of fried eggs and toast, tea and ersatz coffee and then on with the programme before we would be taken to our hotel, wherever that might be. As we drove at a measured pace along its streets, I saw that Peking was still a great city, for something of its dignity and grandeur had survived. The centre was a gridiron of long, wide boulevards, flanked by identical blocks of flats and state bureaux, which still reflected the celestial geometry of the old city. The traffic filed along them in stately convoys whilst an endless parade of bicycles, all pedalled in unhurried harmony, bells ringing out in brief, urgent interjections, drifted along special lanes to the side. Whenever we needed to turn left or right, we had to nudge our way through the flow of bicycles, which continued to wheel about us with serene indifference. What gave Peking its character was its vast scale, the long perspectives that vanished into dusty, glowing horizons and what gave it a touch of humanity was the handful of gorgeous relics from its imperial past that, for one reason or the other, had been allowed to remain part of the proletarian vision. The wind whipped along the Avenue of Eternal Peace, and the rows of coloured flags and the red banners decorated with portraits of Marx and Engels snapped in noisy unison.

But first we were to repay our respects to the Great Helmsman himself, kept in God-like suspension at the heart of the city. Lenin in Moscow, Mao in Peking. In Moscow you joined a queue and froze. In Peking, as honoured 'foreign friends' we were placed at the head of the long lines of wide-eyed peasants visiting the Mausoleum, there at the centre of the square, on the exact spot where once had stood the Great Qing Gate, the entrance to the Thousand Paces path that led to the Gate of Heavenly Peace – the central point of the centre of the centre of the world – and in hallowed silence, but for the whisper of the air-conditioning, we uneasily shuffled past the old devil's waxy corpse. Of course we, too, were objects of curiosity to those same peasants, who gathered and advanced in groups like herds of watchful cattle and stared at us, laughing nervously if we met their gaze, fascinated by our pale skins, our blue eyes and our white hair.

Then we re-emerged, dazzled by the brilliant spring sun, into the great square, rather magnificent in its way underneath a vivid, cerulean sky. Sometimes the cool breeze became a wind, which, scooping up the grit and dust, blew it in billows across the square. I remember the kites – old men flying their kites, conduits for their dreams. I understand that kites – and dreams, too, if Mao could have found a way – were banned at one point during the Great Helmsman's reign. Too frivolous? A threat to national security? Who knows. But I remember so clearly those old men with their home-made kites and their perfect concentration, the freedom in their upturned faces, the unaccustomed stillness and the joy of flight.

What is now the square of Tian An Men and the Forbidden City that rolls away from it northwards in waves of courtyards and pavilions, is the focal point of Peking. It was the centre of the city's celestial geometry, as if the beautiful old city that preceded the vision of mediocrity that came after was a reflection of the firmament above.

The scale of the square was magnificent for its emptiness. Other than the Maosoleum, and the Monument to the People's Heroes, Tian An Men Square was an urban dust bowl. If it were not for the two ancient gates at the south and the entrance to the Forbidden City to the north, the square could just as well have been a vast parade ground.

We walked through the Forbidden City, filing in across the marble bridges beneath the portrait of the Chairman, through the arches of the Gate of Heavenly Peace where the imperial dragon finials had been replaced by sunflowers as symbols of the masses' gaze turning to the sun that was the Great Helmsman. Then we wandered, as mystified as ever, amid the still-dusty, then souvenir-free, vermilion pavilions, and across echoing courtyards, and up flights of steps with intricately carved marble balustrades. It was strange to walk through a palace, until 1911, so recently as to barely seem history, the epicentre of the Chinese empire and where, in a sign of what China was to come, when it was time to take the inevitable 'rest', to slake our thirst we were given not tea, but cans of Coca-Cola.

The empty Forbidden City, a tracery of marble balustrades and gorgeous blazing tiles.

Because of the extreme nature of modern Chinese history, it was hard to connect all the random events we were told of and where they took place into a coherent whole. Peking was a fragmented city consisting of acres of barrenness punctuated by unexpected oases where beauty flourished.

It was like this. Peking had become great under the Ming Dynasty. It was a project. The Yongle Emperor, for debatable reasons, but which surely involved cliques and power bases or perhaps because he preferred the drier, northern climate to the sultry humidity of the Yangtse valley, moved his capital here from Nanking. On the foundations laid by previous dynasties, he built, in 1421 a magnificent Northern Capital that became the object of romantic legend.

I knew nothing of this. I saw what I saw and what I saw was the magnificence of what remained. And what remained was truly fabulous but in comparison to what was lost – the inspiration for *Gormenghast* and numberless fables and poems – if Mao had kept his barbarian hands to himself, the city through which we wandered would be without doubt the greatest in the world. For what the Yongle Emperor did over the following years was to create a material fantasy. Imagine a series of cities one inside the other – the Tartar City, the Chinese City, the Imperial City and the Forbidden City – each surrounded by its own wall up to forty feet high and sixty-two thick, each filled with palaces, temples, pavilions, gardens, arranged in a symmetry that satisfied the Chinese love of the symbolism and magic of numbers. That was Peking, with the emperor at the very centre of the Middle Kingdom, around whom the world revolved:

'So twice five miles of fertile ground
 With walls and towers were girdled round,'

was not so far off the mark. Stand on Coal Hill at the southern end of the Forbidden City and look across the shimmering yellow roofs that remain; imagine that three, four-fold and understand the magnitude of what once stood there. Most of it still stood in the age of photography, so the extent of the vandalism is plain. It is within living memory. I am not recounting a legend. What a loss, what a terrible, heart-rending loss. Not like the loss of a child or a friend; not even, perhaps, like the loss of family photographs to rampaging Red Guards but we are mortal, and Peking could have outlived us all and for always. The irredeemable tragedy is that the sacking was deliberate.

Perhaps only we outsiders are able to luxuriate in nostalgia. It could have been far, far worse, for, by a poignant irony, a plan to construct a road bisecting the Forbidden City's north-south axis was thwarted only by the collapse of the economy following the Great Leap Forward. Sometimes it seems that the Chinese are indifferent to change; perhaps fable is enough for them and should be enough for us. Yet the Chinese are creatures of habit, it is the country of ancestor worship. Eventually they would have come to treasure not just the memory of Peking's grandeur but its tangible relics. There is precious little left now. Rather, from a run-down *proletariopolis* it has been transformed into an air-conditioned, sky-scraping shopping mall, punctuated by islands of historic survivors become museums.

We cannot blame Mao for everything that went wrong in twentieth century China. The Republican administration that filled the interregnum between 1911 and 1949 had exacted their share of spoliation. That was greed and stupidity and chaos and reprehensible though it be – look at many a provincial English town – at least it was not wholesale destruction in the name of ideology. Mao had his way but he failed to eradicate the past, merely render us all the more nostalgic for its beauty and wonder. My mind went back to Warsaw Old Town, reconstructed by its remaining inhabitants not just to recover the buildings themselves, but to recover the memories and a sense of identity and place that the buildings represented and which give tangible meaning to a life.

Once, many years later, I had cause to be in a region of China, which, being a plain of unremitting flatness, and unfamiliar to Westerners, remained wholly unvisited by the tourists who by then were a fixture elsewhere in the country. This region had been so poor before the Revolution that when the call to arms came, many answered and ran away to fight for a better life. In the village that was my destination, apart from the agricultural habits of centuries, nothing remained of old China. Instead, to my amazement, among the trees that clustered about the village, I came across a newly built Christian church and when I looked more closely, I saw that across the landscape, cross after cross stood up against the pale sky above, perched on the roofs of churches just like it. For a while, so out of step with modern China did this seem, I wondered if these were indeed churches or whether what I took to be Christian crosses were not in fact a local symbol with no connection to Christianity at all. The confirmation that they were what they seemed was a surprise, for I was there to pay my respects to the memory of a man I had known, who had been brought up in barefoot poverty in that village and who, with nothing to lose, had set off to join Mao's peasant army. He had survived a civil war; a war against the Japanese; fought in Korea against the Americans; continued to rise through the ranks during the Great Leap Forward and the other madcap schemes and eventually died a general to be buried with honour in Peking in the cemetery reserved for Party heroes. He was a decent man, an atheist, who gave himself completely to what he imagined was the future and never relinquished his faith in the Party. And yet, in that village – of all villages – and, it seemed, in all the villages for miles around, there were now Christian churches, the antithesis of Maoism. His relatives ushered me from the village down to the bank of the river across which the People's Liberation Army had made their way as they speared southwards in the final push for Peking in 1949 and pointed out the family graves and the little pavilion with its upturned eaves sheltering a stele inscribed to his memory. You cannot tell me that in the hearts of those children and grandchildren and nephews and nieces, proud though they were of their village's most illustrious son, there did not linger a yearning for what had been snatched from them by the years of persecution and chaos.

A man who would have seen many changes.

One evening I wandered out onto the streets near our hotel – in which the lobby was festooned with a giant ribbon embroidered with the words 'China has friends all over the world', as if in affirmation of its emergence from decades of self-imposed isolation – with the Australian couple whose passports had been vandalised at the Soviet border. We had just collected their replacement passports from the Australian Embassy. It was dusk. We had eaten our dinner at four o'clock, for in those days in China, meal times were scheduled randomly, which displeased those, like Archie, who believed that in life there was a correct and inviolate protocol for everything. Our poor slip of a local guide had been made aware of his opinion in no uncertain terms; he stood there utterly baffled and embarrassed at the anger of a well-fed man who was being asked to eat at an inconvenient hour. The Chinese are always ready to eat at a moment's notice, responding to the call of the stomach more than the call of the hour. I found Archie's attitude merely impolite but later realised that Mr Zhou, full of youthful optimism for a new China, eager to impress the very foreigners for so long vilified by the Chinese Government, stood before Archie in an agony of uncertainty.

It was these petty confrontations more than the Forbidden City or any of the great spectacles to which we were introduced, that I recall with the greatest clarity. That young man had expected better of us. My embarrassment was as acute as his.

That was how we came to be walking the streets at the dinner hour. Although we were in the capital, the same clothes we had seen in Datong were worn by all; the same faintly military boiler-suit greens and blues, the baggy overcoats and white nylon shirts. A few were in poorly made dark suits and conservatively striped ties. We saw perky babies in shorts with a convenient slit at the back, pushed along the dusty back streets in wooden prams on wooden wheels by grandmothers hobbling on their bound 'lily' feet encased in tiny black shoes. As in Da Tong there was an air of weariness about those streets, as if a storm had passed through, its survivors both regretful and relieved.

As we walked around, trying to separate what was new from what was old, looking for the signs of what China was becoming, we were stopped by an old man, who stood four square before us, slightly stooped, very thin and with the shambling gait that elderly Chinese seem to deliberately adopt at a certain time in their lives. At first he did not speak, just let his eyes wander over us with benign curiosity. Then, after looking calmly about him, he asked quietly, in flawless English, where we were from. On hearing our answer, he nodded slowly before inviting us to take a drink with him at a nearby café. We stopped at a ramshackle building indistinguishable from any other and sat at a bare wooden table on tiny little wooden stools. The old man did not ask us what we preferred to drink, but ordered on our behalf. Shortly, four glasses of hot water were placed before us, for which he paid with a few coins light enough to be whisked away by the breeze and, even in China, of microscopic value. In my embarrassing ignorance I had imagined that we would drink mineral water, or at the very least, tea. But the indigent old man, eager to show some hospitality, bought what he could afford. The Chinese, in the absence of tea, drink hot water rather than cold, partly for reasons of hygiene, partly as an aid to digestion. We sipped distastefully at our water, listening to Mr Ling as he practised his English, asking us about Australia and England, carefully avoiding making any comment about his own country, other than to invite from us respectful observations about the progress it was at last making in the fields of economics and of foreign relations.

Yet his was an act of bravery and defiance because, notwithstanding government policy, there remained plenty of Chinese that resented Westerners, harbouring a visceral contempt for those that consorted with them. Only a few years before his act of courtesy towards us, the simple fact of knowing English would have been enough to have condemned him at least to years of physical and mental abuse. I have no doubt that such was the case with Mr Ling. When he spoke, he looked at us blankly whilst exhibiting an odd tic, which was to roll up his sleeves a little and then briefly hold up his arms as if to flex and stretch his fingers. Each time he did this I noticed a series of livid rings of scar tissue down his wrist, so that I gained the impression that he was trying covertly to demonstrate to us an aspect of his personal history that he could not convey in words. I do not know his background, but my guess was that he would have been classed as an intellectual and therefore out of touch with the toiling masses, a sin that at one time provoked the most terrible repercussions. There was a time when scholarship had been revered in China and scholars respected for their learning and wisdom, but under the Great Helmsman to be one of that number was a dangerous pastime. It could go either way. The traditional skills survived, were even admired; but it was what you did with them that mattered. A poem might be in perfect accordance with the current orthodoxy one day. Or treasonable the next.

By a miracle, throughout the endless campaigns to obliterate it, the beauty of the great Chinese civilisation was sustained in countless small ways. Now that the worst was over, the more harmless arts – the crafts that could be boasted of as the product of the peasant genius – were again in evidence: the miraculous paper-cutters snipping a blank sheet of paper into a crane with a fish in its beak; or a dragon, or a phoenix; the painters in ink who with a few deft stokes create a monochromatic landscape; the chop carvers begging us to buy from them. They seemed to be everywhere, their reappearance owing far less to an individual expression of a creative impulse and far more to an acknowledgement of the country's bankruptcy. But I didn't much care about that. To witness the joy of making and selling made me glad because it was a sign of common humanity that had been absent since West Berlin. To find the beauty in China, amid the interminable grey and blue and green, we had to look at the details that had once been part of the fabric of daily life when every street had a temple or shrine and when families lived around courtyards in the labyrinth of alleys and narrow lanes that clustered about the Forbidden City: the old men playing chess or walking their songbirds in bamboo cages; the dawn practitioners of tai-chi; the solitary musician practising beneath a tree near the Forbidden City moat; the dumplings sizzling in woks at the roadside.

Some in the party had brought sweets and bars of chocolate and photographs of home to distribute, as if China was a country of neglected children and zoological specimens. But I could not help but notice that shining from the Chinese people's eyes was the desire for something else and that, I now realise, was for money. Avarice was not in the Russian blood – their greatest desire was the security of the fortress – but the Chinese preferred the security of gold and jade.

In China what cheered us above all was the food. If it would be trite to claim that the test of a great civilisation is in its cooking, it is certain nonetheless that in China the appreciation of good food was a universal fact. Even in impoverished Da Tong we had eaten better than we had for the several preceding weeks and in Peking we discovered how good Chinese food could be. Although the meal timetable was eccentric, so that one might find oneself eating dinner not very long after finishing lunch, everybody always found an appetite for the plates of fresh greens, garlic-infused meats, stews of aubergine and onion, differently textured bean curds, the occasional whole braised fish surrounded by scallions, the mysterious and visually unappetising dishes of sea cucumber, duck gizzard and webbed feet and the endless

A dancer at the evening performance. The Chinese have a talent for showmanship.

supply of local beer. Whatever else befell us on any one day, at least there was always something delicious to eat. If in Russia the consolation for life's challenges was vodka, in China it was nourishing food.

One evening we were taken to a concert. We had expected an improving Red opera or perhaps, given the open-door policy, a local rendition of a Western classic. Fortunately, as music, too, no longer had to conform to arcane Maoist policy, the concert consisted of new and old tunes played on traditional Chinese instruments, all of which, the *pipa*, the *yangqin*, the *erhu*, were new to most of us. I particularly remember the *erhu*, the two-stringed fiddle, not unlike the similar instrument in Mongolia but sweeter and which when played in unison produced the sound of the braying wind. Just like the kite-flyers in Tian An Men Square, each of the musicians performed with a singular intensity, drawing the horse-hair bow across the strings with a rigid absorption in complete contrast to their attitude after each piece, when they relaxed into a posture of slovenly physical abandonment. It seemed to reflect the duality of the Chinese character, which has the distinction of being able to flit without observable change of gear from unswervable earnestness to cloying sentimentality. The audience members did not sit in rapt attention but coughed and hawked and moved around as if they were unaware that a concert was in progress. That was to underestimate their powers of attention, because it was remarkable how any given moment a familiar melody would provoke a sudden silence.

At the end of the concert, the woman conductor stepped down into the auditorium and to my astonishment made her way towards us, the only foreigners present, with an expression of modest enquiry, as if our appraisal of her work was all that counted in the world. The applause from the audience, I then realised, was not for her but for us, or at least for our attendance as a kind of symbol of reconciliation. The audience looked on with undisguised wonder as the conductor shook hands with me while we exchanged pleasantries; she asking of us our opinion of the performance with the humility demanded by the new government strategy, we with no choice but to convey our pleasure and admiration. Yet, one of the party – I think it was Guppy, who, confusing the demands of Chinese etiquette with a compulsion to give an honest opinion, was unable to resist once again the opportunity to demonstrate his anti-Communist credentials – insisted on having his critique translated by our local guide, who stammered a few words before an intervention by the usually genial Sleeping Buddha ensured that the point was made using a satisfactorily anodyne formula that enabled the conductress to smile without embarrassment and explain that, of course, compared to the wealthy and sophisticated Western world, China was trailing behind and had much to learn. She bowed and left and we and the rest of the audience all clapped some more at each other.

Although to the casual visitor China seemed to be a nation finding its feet, possibly set fair for whatever the future might bring, some areas of life were frustrating for foreigners. Getting about the city was one. According to the same myth that obtained about Moscow, the authorities – whoever they might be – deliberately made independent expeditions as difficult as possible. Certainly, travelling alone outside the major cities was next to impossible for obscure reasons of security and the like, but these restrictions did not apply in those cities open to foreigners. As in Moscow, if you wanted to forego a sightseeing visit you were at liberty to do so, the distinction being that in Moscow there was to hand an excellent and easily navigable metro service that covered the whole city if you chose to make use of it; whilst in Peking although there were two metro lines and a prodigious network of buses and trolley-buses, they were next to useless unless you could read and understand Chinese. Even if you happened to be a linguist with boundless energy and optimism and a talent for orienteering, the difficulties were almost insurmountable because Peking was not only huge, it mostly consisted of one identical suburb after another, with yawning intervals between places of interest. A taxi service did exist, but it was a state-run operation and had to be booked in advance through your hotel. The result of this was that, unless you were ill, in desperate need of solitude, determined to make a point or extremely well prepared for a lack of eventualities, you were better off getting on the bus with everyone else.

It so happened that during our stay in Peking, I had to depend on the taxi service to convey me quickly and efficiently to two embassies, of the Soviet Union and of Mongolia. I forget the precise reason for the visits, but I imagine they were something to do with obtaining visas for future travellers. The taxi duly turned up and we set off. The journey turned out to be longer than expected as the Soviet Embassy sat in fortified splendour in a distant part of the city. This did not worry me as I had the entire day at my disposal and in any case I was enjoying our sedate progress along Peking's avenues in a car branded 'Shanghai', an ungainly pastiche of a 1950s Mercedes-Benz, bedecked inside with curtains and lace antimacassars.

When finally we approached the embassy compound, after a long period when no words had passed between us, the driver became noticeably agitated. Several hundred yards before the entrance he gestured that I should leave the car. I had understood that he would wait for me but instead, pretty much as my feet touched the pavement, he turned around and sped away.

Inside the Soviet Embassy, Vladimir, the genial Soviet consulate, gave a contemptuous sniff. 'You know, when I walk about the city, the Chinese people run away from me when they know I am Russian!' He looked at me unsmilingly. 'I am serious – you laugh, but it is true. The only good thing is that in our diplomatic car, we have the road to ourselves. They are crazy, these Chinese!'

Once our business was concluded, he ordered a taxi for me. When after an hour no taxi arrived, I saw that he was right. It was a very long walk back to the city centre.

As no Peking taxi driver then spoke English or any other language apart from Chinese, it was vital to have your destination made plain before setting off and preferably to have it written down. In the afternoon, I ordered another taxi to take me to the Mongolian Embassy, which arrived as requested and parked outside the hotel, facing the gate. I introduced myself, placed a bag filled with passports and documentation on the back seat, shut the door and went back into the hotel to speak to the guide. When I re-emerged, the taxi had vanished. For some seconds I stood on the steps expecting him to come back. When he didn't I searched the immediate area but he had gone, together with a collection of international passports. Rising panic was mitigated in part by the reputation for exaggerated honesty in those days of the Chinese people. Stories abounded of hotel staff returning items that had been recovered from rubbish bins in bedrooms, mostly I think, to absolve themselves of blame in the event of accusations of theft. Nonetheless, unless the driver were to return smartly, I had a potentially big problem on my hands and I began to think perhaps only death would be preferable to being in Peking with a party of people without their passports because I had been dumb enough to leave them on the back seat of a taxi.

Nobody knew what to do. The taxi driver could not be traced. Eventually, another taxi arrived and took me to the Mongolian Embassy. No sign of the first taxi. I ran next door to the East German Embassy, in case the driver had confused the two, but a consular official told me that there had been no visitors at all that morning. To my surprise, my experience of East Germans being confined to those in the GDR itself, where the protocols of daily life inhibited normal human relations, she immediately comprehended the gravity of the situation. She guessed, as I rather hoped, that this was more of a problem for the taxi-driver than it was for me. It was simple for her to locate the taxi company (there were only two) and then, using her excellent Mandarin, to telephone them on my behalf. Yes, they were glad she called, as they had a distraught driver who had gone all the way to the Mongolian Embassy without realising there was nobody in his car. When he heard the back door close, he had presumed that I was on board and since he couldn't communicate with me, he followed his instructions without looking in his rear-view mirror.

His panic would have been at least as great as mine. China's new relationships with Western countries were still at a tentative, somewhat ambivalent point in the arc of friendship and whereas in later years a bundle of foreign passports might have presented an irresistible temptation, in 1981 they posed nothing but problems for the sleepy driver. My fear was not that he would have stolen them but that in his panic he might have thrown them away. The relief, at returning to the hotel and having the bag returned to me, was indescribable. Naturally, I breathed not a word of this to any of the others apart from Leonard.

'Well, boy, you were lucky there. We could have had a murder on our hands and then we really would be stuck here; would have made Mongolia look like a barrel of laughs.'

Repairing the Great Wall. Years of neglect were finally being addressed.

The stay in Peking passed in a blur of long days, large meals at odd hours and visits to the handful of fabled sites that remained. In the Summer Palace, we had lunch in the Pavilion for Listening to Orioles, where I harboured the delusion that we might see or hear them in a country where fauna of any description was often regarded either as food or as vermin. In this pavilion, where the Dowager Empress Ci Xi liked to listen to Chinese opera, the orioles most likely were not birds but actors and singers. The oriole, too, was the insignia of rank for the eighth grade of imperial civilian officials. In China, poetic names and titles abounded to the extent they often seemed frivolous whimsy, yet often concealed another meaning altogether. Dressing up the unpalatable as exquisite or the ordinary as remarkable seemed to be yet another means of never quite presenting things as they really were. The Great Wall at Badaling, however, was an impressive sight, its battlements and towers snaking like an unfurling dragon across the hills; whilst the Ming Tombs, inserted into the landscape here and there according to the principles of feng shui, were collectively impressive when viewed from afar, but the only one open to the public had nothing much about it. Only the Spirit Way, a sacred avenue leading to the tomb area, reached through a huge marble arch, and lined with marble effigies of fantastic creatures and imperial officials in full court attire, did any justice to one of the greatest of Chinese dynasties. Among this fanciful statuary, that we could touch without censure, where apart from us there was nobody, it was finally possible to breathe in something of the grandeur of China's civilisation even if, as usual, we had no idea of their significance and no way, for as long as we were in China, of finding it out.

The Spirit Way, leading to the Ming Tombs, before the statues were protected with iron railings.

There were some peculiarities to the programme of visits; unexpected enough, indeed, to question the motive behind them. In Peking, secluded among the teeming highways, there were still a few streets where the character of the pre-Mao era was still in evidence. Lined with small shops, purveyors of foodstuffs, fabrics, electrical appliances and so on, that had the appearance at least of being independently run, these streets were on the human scale that was absent in most of a city given over to a delusion of modernism. We entered one such shop dealing in cloth and, as we watched intrigued at the overhead wires that sent bills and receipts whizzing from shop assistant to cashier and back again, a member of staff pressed a button, we were ushered to one side and the floor slid back to reveal a set of steps. This stairway, it transpired, led to a network of underground tunnels that between 1969 and 1979 had been built as a refuge in the event of a nuclear war with the Soviet Union. It was an underground city, designed to allow the city population to exist for as long as it was unsafe to live above. There were entrances throughout the city, and miles and miles of gloomy, damp tunnels that extended beneath the whole city centre and as far as the Western Hills. Although there was not much to see beyond a few bunk beds and written exhortations to remember the Revolution, its very conception and the scale of its construction said so much about what China, until only two years before, had been. That we were shown it was a deliberate demonstration of change, an indication, perhaps, of scorn for old neuroses. Or, possibly, a little extra money for the shop.

Flying kites on Tian An Men at the entrance to the Forbidden City. Mao looks on disapprovingly.

Everywhere we went, if we were not stared at by gaping peasant farmers, we were surrounded by youths clamouring to practise their English, which after a long period of persecution and stigmatisation was now as essential to China's progress as the manufacture of steel had been just a few years before.

'Hello. Where you from?'

'England.'

'Oh.' Pause. 'Not the US?'

'No, I'm afraid not.'

Pause. 'OK, you speak the Queen's English.' Nervous laugh. 'Do you like China?'

'Yes, I do, very much. Life is better here now, I think. What do you think of Mao Zedong?'

Pause. Consultation with fellow student. 'Yes, better now. Mao 70 per cent good, 30 per cent bad.'

For all the petty irritations and the constant appeals to our tolerance, it was impossible not to be caught up in the sense that something dynamic was stirring in China. The natural intelligence of the Chinese, combined with their eagerness to make up for lost time and to grab opportunities while they were there was astonishing. At this stage of China's development, the apparent naïveté of the Chinese cast an enchantment over most visitors, for there were few obvious signs of the prepotent, ruthless economic machine that a few years after was to challenge the world order.

Nonetheless, our journey was long and there was still far to go. China was not the Soviet Union but for all its charms, the years of austerity had suffused the country with a monochrome uniformity that some found enervating. And it was tiring travelling in discomfort on trains for long distances cooped up in compartments with people you did not know well and who you may not like. So, it was no surprise but a great relief when finally the bibulous Len decided to call it a day. He knew that he had come to the end of the road, or rather he had been given a glimpse of it by Sandy, who had informed me that after all these weeks of sharing a room with him, he could bear it no more, brothers in arms or not. On the two overnight train journeys since leaving Ulan Bator, I had shared a compartment with him.

He had taken a bottle of whiskey with him to bed and drunk himself to sleep; woken after an hour or so and levelled a tirade of abuse mostly at me; drunk and slept some more; woken again and so on, all through the night. Although weakened by booze and bitterness he was an essentially good man, but when he announced to me that he was leaving I may not have been able to disguise my relief, for the prospect of further weeks in his company in the inescapably cramped surroundings of a Chinese train was not an inviting one. With a confrontation inevitable, his energy dissipated, his delusions pricked, he took matters into his own hands by taking a plane to Hong Kong. From there, who knows. Sandy expected to meet up with him again in Australia, but I later heard from him that Len had disappeared without trace; there was an allusion to suicide. I suspect that for some this journey represented redemption, which, when unforthcoming, provoked a shattering crisis.

And then there was Bert. Bert's was a different form of unhappiness to that which bedevilled Len. Within Len raged a destructive bitterness; Bert regarded himself as a youthful lothario when really he was a middle-aged husband of German descent dressed as a cowboy. In short, a child-like fantasist whose good ol' boy charm was as unconvincing as it was shallow. He was shy and the drink was his prop for his act. He had been understood in Russia – his maudlin type was familiar there – but in China then, drunkenness was more or less unknown and certainly frowned upon as it implied loss of control of oneself and therefore of one's 'face'. That was perhaps why the solitary, soporific pleasure of opium had once been so attractive to the Chinese.

Everything about Bert's behaviour would have been obnoxious in China. His tendency when drinking to embrace anyone within reach was particularly repellent, especially to Chinese women. Whilst privacy in China was a rare, almost unsought pleasure, with people thrown together physically in houses and buses in a way that Westerners would have found unendurable, while in a crowded street people would barge and bump without qualm, to touch a Chinese woman in public, to single her out with a show of affection, especially by a foreign man, no matter how lightly or innocently, was to compromise her dignity. I learnt that very quickly; when I touched the arm of one of the guides to gain her attention, she shrank from me as if I had poured hot tea over her, gave out a small cry of indignation and threw me a look of ineffable disgust. I was shocked and embarrassed, but Sleeping Buddha, who had witnessed this (he was never far away) hastily explained it all away with one of his many ready aphorisms. 'No anger,' he confided to me solemnly, 'no friendship.' Bert, though, was insensible to the nuances of an alien culture. Everybody, and especially every woman, according to Bert, was there to be cuddled; but when he put his arm around their shoulders, they stiffened and bridled like cats. His advances were not sexual. Rather, he rejoiced in the air of apparent innocence in China that was attractive to those whose own lives were in disarray. He had no idea that behind the beguiling veneer there was steel. Bit by bit, as we headed south and it became warmer and the drinking more uncomfortable, he learnt to desist and simply enjoyed the rest of the journey.

Chapter 7

The Xian Line

We departed Peking the following morning on the twenty-four-hour train journey south west to Xian.

Those trains! Each compartment with its single fan, awaiting the summer heat, motionless above the window. Tin flasks decorated with pink peonies filled with boiling water by the attendant and placed in the corridor outside each compartment door. A strip of worn and grubby red carpet ran the length of the carriage and the smell of jasmine and dust filled the air. The attendants in China, in blue uniform and peaked cap with the distinctive China Railways badge on the crown, took pride in keeping their carriage as spruce as possible, cleaning the windows, slopping out the toilets, brushing with a straw bristle broom the old carpet that would never be clean. The trains of each country had their own odours – in those days I could have been placed blindfolded into any of them and known to which country it belonged. As we sped through the cool night, thick coverlets kept us warm and at breakfast in the dining-car we were given eggs fried fast in a deep layer of old hot oil.

Getting aboard and disembarking were logistical challenges.

Notwithstanding the discomfort – the swaying ride and the treacherous deceleration that flung me to the edge of my bunk and the fact that there were now four to each compartment – I found the journeys across China mesmerising. In contrast to the numberless, drowsy forests of Russia; to the ethereal emptiness of Mongolia; the prospect was busy and filled with life. The landscape was man-made, completely man-made – sculpted, squeezed, strained, pinched, ploughed and dug to the limit of its exhaustion. You did not notice the sky for the creativity beneath it. Far from the stagnancy and complacency of Russia, where comfort lay in the refuge from the wilderness, in China the countryside, properly managed, was various and bountiful. Even twisting our way to Xian across the arid hills of northern Shaanxi, dotted with mud villages, the crops, few of which we knew, were coaxed into fruitfulness.

When I think about it, the train journeys themselves were uneventful enough. They were perfect points of observation, a mobile platform from which to look over the world. Of course, things happened – some of which I probably knew nothing of – but on that particular leg, I recall one of those incidents that could, I suppose, have had awkward consequences. I only heard about it the following morning, when the Chinese woman sleeping on the bunk beneath mine spoke to me as I slid down to the floor in my usual state of dawn befuddlement. She was young, with an unusually full figure and the voluptuous features that would have conformed much more to western than to Chinese taste, which I had been told by our guide in Peking depended on subtle delineations of the nose, the shape of the eye, and of carriage and demeanour.

The mountainous countryside between Peking and Xian.

The rules of beauty, as with every other aspect of life in China, were very strict, as if defined by a sage whose proclamations demanded unquestioning obedience.

The Chinese girl told me what had happened during the night. When, finally, I slept – the army officer in the bunk opposite gave vent to the loudest snores I have ever heard in my life – I slept deeply and unflinchingly. In the party was a small group of elderly friends from Florida. These were people who had been assured by their travel agent, somewhat disingenuously, that there would be showers on the trains, porterage throughout and the kind of service associated with the so-called golden age of travel, an expectation that somehow they failed to square with the very low expectation they harboured of the countries themselves. It was rather charming, in its way, this naïve Western doublethink, which presumed a certain luxury within the trains, and various levels of impoverishment without. But those people were resilient. Although they moaned all the way along the line to compensate for the unexpected discomfort and as consolation for the money they had spent in vain, they were determined to make the best of it, which they did by playing endless card games and by the institution of a regular cocktail hour. Among them, one couple consisted of an acid-tongued wife who had dragged along her much reduced husband – I think he had suffered a stroke – and who came along with her cronies purely to play bridge. He was affable and likeable but prone to confusion and so forced into dependency on his selfish wife, who with ill grace would interrupt her card games to deal with his weak bladder. That night on the train he had made his way safely to the lavatory at the end of the corridor but on his return had become disoriented, entered the wrong compartment and stumbled into bed with the Chinese girl. Her name, she told me in flawless English, was Jade Cloud and she recounted the drama not only with equanimity, but admirable solicitude for the man's welfare. She had, it seemed, gently cajoled him out of her bunk and somehow delivered him to his own compartment, then looked on in sorrow as without any word of gratitude to her his wife had berated her hapless husband. I was struck by her calmness; since casual physical contact was abhorrent to the Chinese, many women would have reacted differently. At first I was not certain whether her composure derived from innocence or sympathy but I concluded the latter, for in China respect for old age is sacrosanct. Jade Cloud had understood instantly that there was no need for hysteria. She impressed me with her humanity, the first instance encountered in China that was not acted out according to the rules but came from within. You see, for all the trumpeting of 'New China' and 'China Reconstructs', which were the government-inspired clichés of the time, and despite the dogged enthusiasm for them cautiously exhibited here and there, spontaneity was almost universally absent from daily life. There was much defensive courtesy but the vagaries of the heart were well concealed.

Most Chinese introduced themselves by their surnames – '*Ni hao*, my name is Wang' - so to hear something as exotic and sensuous as Jade Cloud was captivating. For the Chinese, Jade is synonymous with purity, beauty and virtue. It is talismanic. It glows green like angelica and creamy like mutton-fat and the most revered and desirable pieces demand a discernment that is beyond my abilities. Like the Chinese idea of perfect beauty, it conforms to recondite rules understood only by the connoisseur. It is almost wilfully mysterious. Yet its tactile qualities require no expertise: its smoothness and its hardness; its coolness and its warmth; its resistance to the sculptor; its misty colours, which coalesce into a form that is gaudy and subtle all at once, as well as being, in its finest manifestations, of significant monetary value to the Chinese. At the time, jade was no longer worn by anyone in China for anything decorative was considered immodest and immodesty, in all its guises, was the worst of sins. I mean, even her name surprised me, until I realised that she was the only Chinese I had met who had introduced herself using the English translation. And yet still it seemed to me a modern name, a little daring, a little romantic. I recall, too, that there was about her a hint of perfume, something subtle and watery, like the scent of elderflower in June; and there was a little make-up, the merest burnish that stood out against her silk scarf, roll-neck jumper and her tailored trousers. Her perfect command of English, she told me, was on account of her job, which, she had said with frank pride, was in the export division of one of China's vast government-owned corporations. She was, I now realise, the face of China to come; the eager trader, the sophisticated woman of the world. But you have to be tough to survive in modern China and I wonder if she was devious enough to have made it, once the state-owned monoliths were confronted with competition from the hungry generation that rules now.

The People's Hotel, Xian, built for Russian experts.

Our train finally pulled into Xian in the late morning. I did not know it, but we were entering one of the great cities of the world – you see how profound was my ignorance. I know that with the snap of a finger, Xian has been transmogrified into another parade of sleek glass towers. But hardly anyone except flocks of tourists know it by name; a city of eight million people! When we disembarked from the train, Sleeping Buddha consulted with the local guide, who led us out of the station building to the square outside, where hundreds of people surrounded by plastic suitcases and cloth-bound bundles squatted and slept, awaiting a train to take them to some government-imposed destination, for in those days, for the Chinese, travel for the sake of it was unimaginable. The return to normality after the dismemberment of the country through the Cultural Revolution was a long process. Countless individuals sent to remote villages far from home in order to build socialism were trickling back to their families, once permission emerged from China's cruelly labyrinthine bureaucracy.

Rising before us was a magnificent survivor. Enclosing the old town, the blue-grey Ming dynasty city wall, tapering away into the morning mist, had become an unregarded monument. In places, the brickwork had fallen away to reveal the rammed earth behind that spilled out like an old wound. Bits of vegetation grew out of the sides and the moat water was still and stagnant. Within, Xian was a grid of oddly anaemic streets.

Yet that wall was considered a potential defensive fortification until only a few decades before our visit, when the Japanese Army was threatening to take the whole country and the Communist Army was mustering its forces in readiness for power. Barbed wire had surrounded the city, whilst the heavily guarded ancient gates were kept ajar only enough to allow the passage of a single person at a time.

Xian, like every city in China, had fallen into decline. I was reminded of the slough of a dragonfly, parched and lifeless, leached of colour but somehow holding its withered shape. I believe that it had been like that for a century or more. Once, though, it had been perhaps the most populous city in the world and the place where Chinese civilisation had been at its pullulating finest and its most cosmopolitan. Xian, known then as *Chang'an* – 'Eternal Peace' – lay at the eastern end of the Silk Road, where Chinese traders mixed with Sogdians and Tibetans and Persians and Turks. Kingdoms and princedoms from Kashmir and Nepal to Japan and Korea paid tribute to the Tang dynasty here. Buddhism was introduced to China by a Tang monk who travelled to India from Xian and, returning laden with Sanskrit manuscripts, had the Wild Goose pagoda built to house them. Yet even then, almost 1,500 years before, the Chinese state was fickle in its relations with the outside world, closing its frontiers at the merest hint of a threat to its integrity.

Of the Tang dynasty in Xian, arguably the greatest of all Chinese dynasties, nothing tangible remained, except a pair of pagodas and, away in the countryside, the forlorn imperial tombs. Of its illustrious predecessor, the Han dynasty, during which a palace was constructed that was almost seven times the area of the Forbidden City in Peking, and an imperial envoy sent west beyond the Heavenly Mountains to locate the flying horses of Ferghana, only the imperial tombs remain. But it came to me, with every new day that I spent in China, that the mark of Chinese civilisation was not revealed in the comforting presence of monuments from the past but in its heirs. Whereas in Rome, there is much to see but in modern Italians little to connect them to their martinet forbears, in China the pervasiveness of its civilisation is implicit in the habits of each and every Chinese. Palaces come and go but the patterns of thought were ancient indeed, as unchangeable as the pictograms and ideograms and ideographs of Chinese script. Even the Great Helmsman could not entirely despatch the habits of millennia. If a peasant from the Tang dynasty were to meet a peasant from the Communist dynasty, they would have much in common. If a courtier from the Tang court were to meet a party *apparatchik* from the upper echelons of the Chinese Communist Party, they would understand each other's motives. But, I felt, had a Tang scholar the misfortune to materialise in the China of 1981, his soul would have withered before Mao's vision of an existence bereft of curiosity and irony, merely a cruelly interminable cycle of labour and puritan propaganda.

Yet, what brought us to Xian was a newly discovered relic of another, earlier dynasty, the Qin, whose founder and only emperor, Qin Shi Huang Di, is considered the unifier of China and whose capital, of which nothing survives, was not in Xian but in another nearby city by the name of Xianyang. The Terracotta Army – who now does not recognise those squadrons of impassive, sightless faces – has become the symbol of China reborn, just as when placed in formation 2,000 years before to defend in perpetuity the work of the Qin Emperor. We drove the few miles to pass the anonymous grassy mound beneath which, surrounded by rivers of mercury, lies his unearthed tomb. A path, created by the feet of farmers over the centuries, led to the summit. Some of us followed it to survey the desiccated countryside surrounding the mound, young crops bursting through the yellow friable soil in the pale spring sun, just as they had done when the emperor lived and imposed himself on a fractious land. It was very strange to know that beneath our feet lay without fanfare the remains of one who was the foundation of the Chinese state; a man of myth. Yet again, none of us had any idea whatsoever of his significance. The Terracotta Army was already famous, yes, all set to become an essential stop on the modern Grand Tour but it meant nothing to us. None of it made a true impression. We could not make the connections. To understand Chinese history, we had to understand modern China and we could not. But we could make a few superficial observations. It was Archie who mentioned it, for notwithstanding his visceral loathing of dictatorship, though usually expressed with unfortunate lack of consideration for its victims, he was astute in his judgements. We saw Mao asleep in Peking. Here the first Emperor slept, his fame on the up, one day to replace the Great Helmsman as the true founder of China.

The Terracotta Army lay under cover within a compound, outside which as we disembarked a horde of peasant farmers bayed at us to buy their old coins and folk toys. I remember those toys because of their rare brilliance, red and yellow cats and lions, all made from shreds of cloth dangled and waved at us by the people crowding about the bus, with dogged, shrieking insistence.

Once we were at Pit Number 1, gazing down at those regiments of eternal guardians of the First Emperor, I was transfixed. Here in clay were figures with the same faces, the same stature, as their descendants outside the gates but here marshalled into sinuous order, proud and majestic. The beginning of China, a mere eighty generations or so before, yet present, almost new and current. They looked forward with such astounding confidence, as if they had assembled that very morning, ready to protect the China they had been awaiting with immovable patience, for 2,000 years.

And then there was a commotion. An undercover guard – I came to learn how to recognise them; they, like many others in China were always dressed in a white shirt and black trousers, but were burlier, with filled-out faces that implied plenty of protein – came rushing up to us, screaming – really, screaming – his face distorted into a taut, white rage that I imagine was a familiar sight among the Red Guards at the height of Mao hysteria. 'Leader,' he shouted, 'where is leader?' That was me. Sleeping Buddha awoke and he, too, tense with disapproval, escorted the guard over to me and interpreted as this man, who had been lurking among the warriors in the pit below, stood before us to berate me in an attitude of anger that was close to hysteria. He had seen, it transpired, one of our number take a photograph. We had been warned very clearly and very seriously that photographs were forbidden; that cameras could remain in our possession but were not to be used. We were entrusted with a kind of diplomatic mission. But she, a young woman from Switzerland, one who had maintained a certain anonymity throughout, surreptitiously pressed the trigger of her camera held about her waist and presumed to have got away with it. She had not reckoned with the sensitivities of the Chinese. There is in the Chinese people, when called for, an alertness that is preternaturally attuned to its surroundings. And a sure capacity for the detection of lies. The Swiss woman protested vehemently but in vain; the guard was certain of his ground. He was implacable because he was right! He knew. Although his ravings about 'insults to the Chinese people' amounted to so much cant – the seeds of commercial protectionism were already in place in the People's Republic of China – his insistence on retribution brooked no dissent. She would be escorted to a room where the film could be developed and innocence proven; or she could simply remove the film there and so, on that balcony overlooking the massed ranks of the First Emperor's Army, thus losing souvenirs but – and this is important – saving face. Respect among the Chinese for saving face is of greater force than that for integrity. If face is saved, everything is possible. It is not an appealing trait but as a means of getting one's own way, it is magnificent.

She chose, shamefacedly, grumbling, guiltily, to expose the film there and then. The guard immediately relaxed, his features slackening into a state of bland triumph. He was not of the breed that once the danger passed would turn into an apologetic sycophant. Instead, he muttered something disparaging to Sleeping Buddha and returned to his duties among his forbears in the pit below.

If the guard's reaction to what he appeared to regard as a slur on the Chinese nation by a perfidious Westerner was unnecessarily zealous, another tacit reminder of Western imperialist arrogance, it was not entirely without foundation. There was among our party a certain Ratnob, small, pugnacious, immensely rich (we knew this because he made it plain); a man of uncertain origin, possibly Hungarian, now British, his accent still guttural, who had joined us in Peking with a small contingent of fawning courtiers in tow. He and his bejewelled wife stalked along the galleries above the warriors as if entranced, their eyes aglitter with unconcealed avarice. Finally, unable to contain himself any longer, he ordered me to find Sleeping Buddha. Sleeping Buddha, whose usual unflappable equanimity had been sorely tested by the incident with the photograph, duly asked the charming Ratnob how he might be of service. Ratnob, apparently convinced that he had the measure of the obliging Sleeping Buddha, announced proudly, in the way of one having looked in the mirror imagines that all humanity is similarly built, that he wanted to purchase a Terracotta soldier; or two. I, it goes without saying, was dumbfounded. For he was serious; he thought that his money could buy a slice of Chinese patrimony. At a bargain price, no doubt! All he needed to know was how to ship it back to England. The response to such a request today would be a slap on the back and a peal of laughter. In the atmosphere of the epoch in China, the offer made by Ratnob was crass beyond measure. It was not as if there was any irony intended, for he was deadly serious in his one-upmanship; he believed he was getting in through the back door of the ground floor. Sleeping Buddha, the epitome of the bland and slippery Chinese *apparatchik* of the third rank, a master of the beggarly plea for 'cooperation' from us when our simple requests met with denials and refusals, laughed nervously. He hailed from an obscure industrial town where, since 1949, no European, other than the occasional Soviet 'expert', had been seen. There he enjoyed a certain standing but here, even in down-at-heel Xian, confronted by the anarchic ways of foreigners, he became uneasy. To suggest that one of these examples of the people's art could be for sale! To a Westerner! Had they been discovered during one of the Great Helmsman's destructive periods, I wonder how might they have fared: smashed because of their associations with the imperial past; or saved because of their connections with the foundation of China? Who knew? It was a question of mood. But now, for Sleeping Buddha and for the multitudes, they had become precious relics to be protected at all costs from the grasping hands of foreign exploiters.

Sleeping Buddha went away to the site office. He returned, accompanied by a weary-looking man whose threadbare suit and nicotine-stained teeth belied his position as site director. Cigarette smoke drifted across his face, inciting a tiny palpitation above his eye as he extended his hand. I was amazed that he bothered to acknowledge Ratnob's outrageous bid, but in those days China was a country that oscillated between ingratiating courtesy and bureaucratic despotism. The knack for dealing with matters on their merits had been lost. This man, so Sleeping Buddha told me after, was an eminent scholar. Looking at his nervous hands, from one little finger of which there projected a long nail, filed like a dagger, and his generally strained demeanour, I would never have known this. Far from being a compliant middle manager, he was an intellectual and that had been his downfall; for like all those whose interests could have been described even tangentially as anti-revolutionary, he had been a target for all the resentments and jealousies with which Mao had infected the Chinese masses during the Cultural Revolution. With Sleeping Buddha as interpreter, he politely declined Ratnob's offer, laughed at his responses with modest self-denigration, extended a hand and shambled back to his office. Later, I learnt that the site director spoke impeccable English. That he chose not to use it out of respect or deference to Sleeping Buddha was laudable, as well as a convenient diplomatic barrier.

It is not possible to avoid a summary of the Cultural Revolution, which had come to a close a mere five years before in 1976, if only because so many of the people that crossed our paths throughout our stay in China would have been directly affected by the chaos and destruction that came in its wake. The name, so suggestively academic, disguises a level of turmoil deliberately unleashed that even Mao had not so far surpassed.

Now of course it is classed as one of Mao's 'mistakes'. It is not the Chinese way, at least among the governing classes, to admit to failure or to guilt. That would be loss of face writ large. I will not bore you with the tedious detail and tortuous, specious, sadistic reasoning that impelled the Great Helmsman towards the last of his internecine campaigns. You have heard of the achievements of Uncle Joe and the Number One Brother: Mao Zedong, some might say, exceeded them all, at least in sheer number of victims. But who is counting? He had more millions of serfs at his disposal than the others. That was his advantage. He loved the big picture, the wide canvas, the epic, operatic scale.

There are myriad explanations for the Cultural Revolution. Context should always be considered, it is said. History. Poverty. Ideology. Idealism. These are poor excuses. They excuse nothing! In truth, they make it up as they go along, these intellectuals, thinkers and politicians. So it was that the ageing Mao, in his frustration and in the fulsomeness of his ego, in his quest for the elusive panacea for Man's discomfort with himself, turned again on his people, as if to say 'this time we will save the human race by wiping it out'. Enslavement is the solution. In a dystopia, we can all be equally unhappy. Unless you are a Great Helmsman. Helmsmen, at the tiller twenty-four seven, are exempt.

Here in brief is the philosophy behind the Cultural Revolution or, to introduce it with proper fanfare, the Great Proletarian Cultural Revolution. It all started with a fit of pique. Mao had already done his best to impose his vision on his compatriots by means of the Great Leap Forward and other similar disasters. With his proficiency as an economist very much in question, he resigned as State Chairman and took to philosophy instead. But it was not as if he retired gracefully to a house in the country to contemplate the Middle Way; anyway to innumerable Chinese he was a kind of godhead, a latter-day Buddha, avuncular, rosy-cheeked and cherubic. He was transfigured into the ultimate figure of authority, for he was still Chairman of the Communist Party, itself the ultimate source of policy. The government would not act without recourse to the Party's interpretation of events and so could not act without Mao.

According to him, there were too many in the Party following the Capitalist Road, an army of bourgeois elements aiming to restore capitalism. Mao's solution was 'perpetual revolution' – more of the same, but forever! Again, he had overlooked the simple truth that humanity is fickle. We have a low boredom threshold. Revolution and change is with us always but genuine revolution was not really his aim. What he wanted, as all revolutionaries do once they have overturned a few icons and issued their edicts and proclamations, is for everything to remain the same. For when stuck in a permanent cycle of revolution, humankind will go nowhere and all it will know is eternal turmoil and misery.

In 1966, Mao decided to restore order with disorder. Of course we should not forget that according to him the Capitalist Road was not all about America and Britain – in China memory is long and, feeble though Britain had become, the Opium Wars to the Chinese were only as yesterday – but about Russia, too. I would say, bearing in mind what we had seen of the USSR of 1981, that it is pretty certain that in 1966 it bore even less resemblance to what one might consider a functioning capitalist country. But for the Great Helmsman, these were but fine distinctions.

Mao's method was to isolate the figures who, in daring to criticise his policies, posed a threat to his authority. Never let it be said that Mao bore grudges; yet Peng Dehuai, of impeccable peasant stock who had risen via the triumph of the Party to the rank of General, a decent man as they went, who in 1959 had dared openly to make known his reservations about the egocentric tendencies of his boss, was collared. After years of beatings and interrogations for ten hours at a time, of the visitation on his person of every conceivable indignity, eventually he died in prison. Peng Dehuai's role was an important one. For if he, even he, could be shown to be deviating from the correct path, then clearly Mao's claim that there was rot at the core of the Party could be correct.

Peng's humiliation started in 1959, when he was deprived of high office. He became a figure in the shadows, until in 1965 when he was said, conveniently, to be the subject of a play, *Hai Rui Dismissed from Office*. It seems that there were some in the upper reaches of the government – or of the Party, the two are almost interchangeable – Deng Xiao Ping, perhaps, among others, who felt that Peng was due rehabilitation. It followed that, years later, the Great Helmsman, who once upon a time had admired this play about a hapless civil servant sacked by a corrupt emperor, sensed an opportunity. He suggested to a hack polemicist, by the name of Yao Wenyuan, later to become infamous as one of the Gang of Four, that he publish a critique of the play, in the course of which, in showing that the unfortunate civil servant is clearly Peng and the corrupt emperor, therefore, is Mao, he would demonstrate its seditious nature. He would demonstrate, in other words, that this play was nothing more than a covert attack on Mao himself – for Mao in the eyes of the masses could do no wrong – and, by extension, on the Revolution itself. With this interpretation of the play, Mao was provided with a ready-made excuse to counter-attack his enemies. In that he was a hapless victim, Peng was indeed like Hai Rui; but for Mao, Peng was merely tinder.

The whirlwind was unleashed. University students, encouraged by their lecturers, inspired by Mao's conviction that bourgeois elements were in the ascendant, revolted. They became the Red Guards. A current of chaos rippled across the country. Mao delighted in it – chaos is liberating. He swam in the Yangtze, to show that the winds and waves of imperialism were but feeble obstacles; he said that the people must 'Bombard the Headquarters'. The Red Guards in particular must dismantle the Four Olds; old customs, culture, habits, and ideas. None of these, of course, were to include Mao himself or the government headquarters at Zhongnanhai, in the psychologically impregnable Forbidden City.

New babies were given suitably Revolutionary names, whilst streets with feudal associations acquired new signs, becoming 'anti-imperialist street' or 'anti-revisionist street' and so on. The *Peking Review* of August 1966 said:

> 'The revolutionary action of the "Red Guards" won wholehearted support from the revolutionary workers and staff of the hairdressers, dressmakers, public bath houses and other service trades. In the last few days these workers and staff held meetings, wrote out pledges and issued statements. A cadre in the manager's office of the department stores in the East City said: "As early as a year and a half ago we revolutionary workers and staff of many department stores asked to remove all the old shop names left over from the capitalists, but the former Peking municipal Party committee would not allow us to do so. Our capital's 'Red Guards' have done a good job this time. We give them all our support."'

Then the destruction began. The Great Helmsman decreed disingenuously that the masses should choose the direction of the movement, which was tantamount to saying, 'You can disregard and disobey everyone. Except me.' Over the next few years, China came close to losing its soul. Anything of any historical value was turned to dust. It is a miracle there is anything left that is not concrete and brick.

But that was nothing. You can rebuild a monastery, although you cannot fill the cavity in the soul that its destruction brings. You cannot resurrect the hundreds of thousands of people who lost their lives; or the millions who were mentally or physically crippled; who were imprisoned as a means of settling old scores; who were paraded and humiliated; interrogated for hours and days and months and who in despair committed suicide (if they could) or who were thrown out of windows on upper floors by their interrogators. Those struggle sessions again, a modern Inquisition, from which you could not emerge reprieved because you were always guilty of something, self-criticism bringing no guarantee of safety. The police were forbidden to intervene; in fact, the national police chief is supposed to have said that it was 'of little importance' if Red Guards were beating 'bad people' to death.

Revisionists claim that the chaos brought benefits to the people in the form of rural access to medical treatment and in an improved economy. If there were any benefits, they were rendered worthless by the brutal manner of their conception. Others maintain that the scale of the destruction has been exaggerated; if so, it is only natural in a population in the pangs of mass trauma. There are, anyway, too many personal accounts of suffering and inhumane treatment to deny the facts. Even one person tortured for the sake of a dictator is one too many. Those who deny the Holocaust are in a class of their own. Perhaps it should be the same for those who deny the excesses of Stalin, Pol Pot and Mao Zedong.

I do not believe the accusations of hyperbole. China was running on empty when I first went there. If Da Tong was a desiccated leaf and Xian a ghostly exoskeleton, then the whole of China was akin to a sprig of dead coral, once beautiful and vivid, become etiolated, brittle, and drained of life. Sometimes our guides were former Red Guards. In the course of conversation, they would confess to this in a detached, matter-of-fact manner, as if, like hyper-active teenagers afflicted by uncontrollable hormones, it was just a stage they had gone through. For all that, it was clear that their deadpan confessions were the outpourings of inner anguish. And I met on the street those, banished to the countryside during the Cultural Revolution, waiting to be reunited with their distant families, to return as strangers after months and years of enforced estrangement. None of this was their fault. They had believed and their faith had been betrayed.

We were due to leave Xian for Luoyang the following morning until Sleeping Buddha without explanation informed us that our train was instead to leave in the afternoon. We had exhausted the sightseeing options in the city – the two Wild Goose Pagodas; the Great Mosque; miraculous survivors all of Cultural depredation – and since doing nothing was never an option, we had to do something. From somewhere there came a request to go a little way into the countryside to visit the Xingjiao temple, where the ashes of the Tang dynasty Buddhist monk traveller, Xuanzang, had been placed. The presumption was that such a request would be met with a straight refusal. To everyone's surprise, after consultation with the driver, permission was granted.

We had already driven through the countryside to see the Terracotta Warriors but it had been exactly that – a drive along a purpose-built road, which, rather like the train itself, had insulated us from the crude odours of rural China. Now, we wove our way among bicycles from which hung bunches of fowl head downwards, unprotesting even when their pates skimmed the road surface; we drove over crops drying in the warm spring sunshine; we inhaled the stench of fermenting dung; we saw the toiling peasant poised in mid-hoe amid the bushes to stare with incredulity at our progress.

What impressed me most were the patterns of the crops and the miracle of their abundance in the impoverished soil. At a certain point, we found ourselves on a low bluff just high enough to provide an elevated view across the valley floor. Before us, across miles of exhausted bone-dry yellow earth, ordered rows of unfamiliar plants swayed, their leaves scintillating in the brassy sunlight like bobbing swarms of fireflies. Yellow corn cobs hung in bunches from wooden drying-frames; everything was yellow or a shade of verdigris. In casual defiance of Communist doctrine, armchair-shaped gravestones sat amid the crops that grew on ancestral land. I was overwhelmed by a sense of changeless antiquity, of an attempt at perfection. Whereas in Mongolia, among the rocks and the grassland and the desert, I thought I saw the relics of an abraded Garden of Eden, worn away by time, here in China, I felt as if the sense was a different one, one of man coming to terms with the natural world to make it his own. Even the big-character slogans, the exhortations to work harder and to produce more and to venerate the Party, that were starting to fade into the grey brickwork and tamped yellow earth, had their place. There was in this scene, for all the harshness of life that it represented, something stirring and admirable.

The temple sat on a low mound. We parked and walked up to it along a muddy track. A village of earthen and brick houses hid picturesquely behind a mud wall amid tall slender, shuffling trees. A cry went up – '*waiguoren! waiguoren!* foreigners! foreigners! - and a herd of children stampeded into our path, giggling at our exotic aspect. Of course these children, as children invariably are amid poverty, were enchanting in their humour and frankness, in their vitality and zestfulness. Their parents emerged from within and, standing stiffly on the lip of the track, gaped at us in mute astonishment, then grinned ferociously the moment we caught their eye. The gulf between childhood and adulthood is always great, but in China it is very great. This was the first opportunity any of us had to satisfy our curiosity about Chinese life, because the truth is that we all had sentimental ideas about it. Ineluctably, notwithstanding the feeble protests from our guide and the ever anxious Sleeping Buddha, we made for the village. We were curious, we wanted to see the story-book China, so little in evidence in the tired, proletarian cities. The more practical among us wanted to know about their sanitary arrangements and with good reason because if the fields gave off the perfume of dung, the villages seemed to be remarkably odour free. We walked into the houses, politely but insistently, to see the televisions discreetly veiled with a velveteen cloth, the wok on the fire, the pennants on the walls. We rounded a corner and a woman, lost in her dreams, screamed in cartoonish shock as if we were ghosts and ran from us calling out and looking over her shoulder in disbelief. There were contending schools of thought within the group; those who felt that unrestrained nosiness was our fundamental right, and those who felt that our intrusion was disrespectful.

Americans might ask, 'How can they live like this?'

Britons might say, 'They may be poor, but they have what they need.'

The French might say, 'look, how beautiful is Chinese civilisation!'

The temple was not much, really, considering its venerable history. Only the location, looking over the countryside spread out widely below beneath a lilac haze, lent to it a vestige of sanctity. We were welcomed by a monk in a saffron robe, who led us through the prayer halls, where a small choir of timid acolytes looked at us with doubtless merited suspicion; through the library of ancient scrolls and sutras; and across the courtyard, where some relics of the earthly remains of Xuanzhang rested entombed in a memorial dagoba. Two smaller dagobas concealed the remains of two of his disciples. We tried to make the connection with this hallowed place and the Wild Goose pagodas we had seen in Xian, an efflorescence of the Tang dynasty, built to house the precious Buddhist sutras that Xuanzhang had brought with him to China from the Western Regions. We were in a hallowed place but we did not know it. Yet the image of the Tang dynasty monk laden with sutras supported on his back by means of a kind of ancient knapsack was ubiquitous. His quest had been immortalised in one of the Four Classic Novels, *Journey to the West*, written in the Ming dynasty. Such were the surviving links between modern and ancient China.

In that story, the pilgrim monk is accompanied by three principle companions: Sun Wukong, or the Monkey King; Zhu Bajie, or Pigsy; and Sha Wujing, or Friar Sand. It is a farrago, a mixture of adventure, comedy and epic. The West! Anywhere west of China is not merely foreign but a region inhabited by devils and monsters. But for the intrepid monk, who defied the Tang emperor's prohibition of foreign travel, the west was no less than India and all the places between it and China; and yet it was from India, this barbarous West, that the Buddha had emerged. And as for Monkey, he lives on – he is Mickey Mouse and Harlequin and Faust all in one. A stock character in Chinese opera, he is the fool who is not a fool. He is a creature who, if not reined in, is capable of unleashing apocalyptic chaos. He is an Emperor, he is Mao Zedong, he is all human extravagance.

It is possible that Monkey suffered from a lack of Thiamine – vitamin B1. Some theorise that much of what took place in Stalinist Russia, in Pol Pot's Cambodia and in Mao Zedong's China could have been avoided if the population in each had had greater access to it. It seems that whilst it is impossible to ingest a surfeit, a deficiency of this fundamental substance can have a seriously deleterious effect on the human nervous system; it may lead to confabulation, a kind of delusive state in which the victim willingly projects absurd ideas as statements of fact, with no intention to deceive, but on the contrary with perfect sincerity, in the light of which, dangerous, mad and even suicidal government actions might be seen by citizens as justified and entirely reasonable.

We left Xian. Over the following days, I noticed that a certain fatigue had set in among the party members. As we chuffed eastwards and southwards; as the temperature rose – we were well into early summer by then, and the languor of the tropics engulfed us – and as the end of the journey became perceptible and crept into conversation, a desire for familiar things became apparent.

'Salad!' clamoured the Americans.

'Chocolate!' cried the British.

The French said little, voicing complaints from time to time about this and that while affecting an air of worldly indifference; the others carried on, determined to enjoy themselves at all costs. The Famous Writer came and went on mysterious errands, delivered to the railway station here and there at the last moment; he looked on in amusement, regarding the Chinese and us, his fellow travellers, with lightly-disguised contempt.

China had that effect on us after a while. The fascination of the country lay in three aspects – its ancient past, which we did not understand; its recent past, which was treated as a shameful secret; and its immediate future, which could only be guessed at. The China of all three conundrums drifted past us as we sat sipping tea at the carriage window. For all rural China's exquisite symmetry, sometimes it felt as if there was nothing there. In a landscape that had been moulded by mankind, the truly human element had absconded. In those comely little villages, it was all about work. Nothing more, just work. Over the centuries, love and joy and celebration had been wrung out of Chinese hearts; true feelings would have to be reacquired and relearnt. After those first few days of delighting in the new world that we had entered, the initial sense of wonder fell away before the monotony of daily life. It has been said that, in the end, we humans are here 'just to fart around'. In China, farting around was not an option. That was the problem.

Chapter 8

The Luoyang Line

We stopped in Luoyang, another ancient capital that apparently meant as little to Sleeping Buddha as it did to us. What do I remember of Luoyang? There was the Number One tractor factory, proud producer of the model inevitably known as the 'East is Red'. There was the White Horse Temple, seemingly the first Buddhist temple in China but which had been much rebuilt following the 'Cultural Revolution'. And there were the Longmen Grottoes, like their counterpart in Da Tong, a series of ancient Buddhist caves dominated by towering sculptures of the Buddha.

Construction of the road from the city to the Longmen caves had only recently commenced in expectation of the great tourist boom to come. We wove our way in our air-conditioned bus through the roadworks. Below us was a scene that in any other country would have been regarded with the utmost censoriousness. Between the lace curtains, we looked down on roadside shrubs smothered in dust, and beside them the road builder – or, rather, the human beast of burden. For there was a man, naked from his neck to the top of his army-green trousers, a rope about his waist, another

The crew waiting to board the train.

about his head, leaning as if into a powerful wind, veins and sinews in high relief in the effort to heave on a wooden cart, piled high and weighed down on its bowed axle with boulders. He was one of many, all with barely a trace of fat on them, heaving and straining all day long, creating a foot at a time the highway to the Longmen caves and to prosperity. Without a mechanised device in sight, it was a scene we might have seen had we been present when the statues themselves were being carved over the centuries between 493 and 1127 AD. From our lofty position their conditions of relentless toil indeed seemed medieval. Most striking was how their scarce physical resources were refined into a power beyond the limits imposed by their wiry frames. That ability to channel concentration is a mighty strength in itself and one that the Chinese possess in abundance.

I had seen that ability manifested in the town centre only the day before. The fight came as a surprise; China was nothing if not cowed, then, all natural tendencies curbed before the restraints of government, never more so than in the presence of foreigners, before whom a mask of serene contentment was generally maintained, for fear of losing face. So, when in what was left of the old town, a few wooden houses with their pretty eaves and simple verandahs, I chanced upon a crowd of passers-by standing about like spectators at a bare-knuckle boxing bout, except they looked on in mutely fascinated silence, as if at a theatrical performance (which, by contrast, in those days in China, as we have seen was a noisy affair, with much spitting and hawking), I was intrigued. Two men fought but not in the brawling manner beloved of our own outside the pub,

Entrepreneurs at work. The Chinese relished the new freedom to trade.

but with a steeliness that ran through the whole of their bodies, sprung as if cobra and mongoose. The anger in each of them was palpable. There was no taunting, for both were quite consumed with an intensity that went beyond words and which excluded from their consciousness all sense of the world about them. They saw nothing but the other. They closed, they wrestled, they hit out, they separated. They fought as the men on the roads heaved on their carts, with a deliberation that brooked no interference. And the crowd, both enthralled and afraid, just watched; until my presence was noticed and then a murmur of alarm spread through it, nervous eyes glanced back at me, followed by nudging and whispers and finally the throng, including the two opponents, hustled off and dissolved hurriedly into the streets there about. The undeviating absorption in the task in hand, as with the guard among the Terracotta Warriors, was then a national characteristic that surfaced often, resurrecting each time the vision of unbridled zeal that had been sprung with each wave of political movements.

At the Longmen Caves was the snake. We had gazed for a while on the carvings themselves, which like their counterparts in Da Tong were on an astonishing scale and which had come through the last few decades remarkably unscathed. At last we began to grasp something of the scale and cohesion of China's history, since the first construction at Longmen goes back to the Northern Wei dynasty when it moved its capital to Luoyang from Datong.

The snake was almost the first living creature that I had seen in the wild in China. Until then, no rabbit, no deer, hardly a bird. Not even a pigeon! The day was unusually

The magnificent Longmen Caves, near Luoyang.

hot and behind me above the raucous racket of the crowds of school children and local tourists, all I could hear was the cry of the ice-cream seller – *Bingqilin, BINGqilin! Bingqilin, BINGqilin!* – and following it the sound of the wooden club that she slapped rhythmically against the side of her wheeled tub to gain attention. But as I stood at the shore of the river at the foot of the Longmen Grottoes, something caught my eye; not more at first than a ripple, like a dribble of mercury. Then, I began to make out a small, scaly, eager head, in my recollection a flaming green and red, cleaving through the silty ochre water. Brilliant colour in China, the land of silk, was so rare, that anything not navy blue or army green stood out like a gemstone and the sight of a moving creature that was not a human being so shocking it was as if a God had appeared before me. What was it – a Banded Krait? A Green Vine snake? A Mandarin Rat snake? I don't know; but I remember that snake so vividly. Not just because it was a snake – which under the best of circumstances would frighten the life out of me – but because there was something about that moment, the sacred snake, almost a dragon, swimming unnoticed by all but me, in the shadow of those magnificent sculptures; that was like a supernatural glimpse into another China, one that was not necessarily kinder but one where the vanity of grand Utopian projects was acknowledged.

Chapter 9

The Nanking Line

From Luoyang, the train quit the arid north to enter the moist, green, glistening tropics. At last, we had entered the China of the paddi field and oxen, the fish lakes, lotus flowers and mulberry leaves. Because of the homogeneity of Chinese life, it was easy to overlook China's physical vastness, which did not impinge on one's consciousness in the same way Russia's had. The most obvious division was between the arid north and the subtropical south but the gulf between east and west was similarly striking. By the time we reached Nanking, it was clear that we were entering another country. Perhaps it would be more accurate to say that we found ourselves in another era. In Xian and Luoyang, we had experienced medieval China. Nanking had been a medieval capital, too, but it had also been, twice, the capital of China under Chiang Kai Shek between 1927–37 before he was forced west by Mao's communist forces, and again between 1945–49 before his flight to Taiwan. It still bore the veneer of sophistication that belonged to the mid-twentieth century.

Changing locos. As we travelled south the steamers fell away.

Until our arrival in Nanking we had been in antique China, where the poverty that school had taught us to associate with it ground on as if the promise of a brighter prospect had never been; where the old ways, left over from ancient times, persisted as scarcely understood customs and habits. In Nanking, the Ming dynasty wall still proudly encircling the city's core, there was a lighter touch. The populace were different; I sensed pride and dignity, even a kind of urbanity. I felt that here a great silent collective sigh had been breathed at the demise of the Great Helmsman, as if the real leader, Sun Yat Sen, after the fall of the last emperor in 1911 the acknowledged founder of the Republic of China, whose tomb gleamed blue and white on the slopes of the Purple Mountain that overlooked the city, would be resurrected and take back his rightful place. Within the walls, the old Ming street plan of straight, intersecting avenues persisted, shaded by peeling sycamore trees, their beseeching branches reaching across in a tracery of dappled light. There was something of Peking in it but gentler, less self-important, without the capital's austerity. There were the usual ranks of socialist housing, and a few half-hearted tributes to ancient China – upturned eaves and splashes of colour on concrete – but somehow they did not lessen the city's essential grandeur. Some buildings, like the Nanking Guest House, where we stayed, were in the early twentieth century European villa style. The hotel kitchens, thirty-two years after foreign residents had fled before the advancing Maoist troops, still turned out their famous chocolate soufflé – famous many decades before but now a watery imitation that we seized upon with relish, for weeks of salty Chinese food had inspired a yearning for sugar. The hotel sat in gardens that echoed the pre-war colonial age, with tidy English lawns and shrubberies and trees which one warm afternoon vibrated to the uncanny percussion of the invisible cicada.

Outside the walls, the countryside was lush and warm, the winding roads flanked by feathery groves of bamboo; among them, untended and ignored, the tomb of the first Ming emperor lay. To the north – for we were officially in southern China now – the city was washed by the muddy, churning waters of the Yangtse. All told, Nanking emanated an idea of civilised China. Even in 1981, when the future path that China would take remained unknown, there was something refreshingly cosmopolitan about it.

The Yangtse River Bridge, like the glimpsed arched back of a gigantic sea-monster refracted through a tropical haze, was frequently visible as we trundled from place to place in Nanking. Crystalline days being a great rarity, everything in China was seen through a haze of one sort or another, whether of dust or pollution or humid air, which in the spring heat incubated a languor and vagueness that was hard to resist. The bridge, built as a double-decker for both road and rail transport, was a Maoist shrine. Before 1968, when it was completed, the only way of crossing the river was by ferry, with even trains transported, carriage by carriage, in especially adapted boats over a period of some two hours.

Originally, the Russians were to have built the bridge but when in 1960 after a doctrinal spat, they pulled out, allegedly taking the construction plans with them,

The Nanking river bridge, a double-decker open to traffic and trains.

it was decided to continue without their expertise. Not only that, as a show-piece for the achievements of the Cultural Revolution, the workers are supposed to have ejected the bourgeois engineers and designers and finished the job themselves, aided only by the miracle of Mao Zedong Thought.

After glimpsing it from every corner of the city, we were finally taken to see the bridge itself. In the room from where we took the lift to the viewing platform, there stood an enormous statue of Mao, defiantly clutching his Little Red Book, with the inevitable great-coat flapping slightly in the chill wind of revisionism. In the meeting room, we took jasmine tea and listened politely to the statistics, pausing only when the room gently vibrated in rhythmical sympathy with a train thundering along the railway line beneath, before continuing up to the platform itself. From there, high up and buffeted by a warm wind, we could see the river on one side and on the other, at the entry point of the bridge proper, triumphal statues of workers in overalls striking martial poses, wielding not weapons but sickles, hammers and books, beneath the unfurled, streaming red banners of the Revolution. With its long curving approach roads, and gardens beneath them and the broad, brown, glistening Yangtze sluggish beneath its span, the bridge was almost beautiful, like a poster image of an ocean liner, the white vapour from steam locomotives drifting up among the girders to emerge above the gigantic red flags surmounting the bridge towers. At its opening in 1968, two years into the Cultural Revolution, with the country seething like a maggoty wound, it must have seemed a miraculous vision, one that would surely have been

Nanking river bridge, revolutionary statues and steam locomotive.

roundly cursed by the millions whose lives had been shattered through the egotism of the very man who took credit for every one of the few things that went right.

Whilst we stood upon the tower, the guide pointed excitedly at the river. 'Tourists, look,' he shouted. We saw nothing. '*Baiji*!' the guide shouted, '*Baiji*!' He was referring to the Chinese River Dolphin, which he claimed to have seen frolicking amid the river whorls. At the time I didn't think much of it, none of us did, but it transpires that this species, rare enough then, is almost certainly no more, the victim, like many species in China, of generations of inappropriate industrialisation together with an insatiable appetite for food and medicine.

If the bridge was the chimera of modern Nanking, then the city wall was its medieval counterpart. In Xian, the city wall was withering away, whilst in Nanking it was largely complete, providing the contour of the city just as it did when it was built during the Ming dynasty. Once the longest city wall in the world, it was a magnificent sight, and even though in places breached and razed for one reason or another, some three-quarters of its forty-foot ramparts remained, together with its intricately designed gates, with their systems of portcullises, gatehouses and ramps. Some of the bricks, bound together with a mortar made largely of glutinous rice, were inscribed not only with the name of the foundry where they were made but even of their individual maker.

In the courtyards of the Zhonghua Gate were the city's entrepreneurs selling the polished rainbow pebbles of the local stone which, immersed in water-filled bowls, glistened irresistibly. As they dried, they lost their lustre, like all souvenirs. 'Eastern promise' was not a term just dreamt up by western copywriters.

A climb up the flight of the steps beside the gatehouse led to the ramparts themselves, from where there was an almost uninterrupted view across the city girded by the wall. Across the roofs of the city, beyond the wall, we could see the Purple Mountains, glimpsing the temple-like structure of Sun Yat Sen's Mausoleum.

Every visit to Nanking included a visit to the Purple Mountain, because that was where Sun Yat Sen was buried and a visit to his mausoleum was on every itinerary. Variously known as the 'Father of the Republic' and 'Father of the Revolution', Dr. Sun Yat Sen occupied an ambivalent place in the hearts of the Chinese. Although he had been the inspiration behind the deposition in 1911 of the last imperial dynasty, his attempts to construct a republic united around his version of democratic socialism was a failure. Founder of the Guomintang Nationalist Party, he was persuaded into an alliance with the nascent Chinese Communist Party, with its close ties to the USSR, believing that he would be able to make use of them whilst keeping their ambitions in check. But the divided Guomintang were no match for the Communists, who were able to exploit the revolutionary experiences of their Soviet comrades and after Sun's death, embark on a civil war with his successor, Chiang Kai Shek, who broke from the Communists once he felt strong enough to do so.

Sun died in 1925, in Peking. The Nationalists wanted to claim him for their own and, although he was a Cantonese, it was politically expedient for his mausoleum to be constructed in Nanking, the Guomindang capital. The Communists, too, claimed

An exercise class at school. Mass participation was still the order of the day.

him as an early revolutionary, but the rise of Mao Zedong meant that he could never achieve the illustrious place in Chinese history that might have been accorded to him in other circumstances.

So it was that his last burial place lay in a sort of pantheon, with a lapis blue roof at the top of an enormous flight of marble steps on the slopes of the Purple Mountain. Our guide trotted out the inevitable cliché that after becoming a doctor 'he realised that although he could heal the illnesses of the Chinese people, he could not heal their poverty'.

The day we were there, the rain fell like a curtain; the 392 marble steps that mounted to the mausoleum itself, as if converted by a switch into a set of rapids, became a powerful cataract. I stood at the bottom watching the waters cascade towards us, sheltering under an umbrella with a young trainee guide, who told me with all the authority of a recruit to the Young Communist Pioneers that he knew a lot about Britain.

'In Britain,' he explained, 'the powerful people wear bowler hats and the poor people must do what they tell them. It is always foggy and it rains like this, except it is colder.'

We were to leave Nanking with some regret. Since 1981, Nanking, like many other cities in China, has changed out of all recognition. The skyline, then still dominated by the great encircling wall, is now a clutter of glass and steel silhouettes, and the city has expanded far from its medieval core. Squeezed into the fabric of the suburbs, the wall still runs its aimless course but is no longer the city's physical boundary; rather, it marks the division of two eras of China's history.

Chapter 10

The Shanghai Line

It was a brief daylight shuttle across the canals and paddi fields of the eastern plain to Shanghai, that most evocative of Chinese cities. Which is odd, given that of all the cities we passed thorough, it was the least properly Chinese. My travellers were by now intellectually comatose but the notoriety, or is it infamy, of Shanghai, revived their interest. I discovered in Shanghai how tenuous is the line between fact and fiction, between illusion and substance, how reputation clings on long beyond its maturity.

For Shanghai was a ghost town. It was not empty of people – far from it. There was in the streets of Shanghai all the paraphernalia to which we had become used in the preceding weeks: the teeming bicycles; the army-surplus lorries with their 1950s snouts, their loads a mattress for sleeping workers; the tinny electric buses that whined and stuttered across the city centre; the whole nine-to-five state apparatus in the hands of an endless supply of jobsworths who pedalled in their methodical way from home to work and work to home.

Shanghai's skyline, a world of smog and art-deco, unchanged from 1949.

The ghosts were those of the city's inhabitants until 1949. If you were to look at a photograph now of a panorama of Shanghai you would not, at first sight, see much to distinguish it from any other of the great Asian metropolises. But in 1981, there was not a steel skyscraper in sight. The roofscape was more akin to Mary Poppins' London. Rows and rows of villas built in the European style, chimney pots and all. We looked on in wonder as we drove along Avenues and Boulevards of Gothic, Mock Tudor, Art Deco, Art Nouveau, with the remnants of their neat gardens, borders intact, lawns trimmed; it was hallucinatory. A swathe of genteel Western suburbia transplanted to the seaboard of the East China Sea. We passed along the Bund, where the great buildings of pre-war capitalist enterprise towered over the Whangpu River, which flowed into the ocean at the yawning mouth of the mighty Yangtse and where they roiled like two shades of melting chocolate. These buildings, inspired and financed by the enemies of Mao's New China, spoke of power and luxury and were now for the most part the offices of various state institutions – The China Import & Export Corporation, and the like – but their exteriors spoke of New York, London, Liverpool, of empire and trade and entrepreneurs.

Shanghai was a fable, the name instantly evocative of glamour, riches, poverty, despair, hope, ambition, love, depravity – the human condition. It had been like a licensed netherworld, where the adventurer could indulge his lusts with official approval.

Shanghai's infamy derives from the time – 1840 to 1949 – when it was effectively run by foreigners. The Americans, British, French, Japanese, between them built a city in their own image but with the advantage of exempting themselves from the laws of China and to a large extent from their own. It was an extraordinary set of circumstances. Anything was possible in a city where the chief detective of the French *Sûreté* was also Shanghai's most infamous gangster. As a guidebook of the era said of Shanghai's bars, 'There are the three categories: high class, low class, and no class.' Naturally, the Chinese Government from 1949 laid the blame for the excesses of pre-war Shanghai entirely with the western imperial powers, although the truth was that there had been many Chinese complicit in the abuses heaped on their own people. It had been the piquant mix of two distinctive cultures that had imbued Shanghai with its peculiar quality of fantasy.

My travellers, for that was how I saw them now that the end of the journey was at hand, my travellers were unusually quiet as our bus sighed its way about Shanghai. I think, as with dreams where everyday events follow each other in an unnatural and unsettling sequence, they were momentarily confused to find themselves in a place that was simultaneously exotic and familiar. Shanghai was taken by Communist forces in 1949, but since that event, so unchanged was the city it could have happened the day before our arrival. Shanghai in 1981 was exactly as it had been in 1949. It seemed that, had we knocked at a front door of one of those villas, it could have been opened by a Chinese maid who would have ushered me into the presence of her Western employer, smoking his pipe at a fireside armchair, reading the local English-

One of the last of the traditional Chinese ships on the Huangpu, Shanghai.

language newspaper with the BBC or *Voice of America* issuing forth from a wireless set; as if to be living such a life in a corner of China, so far from home, was the normal way of things.

We arrived at our hotel, overlooking the river on the corner of the Bund and the Nanking Road. The Peace Hotel in its heyday had been the quintessence of luxury, a plutocratic refuge from the filthy streets outside. Then, when it was known as the Cathay Hotel, it attracted all the celebrities of the time, from Charlie Chaplin to Noel Coward, who wrote *Private Lives* during his stay. The name change came about in 1956, when the Great Helmsman, by now untouchable, decreed it, 'peace' in China, as in the Soviet Union, being a concept apparently limited to the Communist world.

Like the streets outside, the interior of the Peace Hotel had retained its essential character whilst losing most of its vitality and flavour. The bell-hops in the lifts wore the uniforms of another era above their scuffed plastic shoes; the light along the corridors was diffused dimly through handsome art-deco shades and lanterns, their yellow gleam falling on polished brass and copper fire-extinguisher casings that had been manufactured in San Francisco many decades before; the indestructible, noisy, chugging taps and the capacious basins and baths of Western manufacture were all left over from when the hotel was still the Cathay; and the cutlery at breakfast included a cruet, sugar bowl and tongs all emblazoned with the old hotel symbols. There was a barber's shop and you could leave your shoes outside your room to be polished. All told, the hotel reflected in many ways aspects of the Chinese psyche; an addiction to habit and tradition and yet, judging by the cheap glass sales cabinets that dominated a large part of the magnificent lobby, a peculiar indifference to surroundings.

And there was the celebrated jazz band. The Peace Hotel Jazz Band had become, even then, a kind of trendy institution. But the ageing band members were genuine survivors, emerging from banishment for the first time probably since the 1940s. I presume that during the Cultural Revolution, when they somehow succeeded in practising in secret, they must have paid with great hardship for their unarguably Western associations, not that you would have known it unless it were from their faintly leaden rendition of period swing classics – *In the Mood*, *Begin the Beguine* and a host of other tunes from the early twentieth century. There was something both poignant and faintly eerie about their stone-faced performances. Because of the veneration for tradition that is integral to Chinese culture and which had survived the many attempts to expunge it – to the point where you could almost say that such attempts were themselves traditions – and because the city's character was formed during the Jazz Age, in Shanghai it was permissible to play jazz. Nobody would have thought of playing jazz in Peking, or Xian, or Luoyang; they lacked the sophistication that had always been associated with Shanghai, which, for the Chinese, had for generations represented a certain 'cool'. Outside Shanghai, apart from the concert in Peking, attempts at musical entertainment had consisted of a room in a hotel temporarily turned into a bar, decorated with chains of twinkling fairy lights among which speakers thundered out local versions of disco music. Chairs would have been placed around the perimeter of the room and a gaggle of excited members of staff would hang around in nervous anticipation of Western magic.

Given that it was the most Western of all Chinese cities, it was remarkable that Shanghai was not razed during the Cultural Revolution. The old pre-1949 street names, featuring European statesmen unknown to the Chinese, had long been exchanged for names in keeping with the mores of the day and during the Cultural Revolution they, briefly, changed again, so that, as an example of the thinking of the day, the street where the Soviet Consulate was located became 'Anti-Revisionist Street'. But unlike every other city in China, it was not ransacked or where there was vandalism, it was comparatively superficial. And yet Shanghai had for a long time been a cradle of revolution. It was in Shanghai, conveniently outside Chinese jurisdiction, that the Chinese Communist Party held its first congress; it was in Shanghai that the 'Gang of Four' hatched their plots, using the Peace Hotel as their sometime headquarters. In their way, they, too, were *compradores* just like their ancestors, inspired by the Shanghai entrepreneurial spirit.

As we sat and listened to the jazz band, one of the elderly American couples was moved to hit the dance floor. As they shuffled about with surprising panache, I noticed a foreign woman dressed in black lace sitting alone in a corner and drinking steadily, with the glassy eyes and permanent smile of the lush. When one of our party invited her to join us, it transpired that she was an English divorcee from Hong Kong in search of a Shanghai that had long gone – no Humphrey Bogart there, not even his shade. Sitting almost silent among us, in a mist of perfume, her brilliant red lipstick glistened in the low light as the band pounded out tunes of old Shanghai.

She was not alone in her delusion. A couple of middle-aged men in the party, convinced that I, being comparatively young and, presumably, with an air about me of loucheness, should have a nose for the real, underground Shanghai, had urged me to show them a good time. But I guessed, even without knowing Shanghai at all, that the Shanghai of White Russian courtesans, of Taxi Dancers, of green cocktails and green nail varnish, cabarets, opium and gangsters was not there, not even, I was pretty certain, as a treat for the Party supremos. There were no beckoning fingers and seductive whispers from the shadows of old Shanghai. Anyone expecting to find some scraps from Shanghai's former incarnation as variously the Whore of the Orient, the Paris of the East and a Paradise for Adventurers was to be disappointed. When it came to it, there was no more life in Shanghai than there had been in Da Tong.

Instead, we could walk along the Bund, a vast curving terrace of domed and towering institutions in colonial and art-deco styles. There, at one end, was the Soochow Creek, spanned by the iron-girder bridge that effectively separated the International Settlement, where British rule had prevailed, from suburban Shanghai. On the far side of the bridge facing the Huangpu River was the Soviet Consulate, before that the Imperial Russian Consulate and on the other side of the street from it stood the former Astor Hotel, near neighbour to a ziggurat that in its time had been known as Broadway Mansions. Along the Bund itself were the former offices

Crowded Shanghai streets – a sea of white shirts.

of the companies, like Jardine Matheson that made their fortunes on the opium trade; or of the *North China Daily News*, the premier English-language newspaper of its time. The clock on the top of what had been the Hong Kong & Shanghai Banking Corporation no longer rang out the chimes of Big Ben. The Bank of China rose up like a miniature Empire State Building. The Old Shanghai Club, a bastion of British back-slapping colonialism, was long closed and turned into a hostel for oversea sailors. All of these fortresses of international capitalism would have bustled and hustled with the mannerisms and language of Europe, Japan and the Americas, as if it had been Paris, London, Tokyo or New York; and, in a city on the edge of what was first Imperial China, and then the Republic of China, in the swelter and torpor of the tropics, it was considered perfectly normal.

We peeked into the old haunts of the Taipans to admire the intricate iron work and the mosaics and stained glass their money had sponsored; where once the buildings along the Bund had housed gentlemen's clubs, newspaper offices, banks and the offices of the great trading companies, they were occupied now by branches of China's state bureaucracy. No longer expressions of private power, they had simply become receptacles for workers, who, with a marvellous talent for obliviousness to their surroundings, had just moved in and carried on, with the result that most of Shanghai's architecture, though somewhat soiled through time and neglect, remained essentially unchanged. We watched the teeming Huangpu River, ceaselessly crisscrossed by sampans, steamers and junks. Beyond the far bank lay Pudong, which then, apart from a few factory buildings and warehouses, was a wasteland. We braved the guard at the gates of the old British Consulate and found the old rusting roller abandoned at the edge of the coarse lawn, which was kept trim by state employees on their hands and knees, picking out weeds. We followed a line of worshippers into a surviving Episcopalian church, where we listened in amazement to an American preacher speak of fire and brimstone. In the old French Concession, at 'Chez Louis', renamed the 'Red House', it was possible, even then, to order a dish of Soufflé Grand Marnier, which, much like the Jazz Band in the Peace Hotel, survived more in the spirit than in its execution. Bakeries, the origins of which could be traced to their Austrian and German founders who had washed up in Shanghai in flight from the Nazis, still produced pale imitations of the glories of Central European breads and cakes. In the tailoring shops that abounded along the main streets, I would not have been surprised to have been able to order a suit cut to patterns favoured in pre-war Hollywood. There were even shops selling Siberian furs, as if the old days and their glamorous former clientele had never really gone away but had grown old in stately seclusion in dusty villas. The memory of what Shanghai had once been lived on, for despite all its faults, Shanghai had been something, and to be from Shanghai was still to be someone.

In Shanghai more than ever, you could feel which way the wind was blowing. The locals had no time to stand and stare at foreigners; they had other things on their mind and, anyway, this was cosmopolitan Shanghai, where foreigners were no big deal.

China's destiny was written for all to see; the pulse was faint, but it was there and it was quickening. The Bund was bisected by the Nanking Road, the most famous shopping street in China, and as you walked up it towards the old Race Course (renamed the People's Square) and its remaining grandstand, hangovers from Shanghai's past survived like a habit. The Nanking Road's reputation dated from the time when the Sun (since 1949 the Number One Department Store), the Sun Sun (Shanghai Number One Provisions Store), the Wing On (The Number Ten Department Store) and the Sincere department stores (Shanghai Number One Clothing Store) had been among the finest in the world. Now they offered more or less what was on offer in all Chinese cities, albeit on a giant scale – cheap cosmetics with names like Panda Brand or Plum Blossom or Maxam; thermos flasks; nail clippers; key rings; and luridly coloured clothing – reflecting the priorities of an incipient consumer society. There were shops selling books the Europeans had left behind, shops selling ink stones and calligraphy brushes, shops selling Chinese opera costumes. Nearby were the densely packed Shanghai Lanes into which the local Chinese poor had been squeezed by the foreign occupiers and a street where Chinese Moslems lived in traditional Chinese houses distinguished by subtle arabesque flourishes. Here and there were quixotic signs ('Famous & Special Shop'), or the remnants of the Temple of the City God that once dominated the so-called 'old Chinese town' that had been all that Shanghai was before the arrival of the foreigners and the Catholic cathedral distinguished by Buddhist symbols in the stained glass.

Away from the old commercial centre, the sycamore-lined streets were adorned with houses and villas lifted out of English and French suburbs. Some, the former homes of the Taipans, built on a palatial scale, were now divided into offices or schools or dilapidated flats festooned with washing lines. Inside, parquet floors, elegant staircases and wainscoting were all still in place, scratched and buffeted, unpolished but in use. There was the shell of a Russian Orthodox Church, its cluster of pale blue domes bubbling just above the skyline of chimney pots and Ruritanian turrets and spires, now used as a warehouse for washing machines. Peer into one of the old terraced houses and you might see a fully made-up actor in costume, practising the sinuous movements of Chinese opera before an ornate fireplace that for a family of refugees or expatriate employees would have been the homely reminder of somewhere far away. For some before 1949, notwithstanding its fabled mystique, the allure of Shanghai must have been illusory, just another posting turned into a lonely exile in a disagreeable climate amid extremes of squalor and opulence.

A curious thing happened to me. I was sitting in the anaemic cafe of the Peace Hotel, eating a sugary imitation of a Western sponge cake and drinking the nearest thing, though not very near, to coffee that I had drunk in several weeks, when a Chinese man – young, about thirty, I would have said – sat himself down before me. He was very thin and although he had the black hair of all Chinese, it was neater and more care had been taken with the cut. So, too, his clothes, the like of which I had not seen on any Chinese man throughout our journey – you would have to say gaudy, with a pale yellow jacket, slacks and a striped tie that was as wide as it was long. A vision of America from thirty years before.

He spoke to me in fluent English with a strong American inflection, asking me with a sly confidence that betokened, I thought, some kind of criminal intent. But, if criminal he was, his reason for approaching me was purely for the sake of talking with a Westerner somewhere close to his age. But he was sly and when he laughed, as he did often, his eyes rested on me through the smoke that curled from an unbroken sequence of cigarettes.

He was from Taiwan. Taiwan, as it still is, was the other China, the small, independent capitalist China that Peking claimed and claims for its own. His name was Johnson. He told me, in his casual way, as if it were all perfectly normal and natural, that he had relatives in Shanghai and that he intended to marry and settle down there. I was taken aback, first that a Taiwanese could even visit the People's Republic of China, given the diplomatic stand-off between the two territories and, secondly, that that person might choose to settle there. But Johnson, whom I rather suspected of fleeing his country on account of some nefarious personal history, made light of my questions. He told me that since China was certainly on the way to putting its foolish dalliance with Communism behind it, he could have a new life there – that he would be welcomed as an experienced capitalist. All uttered with his peculiar silent snigger that would have been endearing had it not so obviously concealed a calculating nature. Considering that only a short time before, the presence of a Taiwanese citizen on Chinese soil was inconceivable – unless it met some propaganda purpose – and although it is true that universal Chinese brotherhood throws up unexpected alliances, his optimism was intriguing. I knew then that however long it took, one day China and Taiwan would be as one.

Johnson rose, gave his card – Johnson Wu, Business Consultant, Taipei, Republic of China and Shanghai, PRC – and left. I watched him framed in the doorway of the Peace Hotel as he lit another cigarette, his yellow jacket attracting curious glances from passers-by, covertly scrutinising his surroundings through dark glasses, before turning along the pavement with the purposeful, faintly stooped gait of a man of business.

When I mentioned this encounter, the reactions were telling. Only the Americans took it for granted that it was in the nature of things, that you seek out opportunities where you can. Some others, in love a little with a sentimental hope for a China that might learn from the failures of Western avarice, were a little taken aback. There was, it was true, something engaging in the apparent simplicity of Chinese life and the sense of order reflected in the gangs of giggling children who, with their white shirts and red neckerchiefs, performed for us with such innocent enthusiasm. But it could not last.

Although it was far from 'life itself', as it had once been described, I must admit that I fell for Shanghai, with all its etiolated charms. I suppose I hankered after the world suggestively implied by its ghosts and skeletons. But with the final leg of the voyage before us, I was brought roughly to my senses with a material reminder of the brutal present and of the even more brutal recent past.

Most of the party had gone into a department store to do some shopping. Shanghai was almost the only city where the shopper might stumble on something interesting to buy outside the so-called Friendship Stores, government operations aimed exclusively at Westerners, who were expected to purchase using so-called Foreign Exchange Certificates that were given in exchange for Western currency and which were not supposed to be in general circulation. I hung about outside, watching the Chinese world go by. Opposite stood the grandstand, all that remained of the former race-course, now redundant and which instead, like a pared-down Tian An Men Square, had become a great space used only for flag-waving and military parades. As I stood absorbed in the toing and froing, there came a persistent tug at my elbow. I turned to face an elderly man, gaunt and thin, with a wispy beard, in the universal threadbare blue tunic. He gave me a cautious beseeching look that by now I had come to recognise as the mark of someone with a story to tell. Careful to attract as little attention as possible from the crowds passing around us, he spoke perfect English in a sorrowful, even cadence. Could I, by chance, he asked, find him work elsewhere, perhaps in Hong Kong? I am strong, he said. I have a good employment record, for I worked as head gardener in one of the parks in the old days. I worked, too, for an English family. They were good employers, he said ruefully. Then he pointed sadly along the road and up to an anonymous office building. There, he said. There, during the Cultural Revolution, they threw my daughter from the window. His eyes followed an arc down to the pavement and his gaze lingered there. Because of me, he said. Because of me. He looked up, his eyes strained with suppressed emotion. A job, he said, just a job. He slid into my hand a crumpled scrap of paper on which he had written in ink in scholarly English his name and address and a summary of his talents, before slipping away as Sleeping Buddha and the others, clutching their silk purses, emerged. Sleeping Buddha glanced at me and then at the old man, a shadow of suspicion passing rapidly across his features – for a moment I thought he might say something but he checked himself, confining himself to a sudden giggle and, turning to the others, repeating his favourite joke about foreign friends buying up China.

The episode on the street with the old man had been upsetting. In Peking, still in the grip of naïf enthusiasm for a new place, shielded from reality by the theatre of organised tourism, shamefully I had laughed inwardly at a glass of hot water offered as hospitality by a man with a similar story. And now I had met with tragedy again. Only this time, after weeks of a long journey across a totalitarian landscape, it made a greater impact. Here, on the most celebrated shopping street in China, I had come face to face with sorrow in its tenderest form. The very thing that makes sense of life had been stolen from him, as if it were, well, nothing. We had stood together on the very spot where his daughter had landed lifeless like a rag doll because she had dared to have been born to a father who, consorting with foreigners, was marked with the stain of treason. It was chilling. I thought of his wife, his parents, his family, the framework of hope and love upon which we hang a life. I thought of how the Chinese have a reputation as a people without emotion and realised that they just cope with tragedy differently. Over the centuries, through the changes of religion and philosophy that percolated into daily life or through their violent imposition, they had mastered the art of self-discipline. Pain was to be endured by channelling it into a mental recess and locking it away there. This man felt his tragedy objectively, as if he were holding it in the palm of his hand. And this ability was abused, again and again, by his own people. As if it did not matter; because all that had mattered then was the Revolution and all that matters now is the new revolution and the new China. As if the experiment had been worthwhile.

Chapter 11

The Canton Line

We had one more journey left in the People's Republic of China. The weather had become hot and humid. There was a peculiar intensity to the heat in China. It did not burn like a dry desert sun or even a rare hot summer sun in England. The air itself was like an immense cloud of diaphanous vapour. Sometimes, when you first stepped out, the temperature could seem pleasantly warm until, after strolling beneath a pale innocuous sky, nothing would staunch the flow of sweat that bubbled up and dribbled down your back. There was no air-conditioning in China then. Where there was shade it offered no protection from the pervasive humidity. Only those few remaining ancient buildings, cleverly positioned to funnel the slightest breeze from the still, tepid air, or the grandiloquent structures of the age of the Great Helmsman with their dark interiors, could bring relief. At night a dunk in a deep cold bath was the only remedy.

So, this last journey from Shanghai, into the tropical south, the longest and hottest we made in China, was never going to be a comfortable one. It was, however, the most beautiful, as the railway track meandered through the lush vegetation of the tropics, among banana palms and peanuts and soya and tea. Above us were grassy ridges, where lines of slender shrubs rocked in a breeze we craved, milky green leaves glimmering in the misty sunlight. Around us there were glistening paddi fields and green and gold rice terraces rising in tiers up the hillsides in an exquisite staircase of gently scalloped curves. I can smell it again, the smell of confined, broiling heat on the train, of smut-ingrained metal, as we stood listlessly in the corridor by the open windows desperate for a breeze; and when finally we set off, we leaned back in relief only to find that the circulating air failed to keep us cool, merely serving to stay the beads of sweat from our brow so that the moment the train slowed, they popped out and streamed down our cheeks like sooty tears on our permanently glistening skin. Yet for most of the Chinese, whose habits were seasonal, just as their lives were ordered according to their years on earth, this early summer heat did not warrant the shedding of many layers. The washed-out blues and pinks of woolly combinations peeped from beneath their trousers as they had done throughout the winter and not the slightest trace of perspiration moistened their features. When we halted, the Chinese would take their flannels and head for large circular basins fringed with taps on the platforms where they could peel off their nylon socks and wash their feet. In matters of hygiene the Chinese were almost neurotically fastidious but only within their personal space. Spitting, for example, was a national vice, resistant to every campaign the government sponsored towards its eradication, because to rid the body of poison was considered healthy, whatever the consequences for others. In theatres and restaurants, the air was rent by the noises of violent expectorating and hawking, followed by a liquid splat as a globule of frequently bloody mucous fell to the floor. In theory, spitting could lead to a fine; yet the only victim I witnessed was a member of my own party, who lost in thought stood spitting out sunflower seed husks in a circle around his feet at the exit of the Forbidden City.

The first part of that eventful final leg of the journey passed in a sultry daze. Just the sense of heading south, the deepening greens and yellows of lusher vegetation; the tinny whirring of the little wall-fan in the compartment that brought a few seconds of relief as it played over me during its orbit; the long night enveloped in a long, damp towel soaking into the rattan mat.

Late that night, the doorway to the compartment that once again I was sharing with a trio of local people was filled with the gamine shadow of one of the French girls in the party. She stood there, cigarette in hand – in those days smoking was permitted aboard – wearing that look of casual disgust fundamental to the French persona and told me that she had a problem. The problem was that she wanted to keep the main light on so that she could read; whereas her compatriots (for I had foolishly, as it turned out billeted all the French in the same compartment) wanted to sleep. She asked me to intervene, which I duly did, by pointing out to her that she had her own reading lamp above her bunk. Furthermore, it actually worked. She shrugged her shoulders as she blew out a stream of disgruntled smoke and took

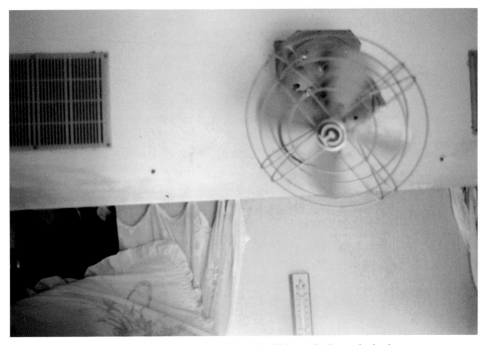

Useless fan in a carriage compartment, complete with Chinese Railways insignia.

to her bunk. The train rattled on through the night. The heat became fractionally less oppressive. Just as I was dozing off, another of the French contingent appeared in my doorway, this time the husband of a couple from Marseilles. 'She insists,' he said in an exasperated tone, 'she insists,' referring to the same girl, 'on keeping the window open but my wife has a sore throat.' So I descended from my bunk and went again to their compartment to remonstrate. The compartment was a maelstrom of smoke and humid air and the pink nylon curtains blew wildly across the window. Before I could find some diplomatic way of saying 'grow up' the husband, sitting next to his wife, who sat in silent contemplation of the girl who admittedly was one of those people whose very presence was provocative in itself, launched himself across the room and wrapping his hands about her neck threw her down onto her back. Shocked, I stood transfixed. Then the rest of us all fell on him together and dragged him off. He sat again beside his wife who looked on protectively, whilst he sat back, still seething with aggression.

The girl, to her credit, was hardly perturbed, merely rubbing her throat contemplatively and mentioning casually that she would be suing her assailant on their return to France. The assailant's wife looked away, muttering, 'Now you know what it is like to have a sore throat.' Then she stood up and shut the window, primping the curtains as she did so.

Clearly, either something that I had not noticed had been smarting there for a long time, or this was just the French way of dealing with adversity. The girl took her towel and slept in the corridor, which was understandable if incommodious for everyone else, who had to step over her each time they went to the lavatory.

After that, calmness reigned. As I lay on my bunk, I became aware of a powerful noise above my head. It was rain, rain of a quality I had never heard before; fusillades detonated on the metal roof and raked across the windows. At least it brought some relief from the heat and sleep came easily at last.

When the morning came, it was still raining. All night the rain had beat on the carriage roof and teemed down the windows in streams, pouring in the gap left for ventilation to form pools on the compartment table. We joined the main line from Peking and still it rained. It poured throughout the whole day and as we settled down again that night, the thrashing went on. We were due to pull into Canton early the following morning and I wondered what we were going to do there if the downpour persisted.

I need not have worried. When we awoke, it was because of the stillness. The rain had ceased. The train had come to a halt and I knew, in the way that one's senses can detect subtleties of mood and circumstance, that all was not as it should have been. I felt that we had been motionless for a very long time. I leant down from my bunk and knocked apart the little starched curtains. For a moment I imagined we were on the coast near Canton, and I thought, good, we have almost arrived. Then my senses cleared and I knew that we were not by the sea, or on the banks of a river or of a lake but stranded above a vast flood. The heat had returned, and there was a faint miasmal odour; I slipped down to the floor and went out into the corridor, almost tripping over the slumbering Parisienne. Peering out, I saw that we were at a small station – no more than a halt – with a tiny platform and two small station buildings. I presumed that this was one of those occasional unscheduled stops and that since we were above the surrounding waters, we would soon be resuming our journey.

I was wrong. An hour passed. We took our breakfast. Another hour passed. There was, of course, no information, and no interpreter. Sleeping Buddha had waved us off from Shanghai, with his usual humourless smile. I had watched as he had turned away when we chugged out of the station and emptied his nostrils onto the track. Now there came the sound of an engine powering up, the train clanked forward, accelerated, before slowing down and coming to a halt. A loud groan came from everyone in the party, apart from La Parisienne, who slept on with peerless unconcern. There we stayed for a further hour, before shunting back slowly to the little station.

By now it was midday. The fans had been turned off in order to conserve power and the heat was intolerable, the humidity suffocating. In those circumstances it was inescapable, especially in the carriage. I could not sit still and yet movement was even worse. Outside the window of my compartment, blocking the view, was a goods train, from which emanated the overpowering stench of pigs' urine. And when, having dozed off, a bloated insect – it must have been a stray cicada – woke me by taking off from beneath my legs, I decided that it was imperative to get out from that tin can. The conductress made a half-hearted attempt to restrain me; she, too, could see that for the foreseeable future we were going nowhere.

Outside, the scene was a dismal one. The platform quickly gave out to a narrow strip of dry land that meandered between the railway line, conveniently raised on an embankment, and the flood water that lay flat and ominous as far as I could see. A steaming mist hovered above it, in and out of which crudely constructed boats bobbed uncertainly between the upper branches of skeletal trees and village house roofs. Telegraph poles poked out of the grey sheen like the masts of sunken ships in a flat calm. The path I had been forced to take – and, I noticed, some in the party that had also evaded the attentions of our carriage attendant – must have been the main street, for it stood a little above the waters and was flanked by the simple shops that characterised every Chinese village then, all concerns dealing either in spare parts for agricultural machines or in foodstuffs. As soon as we were identified as foreigners, the irresistible Chinese talent for commerce asserted itself, unleashing a swarm of salesmen who emerged from all directions (even seaward, as a little dinghy beached hastily right before me) to set up stall. Fires were lit, woks settled above them, and soon the filthy oil bubbled fiercely. Twists of dough were dropped in and within minutes fished out with chopsticks, wrapped in greasy squares of paper and proffered to us as we ambled by. In the circumstances, with food supplies on the train running out, we bought them, but the bread sticks, drenched as they were in oil that had been used over and over again, week after week, were almost inedible.

Scrutinised intently for our reaction to these delicacies, for approval would have meant more sales, we stood in the midst of disaster, for the first time truly part of daily Chinese life.

We shuffled back towards the train without much enthusiasm. Among the rest of the party, a certain restlessness was brewing. In the absence of Sleeping Buddha, this was all directed at me. After my experience in Ulan Bator I was prepared for mental disintegration. More unexpected was the reaction of those who until then had barely uttered a word of complaint from the moment that we departed London. As we mounted the platform, a woman exited a small edifice at the rear of the platform that I now recognised, partly from the Chinese written characters denoting women and men, but mostly from the appalling smell that followed the woman out into the damp air, as public toilets. The woman was convulsed with revulsion. 'Have you been in there?' she asked through pursed lips. 'Well,' she said, 'I suggest that you do not even think of doing so. It is,' she said, 'nothing short of disgusting. And I thought the Chinese were a civilised people. You,' she said, waving a fat finger at me, 'you should tell someone.'

I resisted, just, the urge to tell her to fuck off. I was not at the end of my tether, but I was bored by these bursts of selfishness that erupted when the going got a little tough. You only had to look about you; the poverty, the stoicism, the mess.

I forced myself to have a look inside the toilet block. Never was the term shit-hole more appropriate. It was like a farmyard without the animal appeal. But the fact was that choices were limited now that the toilets aboard were rammed full; it was the station toilet block or a private dry corner in what was left of the village. But no such corner existed.

The absence of protest from those who had imprisoned me in Ulan Bator had surprised me. In my innocence, I had presumed that the awful scenes around us had brought them to their senses when the truth was that they had hunkered down in one of the compartments drinking the only unboiled liquids that remained available, tins of local, very lukewarm beer and a cheap interpretation of the national spirit; a combination that could do nothing more than generate thirst, churning stomachs and hot air.

So, as the day came to an end, our meagre dinner consumed by the few among us who retained an appetite, we sat in our various compartments in preparation for a night of discomfort and uncertainty. No one relished the prospect of lying on bunks oozing like butter on a hot plate and so everyone sat slouched in their seats, stupefied in the gathering darkness, reading or dozing with febrile fitfulness. The smell of pig infected the flat air. Outside, from time to time, the sound of loud Chinese conversation, hawking and spitting ripped through the silence.

Then a shadow fell across the doorway to my compartment. Other shadows joined it coagulating into a dark patch against the light from the station behind them. There they were, the gang from Ulan Bator, the self-appointed committee, our very own politicians, intoxicated with self-importance and cheap booze.

I wished them good evening, a gesture not calculated to endear me to their finer natures. It was true that my tone was one of weary resignation, as I could see that they were in a mutinous frame of mind.

'Oh,' said one of the Americans, 'we have an American hater amongst us!' I don't know from which mouth the insult came but whoever it was had forgotten the other occasion when events provoked a similar reaction. It could have been Slim, the Vietnam Vet that ran riot at the Polish-Russian border, still there, tin of beer in hand, leering and teetering slightly from side to side with his drunken lopsided grin. 'Yessir, an American hater,' someone repeated, as if there were a special category of people known as American-haters. I smiled at them. And then I said to them, 'It is not me that is the American hater. It is you. You are ashamed at your own good luck. You feel disgust when confronted by the human condition. Well, please don't. Relax; it is not your fault. But, come on, a little empathy, that is all that is needed. A little patience.' That is what I should have said. I refrained but I think the judgement is accurate. In the suffering of others, they saw only their own mortality; they were under the illusion that Western democracy conferred immortality. They were innocents, really, and generous in their way. They meant well. They wanted those poor unfortunates we saw about us to have what they had. But they did not see that when you hit the wall, you hit the wall.

One of them said, 'Look, we are trapped in this Communist DICKtatorship. You gotta get us out of here! Call the American consulate in Canton or wherever the hell it is, get them to send out a chopper.'

'And where exactly, do you propose it will land', interposed Leonard, who, as he had done in Ulan Bator, appeared at my side as the spirit of old America.

'You,' the others said to Leonard, 'you are just the same as this guy. Hell, are you in the pay of the comms, too?'

Lionel just laughed. He didn't address the committee at all. 'Did you ever hear,' he asked, by way of passing the time 'of the Shanghai Silk Wrap?' He sniffed at the air, seeming to take pleasure in the porcine stink from the neighbouring wagon that hung in the heat like rancid bacon fat. 'It was a method used by Shanghai prostitutes to enhance the pleasure of their customers. They would lie together and someone would bind them in silk like mummies, in the most complete intimacy possible. Only the Chinese would come up with that, don't you think? Always something new to sell, always one jump ahead.'

Leonard had been impressed with the Chinese. He realised that the possibility of China reverting to Maoist politics was negligible. As for our present plight, there was, he felt, nothing to be concerned about. The Chinese would take care of it. Then, glancing at me as if to apologise for his compatriots, he sat back languidly in his seat and fixed the committee with an appraising look. 'Seen all those people out there? The ones without their houses? Rain, my friend … rain. Just the same as we have at home, and with just the same consequences.'

The committee had no idea what to make of him. 'Damn pinko,' someone muttered.

The chorus melted away. Leonard took his leave and silence descended on the carriage. I looked along the corridor. La Parisienne, engulfed in a towel, lay on the floor near the attendant's compartment, like a rolled carpet. The only light came from the single lamp on the platform outside. The air was heavy and stifling. I must admit that I, too, was beginning to feel a little concerned at our state of inertia. With nothing to be done, I stretched out on my bunk and fell into a light, feverish sleep.

When I awoke, we were moving. The dawn had broken. A warm breeze ballooned into the compartment, washing over my oily flesh. If we were on our way, soon we would be in Canton; the satisfaction was as refreshing as diving into cool water. In the corridor I stood at the window, looking over the passing countryside of cockaded hillocks and smoking villages, where the floods were no longer to be seen, as my furred-up mind gradually cleared. Bit by bit, the sense of relief gave way to confusion and then to displeasure at the realisation that we were not heading towards Canton but away from it. We were heading north. Back to Shanghai! Another day and night on that mobile oven was not to be borne. My whole being began to heat up at the very thought of it.

As it turned out, we were not returning to Shanghai. Or so I learnt from the carriage attendant, who, when I expressed puzzlement to her as best I could, replied with words I could not understand; wrote on a scrap of paper characters I could not read; and finally obtained the services of a student from a neighbouring carriage who said, 'You get off Changsha. You know Changsha? Chairman Mao?' Well, I didn't know what Changsha was, but it turned out to be the city where the Great Helmsman saw the light.

I broke the news to everyone in the party. They wanted to know more – so did I, but at least it was clear that arrangements of some sort were being made for us. I had learnt over the weeks that in the world east of Berlin, when it came to the welfare of Westerners, the administrative wheels turned with surprising smoothness. If the attendant knew we were to disembark at Changsha, it was because someone in authority had told her as much.

And so that was how it all ended. The journey to Changsha took all day, as the dozens of trains behind us that had departed Peking and Shanghai before the rains had come had to be reversed ahead of us. When finally we reached Changsha, we tumbled out onto the platform to be met by a representative of the state tourist agency, who escorted us to a waiting coach and in the fading light by what seemed an unnecessarily circuitous route on to an airfield that resembled a wartime landing strip. We had to await the complete enclosure of darkness before entering through the heavily guarded gates, for security reasons that remained unspecified by our representative, a man who spoke unintelligibly but garrulously over the course of the hours it took to finally board our plane, a small Russian turbo-prop that rattled and shook all the way to Canton. Of that flight I recall only that the frayed seat belt, shortened time and again over the years as the material wore out and the buckle retreated further and further from the metal tongue, could not reach across my then slender frame.

Just as Peking was beginning in the English-speaking world to be known as Beijing, so Canton was making way for its Chinese name, Guangzhou, which foreigners found unpronounceable and which provoked some misunderstandings.

'But I thought we were going to Canton?'

'We are.'

'No, we are not – we are going to Gwainjoo, or somewhere. That brochure was wrong. I didn't pay good money to be fobbed off with ... whatever it is.'

Detained by floods or not, Canton was regarded as little more than a stopover. In Canton, because of its proximity to Hong Kong, it was one of the few places in China since the foundation of the People's Republic in 1949 that had sustained some sort of relationship with the outside world so that even in 1981, foreigners were no longer curiosities. Beneath its humid, grey skies were streets of traditional houses with peeling stucco flanked by banyan trees, whose aerial roots dangled from lower branches like skeins of material hanging out to dry; an island of European architecture dating from the nineteenth century, when foreign traders had been forbidden to mix with local people; a handful of avenues of poorly-built, contemporary corporate-style constructions; parks and gardens rich with the perfume of jasmine; and a food market as fascinating as any in the world, with its snakes, bamboo rats, terrapins, kittens and dried insects and seafood, spices and herbs all for sale along a stifling, dusty, raucous couple of back streets in the city centre. On the fringes of the city a blanket of steam hung over acres of palm plantation.

The restaurants of Canton were said to be the best in China, because Chinese tradition decreed it so. If you told a Chinese that you were going to Canton then automatically they would give a knowing smile and make reference to the food, although it was more than likely that they secretly preferred the cooking of their home town. But, according to the old saw, you lived in Hangzhou (earthly paradise), married in Suzhou (most beautiful women), ate in Guangzhou (best food) and died in Liuzhou (best coffins). The people of Canton were said to eat anything with four legs, 'except tables'. This was true. This, after all, was a place where beating a dog to death was supposed to enhance its flavour.

More noticeable than the quality of the food was the professional level of the service, which elsewhere in China had been willing but inept. From this point of view, it was hard to believe that Canton was in the same country as Peking and Xian, or even Shanghai. Those places were still being schooled for change (it was possible to believe there that the revolution might live on), whereas the atmosphere of Canton was of a done deal. The Cantonese seemed unconcerned with what was happening elsewhere. As far as they were concerned, the future had already arrived. Compared to the rest of the country, Canton was like the supermarket that moves into a village of staid corner shops.

Chapter 12

The Hong Kong Line

Canton was of little interest to us. Home, in the form of Hong Kong, where the restaurants promised at least as much and where you could get a decent salad, was just a few miles beyond the Pearl River delta. It hardly seemed credible that only a few weeks before, we had been trundling across the high plateaux of Mongolia and now all that remained of the journey was a short run across the southern tip of China to the border and beyond it to the New Territories, Hong Kong and the South China Sea.

But we were still in China and to reach Hong Kong we had to cross a border. By 1981, passport and custom formalities were no longer dealt with at the border itself but in Canton station, from where most foreigners exited the country in purpose-built trains. It was here, in the stifling immigration hall, that one final drama took place, a major skirmish with a party of French tourists.

Since our visa was a group document, we had to line up according to the sequence of names on the visa before the immigration officer, who could not read or speak English. The room was packed with groups of foreigners, pressed together with their luggage, tripping over each other to get into position in the breathless heat. Above us a bank of fans turned with slow, precise impotence.

In the crush of a narrow corridor, an Australian man in my party brushed the leg of a Frenchwoman with his bag. He apologised; she responded by spitting at him and then, screaming '*Espèce de cretin Americain! Espèce d'Americain!*' stubbed her cigarette out on his neck. The shock took him aback briefly but as the pain grew, presuming her to be a madwoman, he wrestled her to the floor, as dozens of bewildered tourists looked on in astonishment. The police panicked, for unless foreigners were posing a threat to national security, they were not sure whether it was their role to interfere. Eventually, however, they stepped in to separate the pair, grateful to have discovered that internecine war was not confined to the Chinese. What had untapped the woman's furious attack we never knew, unless it had been the horrifying sight of Coca-Cola bottles as, once again, the USA usurped France's rightful place as a model for civilisation.

The final train was brand new, purpose built and air-conditioned. Although we had to endure videos featuring winsome girls twirling parasols and singing saccharine songs of yearning for the mother country that we were now leaving, this train, more than anything we had seen since leaving Berlin, foretold the future. It embodied China's commitment to change and to a fuller relationship with the world beyond. Already, in 1981, the short shuttle between Hong Kong and Canton was almost a commonplace. In Peking and in Xian, the very wellsprings of revolutionary conservatism, there prevailed a nervous suspicion of change, but here in the south it was clear that there was no going back.

At the border, there was a brief stop as we passed through the Bamboo Curtain at Shenzhen, now a city of millions but then a tiny frontier town of almost invisible insignificance. The two parts of China were separated not by a wall, but by a wire fence, which just as in Berlin, the train pierced to move us unobstructed from one world to another. As we left China behind, from somewhere in the train we heard hear muted cheers of relief. Yet the Bamboo Curtain was a misnomer for, unlike its grim equivalent in Berlin, the wall was here a high mesh fence, as much a psychological barrier as a physical one. The Chinese understood that to be able to glimpse the motherland also served a political purpose and on the Hong Kong side of the border, a huge burial ground climbed up the hillside filled not with unlucky escapees, but with the remains of those parted from their ancestors by poverty and politics, who had asked to be buried as close as possible to China.

'Why don't you guys let Hong Kong be independent?' The question was addressed to any Briton within hearing on the train. 'Let the people here choose – give them democracy!'

The proposition seemed naïve, for Hong Kong was a British colony only institutionally. Power in Hong Kong, a self-generating bank with gigantic resources manned by money-makers from across the world, including the local Chinese

Fragrant Harbour – Hong Kong.

magnates and, invisibly, their cousins on the mainland, came from within. With the handover of Hong Kong to China still far enough in the future to be safely ignored, systemic change seemed unnecessary. As things have turned out, perhaps the speaker's instinct was correct and perhaps the gift of proper democracy should have been Britain's final bequest.

Just as all those weeks before, we had felt a pang as we caught a glimpse of gaudy West Berlin before entering the darkness of the East, so now a curious sense of dislocation, relief tinged with nostalgia, beset us as we pulled into Kowloon station and the harlequinade that is the capitalist world. Hong Kong, teeming, hot, comfortable, absurd, opulent, greedy, cheerful, efficient and addictive, welcomed us.

And then we dispersed, just like that. After weeks of unavoidable, occasionally undesirable intimacy, the peremptory separation was unsettling at first. For all the complaints and discomforts, I like to think that each of those people would come to regard that journey as a unique insight into the intricacies of humankind's attempts to organise itself and the enormous cost of its failures to do so. There were, it is true, times when I could cheerfully have left one or two of them at various benighted spots between Berlin and Canton, but these moments of frustration and anger quickly faded when something turned up to pique our curiosity or puzzlement or, occasionally, wonderment, whether the inexpressible grimness of East Berlin and the overwhelming pantheistic beauty of Lake Baikal or sympathy for the restless Poles, affection for the Mongolians and admiration for the ever-optimistic Chinese. These travellers, of all ages, backgrounds and nationalities, were individuals, with their own minds and opinions, who had chosen to join with others to look at what was otherwise invisible. Most were patient, thoughtful, genial and likeable people who dealt with the challenges with equanimity and good humour. Only on a train was it possible to see what we had seen, as we were briefly part of the daily life of half the world.

As we were waiting for our bags to come through customs at Kowloon Station, I saw that Slim, one of the Vietnam Vets, was in conversation with another recently returned visitor to China. I edged closer to listen, certain that he would be pontificating about the iniquities of the Communist world.

'Russia … what a country' I heard him say. 'Fantastic, such great people. If only they could get rid of that guy Brezhnev. And China, what a future. You really should consider doing a trip like the one we just did. OK, it wasn't a bed of roses but, you know, when it's tough, you gotta adapt!'

I flew back home. I had revelled in the experience, for it had been for me like an initiation. Life could never be the same. In a few hours I would be reinserted into the familiarity of home. In the meantime, I sat encased in another metal package, inhaling the artificial aircraft air, while far beneath me, below the clouds, across the great open spaces that made up the domains of Uncle Joe, the Great Helmsman and all their disciples, the trains we had taken, filled with the people whose lives we had brushed against, nodded from place to place.

Within eight years, the Communist world would largely fall apart, leaving behind the detritus of history to be slowly cleared up over the ensuing decades. Computers, the internet and mobile communications would render obsolete theories of the dictatorship of the proletariat. In Britain and America, 'no-platforming', by which eminent thinkers and writers would be denied the right to speak when their opinions conflicted with those considered acceptable by self-appointed arbiters of moral and political values, would become a feature of public life. Attempts would be made to dismantle statues and memorials connected with controversial historical figures. Just as in the Soviet Union and the People's Republic of China.